MW01259296

PIONEERTOWN, USA

The Definitive History of Pioneertown, CA: Where the Old West Lives Again

BY
KENNETH **B.** GENTRY

P I O N E E R T O W N ,   U S A

ISBN Number 9781513633114

FIRST EDITION
BLACK & WHITE
FIRST PRINTING
MARCH of 2o18

WRITTEN & PUBLISHED BY
KENNETH B. GENTRY

www.HighDesertVarnish.com

www.VisitPioneertown.com

Foreword:

Pioneertown, California. A home of true western history, a source of great mystery and a town truly unlike any other in the USA. I have often referred to Pioneertown as "the American Dream come true" and "My slice of heaven". When I sum up the whole-story of the town's history for people, I honestly tend to feel a little jealous, excited and oddly inspired, all at the same time.

I am a California kid; born in Santa Monica and raised in the greater Los Angels County. I'm an old soul at heart and I have always felt out of place while living in the city. My Father moved to Palm Springs late in 2oo5 and I followed shortly after. I thought I was getting out of the big city.

Please note that I mean absolutely no offense to Palm Springs or the surrounding cities. I love 'em. They're all great. But I found the greater Palm Springs area to be very much like Los Angeles. It is just as heavily populated, there are lots of red traffic lights, cookie-cutter houses and the same repeating franchises. The only significant difference I found in Palm Springs was that it is a lot hotter than LA and the whole city is surrounded by the desert.

I moved back and forth between the desert cities and Los Angeles County for a few years; never really enjoying either one. Any time that I enjoyed in the desert was spent far outside of the city, in the surrounding wilderness. One night while living in Palm Springs I was ranting to a friend about how much I disliked the city when she mentioned a house up the hill in Morongo Valley that her father was helping to renovate. It was almost finished and was then going up for rent. I was sold just by the way she'd described it, well before I saw it, and I actually signed a lease within 48 hours of her mentioning it.

As it turned out, the date that I was able to move in happened to be just a couple of weeks before I turned 3o. I had experienced a hard year of very complicated medical issues when I was 29. My health was finally returning and I finally lived in a house outside of the city. Without even realizing it, I had become a resident of the High Desert. There is a big difference between the low and high deserts of southern California. I felt reborn here. I can not express to you how lucky I feel for having been blessed with that opportunity. I can honestly say that I never want to turn back.

I have always been artistic and enjoyed the outdoors, but I blossomed here. Shortly after moving, I created an art & science focused small business, staked a 2o acre mineral claim, designed numerous highly rated products and started selling art and prospected minerals around town. I quickly soaked up the local culture, entertainment and history in the area. But the fun was really just getting started.

It wasn't long before friends said that I had to meet Christy up in Pioneertown. I had been up there a couple of times before. But, like so many other people, I had only randomly passed through during the middle of the week when the town was empty. As far as I knew, it was just an isolated bar up in the hills next to a few blocks of fun looking false fronts that were mixed in with some real houses. Boy was I wrong!

I'll never forget the first time I met Christy and Roger. My friends introduced us on Mane Street while they were using a tractor to level out dirt that had been brought in to replace what a rainstorm had washed away earlier that month. They stopped working just to come hang out and talk. Everyone in town was so nice and inviting. I instantly felt right at home, just like I had in Morongo Valley. So I started volunteering to help when they had big events and then started working at the Jack Cass Saloon soon after.

My love for Pioneertown developed quickly! I started working at the Jack Cass regularly and really enjoyed the opportunity to have lots of fun, learn about local history and display some art at the same time. Some of the best memories I have were spent right here in town. Getting to see the Melvins at Pappy & Harriet's with My sister and hanging out with them afterwards.. being half of the elephant in the Shodeo Rodeo Parade.. staying up until the crazy hours of the morning out back in the campground with a bunch of friends. I literally get to meet people from all around the world every weekend!

A big part of running a shop on Mane Street is filling visitors in on the history of the town. I learned the general story quickly, both out of genuine curiosity and also so that I could recite it when people asked. Over the years I started to develop a bit of a script on Pioneertown that I updated every time I learned something new, so I could get out all the fun historical facts without talking people's heads off. But it seemed like I was learning something new about the town every day and eventually I had to start sticking to just the coolest facts, elst I'd be talking for hours every time someone was curious about Pioneertown's history.

There was a two page pamphlet on the history of Pioneertown which was written by Ernie Kester in 2o1o that we gave out when visitors wanted more information, but it was an almost decade old photocopied copy of a copy that was in dire need of an update. I like to write. So I decided I was going to rewrite and update the information and I set out to make a new Pioneertown guide. I had absolutely no idea what I was starting.

I had two pages of new information in no time at all. It was even shrunken down to size 8 font so I could fit in as much information as possible, without making it impossible to read. The history of Pioneertown is amazing! For every interesting fact that I already knew, I found ten more while doing research. I started noting some discrepancies between reports, inaccuracies and unanswered questions. I also learned some truly jaw-dropping facts that had simply been forgotten over time. I wanted to do more research, but as it was, I had already compiled way too much information for a small visitor's guide. There is a wealth of history here that had huge effects on the Hollywood Scene, the State of California and the greater United States. I felt that it should be properly documented.

My family and I went out thrifting in Old Town Yucca Valley one weekend and I came across a local book that you can find all over the High Desert. Its a simple little book; self illustrated and published. It was the last bit of inspiration and motivation that I needed. I bought the book. Well.. My sister bought it. I didn't have any cash. But I took it home, I put it next to the research that I had already compiled while writing out the new Pioneertown guide and then I started working on this book.

My goal here was to compile all of this town's history, answer those unanswered questions, settle those discrepancies, correct any inaccurate reports, highlight all the interesting facts that have faded away over time and compile everything into one neat presentation. I aim to help preserve the history of what I consider to be an amazing example of the American Dream come true. I hope you enjoy *Pioneertown, USA*!

Contents:

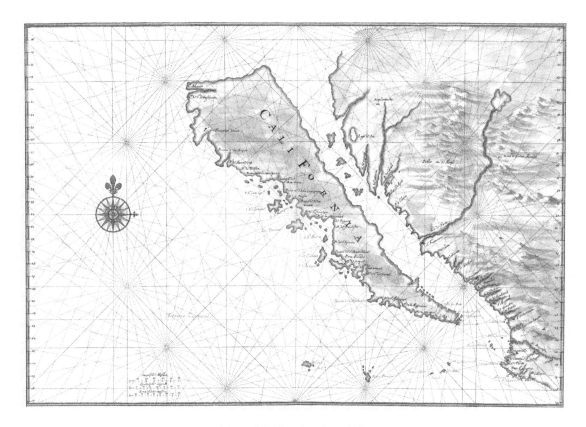

Map of California, circa 1650

Chapter 1

A Land Before Pioneertown

Pioneertown sits in the south eastern corner of the San Bernardino Mountains. These mountains are part of the Transverse Ranges which are a group of mountains in southern California with an east-west orientation, which is opposite of California's general north-south running coastal mountains. The San Bernardino Mountains reached their current height about two million years ago and are the result of the extremely complex tectonic activity in the area, as the San Andreas Fault lies less than 25 miles to the west. For the past 28 million years the Pacific Plate has slowly been moving underneath the North American Plate along this fault line, pushing up the San Bernardino Mountains and many others in the process. The San Bernardino Mountains became a part of the San Bernardino National Forest when it was established in 1925.

They are home to some of the most diverse wildlife in California, including Bald Eagles, Bighorn Sheep, Black Bears, Bobcats and Beavers, just to name a few. The San Bernardino Mountains encompass some of southern California's highest peaks, such as Mount San Gorgonio, which stands 11,489 feet above sea level. Its wide range of different ecosystems include some 440 different wildlife species and thousands of plant species, over 30 of which are listed as threatened or endangered. These mountain ranges include a diversity of flora and fauna that is so different from surrounding areas that they are known technically as a Sky Island. Indigenous people have populated the area for over 10,000 years.

No tribes are said to have set up permanent residence in the area now know as

Pioneertown. But it was used as prime hunting and gathering grounds and as a cool retreat during the summer months, much like it still is today. The area also hosted some very heavily trafficked trading routes, as it made for a direct link between many different local tribes. The Tongva, also known as the Gabrieliños or the Fernandeño, lived to the south west, near what is currently the Inland Empire. The Cahuilla lived to the south, in the Coachella Valley & Salton Sea Basin. The Serrano & Chemehuevi lived mainly in the areas north and north east. The Serrano tribe inhabited the area now known as Big Bear and originally called themselves the Yuhaviatam. It was Spanish settlers who called the tribe "Serrano" which means "Highlander". Although none of them actually called the land that makes up Pioneertown home, each tribe had a good deal of interest in the area.

In 151o, the fifth book in a series of Spanish chivalric romance novels, Las sergas de Esplandián (*The Adventures of Esplandián*), by Garci Rodríguez de Montalvo, described a fictitious island: "Know, that on the right hand of the Indies there is an island called California very close to the side of the Terrestrial Paradise; and it is peopled by black women, without any man among them, for they live in the manner of Amazons."

Some of the first European explorers to the western coast of North America were Diego de Becerra and Fortun Ximenez in 1533 at the behest of Hernán Cortés. They left the area thinking that Baja California was actually a large island. It is highly probable that Montalvo's description was the motivation for naming this area California, which was first found on a map in 1562. While it was proven more than once that Baja California was not an island, maps would go back and forth between island & peninsula up until the late 17oo's.

Juan Rodriguez Cabrillo of Spain was the first recorded European to explore what we now call California in 1542. He died from an infected leg injury he sustained while trying to rescue some of his men from attacking Tongva warriors. At that time, California was under the rule of Spain. But most of the igneous people continued living freely as the land was not of very much interest to Europeans until the 16oo's when Russian & British explorers began to settle in the area.

In 1769 Alta California was established as a polity of New Spain. It included present day California, Nevada, Utah and parts of Arizona, Wyoming, Colorado and New Mexico. While looking for deserters of the Spanish Army in 1772, a Military Governor of Alta California named Pedro Fages became the first known European to visit the San Bernardino Mountains. Then in 1774, Juan Bautista De Anza's expedition explored the area.

The 18oo's saw the start of big changes in the areas surrounding present day Pioneertown. Spanish Missionaries established a church at the village of Politania in 1810. On May 2oth of that year, Father Francisco Dumetz named that church "San Bernardino", after the feast day of Saint Bernardino of Siena. Missionaries also gave that same name to the snow-capped peaks nearby, in further honor of the Saint. It is from Father Francisco Dumetz and Saint Bernardino of Siena that the California county of San Bernardino derived its name.

In 1821 Mexico gained its independence from Spain and became Independent Mexico. Celebrations of their independence were short lived however, as conflicts between Mexico & the U.S. lead to the start of the Mexican American War in April of 1846. Later that year, while struggling under Mexican rule, a group of people in northern California formed the California Republic and revolted from Mexico for twenty-five days. On January 24th, 1848, while helping build a lumber mill on the American River for Sacramento pioneer John Sutter, a foreman named James W. Marshall discovered gold. This discovery would change both California and the world alike as it single-handedly sparked the California Gold Rush.

Just a week later, the treaty of Guadaulpe Hidalgo was signed on February 2nd, 1848, ending the Mexican American War. The U.S. was granted the Rio Grande as a boundary for

Texas along with ownership of California and a large area comprising roughly half of New Mexico, most of Arizona, Nevada, and Utah, as well as parts of Wyoming and Colorado. California residents immediately started working towards entering the Union. They hosted the first California Constitutional Convention in 1849 and sought Statehood shortly after. This heated nation wide debates over the issue of slavery in newly acquired U.S. territories. The Compromise of 185o was a set of five bills which defused these slavery disputes in territories acquired by the USA in the Mexican American War. With that, California became the 31st State of the Union on September 9th, 185o. Records are rough, but the estimated population at the time was 1oo,ooo non Native Americans and 2oo-3oo,ooo igneous people.

In 1852, Col. Henry Washington, a distant nephew of President George Washington, was the deputy surveyor under contract with the U.S. Surveyor General of California and was assigned the task of establishing an Initial Point for all future surveys, where the Baseline & Meridian would intersect at a highly visible point in Southern California. Even with 11 barrings taken to help define the location of the Initial Point Monument, it was difficult to obtain true fixes on triangulation marks due to the shimmering heat waves of the San Bernardino Valley. To overcome this problem, huge bonfires were built atop the peaks that surrounded the valley and the surveys were made at night time.

Col. Washington, with the help of 12 assistant surveyors, established the Initial Point half a mile west and a few hundred feet below the peak of Mt. San Bernardino, at an elevation of 1o,3oo' above sea level. They erected a monument that stood 23' and 9" from the ground, complete with tin flashers hanging from each side, which could easily be seen from land below. With the establishment of the Initial Point, land surveying boomed until all of Southern California was mapped out and thoroughly recorded. In 1853 the U.S. Government was then able to survey parts of the Palm Springs area for the first time while mapping the first wagon route through the San Gorgonio Mountains. On April 26th of that same year, the county of San Bernardino was established.

Back in the Mexican American War, the Mormon Battalion, a volunteer unit and the only religiously based unit in U.S. military history, occupied Los Angeles & San Diego. Members of the Mormon Battalion, an estimated 534 - 559 Latter-day Saints men, made the long and grueling trek from Council Bluffs, IA, to San Diego, CA. Company C of the Mormon Battalion was detailed to guard the Cajon Pass from Indian horse raids in April of 1847. Even in the midst of war, the members of the Mormon Battalion were overwhelmed with the sheer beauty and rich potential of the land that they were sent to protect. They soon requested that Brigham Young, the second President of The Church of Jesus Christ of Latter-day Saints, allow them to establish a colony there in California.

Their request was granted and in June of 1851, 5oo Mormons in a 15o-wagon caravan reached a sycamore grove just a few miles north of the Cajon Pass. They stayed in this area while they negotiated to purchase the Rancho San Bernardino, just 15 miles to the south. In 1851, they agreed to purchase the Rancho, a total of 4o,ooo acres that included much of present day San Bernardino, for $77,ooo with a $7,ooo down payment. They began to build and farm in the area well before the final paperwork was registered in February of 1852, due partly to the fact that they feared attacks from the native desert Indians. They decided to build a 75o' by 32o' stockade similar to the one that they constructed when they had first arrived at Salt Lake, in Utah.

Fort San Bernardino was erected in the heart of present day San Bernardino and was guarded by a wall made of cottonwood and willow tree trunks which stood 12 feet above the ground. Lytle Creek, which ran nearby, was diverted to run through the center of the Fort, which also encompassed two water basins for domestic purposes. Fort walls were reinforced on the inside by rows of tightly packed houses & buildings that skirted the perimeter. Every effort was made to ensure that they could hold out against the harshest of Indian raids. Fortunately for them, their hard work paid off. It is said that after seeing the elaborate preparations, the nearby Indians made no attempt to raid the Fort or the valley it lay in. By 1853 the walls were dropped and the Fort layout was replaced with a more common city-type grid layout which was designed to resemble a miniature Salt Lake City.

While traveling back and forth between California, Utah and their ties in other States, the Mormons used the Old Spanish Trail which was already well mapped during the expedition of Antonio Armijo in the 1820's and later publicized in John C. Frémont's Report of his 1844 journey for the U.S. Topographical Corps. "Cañon de San Bernardino", an area encompassing much of the San Bernardino Mountains, was just a small part of the Old Spanish Trail that stretched far to the east in the footsteps of original Spanish explorers. During California's gold rush, this route was known to the 49ers as the Southern Route of the California Trail; the trail which lead prospectors to the golden opportunities in northern California. In Utah, Arizona and Nevada, this southern route through California was known as the "California Road". But residents of California referred to it as the "Old Mormon Road", the "Old Southern Road", the "Immigrant Road" or the "Old Mormon Trail" which became the most commonly used name as the Mormons were the most frequent travelers across its path.

In 1859 a prospector and sharpshooter by the name of William Francis Holcomb heard about gold being found near the Old Mormon Trail in Yuhaviat, the Serrano name for "Pine Place" and what is now known as Big Bear, CA. After arriving at a small settlement known as Starvation Flats in Yuhaviat, Holcomb was hired by the locals to kill off the aggressive grizzly bears that plagued the area. His skill with a rifle earned him the name nickname "Grizzly Bill". Less than a year later, Grizzly Bill Holcomb and his partner, Ben Choteau, filed five gold claims just a few miles north of present day Big Bear. Within a year their claims in the area now known as Holcomb Valley attracted enough attention to spark a boomtown known as Bellville, CA. In 1860 Bellville had a population of nearly 1,500 and was actually proposed for the county seat. The September Elections of 1860 instead gave that title to the small town of San Bernardino who narrowly won the election by a mere two votes. It is interesting to think about how different southern California might have been had Bellville won the county seat instead of San Bernardino. The county in question is the largest in the Continental USA.

At one point in time Bellville was the largest producer of gold in all of Southern California. Operations nearby, like the Rose Mine, produced gold ore valued at $40 - $225 per ton while the average for the greater Morongo Basin was around $40. The gold rush which swept through the San Bernardino Mountains only lasted a couple of decades and by 1870 many of the prospectors & miners had already left. Due to its large population of secessionist sympathizers during the national crisis of 1860 - 1861, the U.S. government actually sent a Federal troop to Bellville, fearing a secessionist revolt might break out there. No such incident occurred. But, fearing an ambush, the troop secretly traveled through the San Bernardino Mountains only at night. Records from the time don't provide very much detail; but it is highly probable that Federal troops on an early Civil War mission once traveled along the Old Mormon Trail through the land that we now call Pioneertown.

The country was well into its Civil War in 1862 when President Abraham Lincoln signed the Homestead Act into effect, encouraging Western migration by offering homesteaders each 160 acres. The desert population then suffered in 1863 when a Smallpox epidemic rattled through the area and killed a large portion of the indigenous people. The following year brought news of more big changes in the area. The Pacific Railroad Act of 1864, a revision of an Act established earlier in 1862, granted Southern Pacific Railroad more Federal land for every mile of track they completed. For every mile of track they laid down, they would now receive 20 square miles of land, on alternating sections, on either side of the tracks.

Following statehood, California saw the start of the California Indian Wars which lasted from 1850 - 1880. These conflicts arose for many different reasons but none more-so than the large western migration through Native American territories, inspired by the California Gold Rush. The American Civil War ended in 1865, but civil conflicts were still abundant in the land. The Mojave Desert Indian Campaign, a retaliation from a San Bernardino County Posse against Chemehuevi raids on miners & ranchers in San Bernardino, lasted from 1866 - 1870.

On May 15th, 1876, President Ulysses S. Grant, by executive order, created nine reservations in the area, including Potrero Ajenio, also known as the San Gorgonio Agency. Originally established in 1865, the site lay at the foot of the San Gorgonio and the San Jacinto Mountains, in present day Banning. Its name is derived from *Potrero*, meaning 'Horse Pasture' and *Genio*, the name of a Cahuilla chief. The first official "Captain" of Potrero Ajenio who acted on behalf of the Bureau of Indian Affairs, known to Americans by his English name, John Morongo, was the hereditary leader of a Serrano clan called the Maarrenga'. What we currently know as Morongo Valley was first shown on maps in the late 1850's as the "Marengo Pass".

The valley was originally a Marrenga' village and home of the Serrano Shoshonean clan until 1876, when the U.S. government began relocating local Indian tribes to reservations. As settlers to the valley began to replace the native Americans, they preserved the historical name, but modified it to sound more English. The natives to the valley moved to the reservation in Banning and, as time went on, the Bureau of Indian Affairs began to referrer to the tribe as the Morongo Band of Mission Indians. That name grew to encompass many different Indian tribes in areas spanning from the mountains just north of Palm Springs all the way up to U.S. Route 66. It was John Morongo who, in turn, is responsible for the name of the great Morongo Basin in Southern California.

Later in 1876, the land composing Section 19, as well as the other odd numbered sections, of Township 1 North, Range 5 East, in California Meridian 27, was granted to Southern Pacific Railroad. That land is present day Pioneertown. Just a year afterwards, in 1877, the Desert Land Act was passed which helped promote the idea of populating the deserts of California. But even with new trains now running within a day's ride and homesteading being heavily promoted; homesteaders took a backseat to all the prospectors who took notice of the High Desert in a very big way.

In 1881 the Dale District, a gold hungry boomtown near current day Twentynine Palms, was established. Now a ghost town like Bellville, the town was once home to over 3,000 miners and was responsible for much of Twentynine Palms' early growth and development. H. A. Landwehr owned the most successful mining operation in the Morongo Basin through the 1880's: the Supply Mine. In its prime early days, the mine employed over 80 men and produced many millions of dollars worth of gold ore. Landwehr later sold to a company by the name of United Greenwater Co., who continued to successfully work the operation for many years.

The Morongo Basin and the land surrounding it saw four main large mining operations in the late 1800's, including the Gold Park Mining Co., Seal of Gold Co., the previously mentioned United Greenwater Co. and the Virginia Dale Mining Co. By 1900, the area was, or had been, home to many famous (in their time) mines such as Barker, Bonanza, California, Copper World Iron Mine, Deadman's Hole, Desert Queen, Eagle, Good Hope, Gold Coin, Gold Crown, Gowman Frying Pan, Iron Age, Iron Chief, Last Chance, Little Giants, Little Joker, Lone Star Lode, Lost Horse, Monitor, Morongo King, Nichols, Poor Man, Pride of the West, Rattlesnake, Rose, Scandalosa, The Capitol and many more.

In 1870, Ollie Smith was the first of many cattlemen recorded in the Morongo Basin.

Smith brought a herd of Texas Longhorn cattle to Quail Springs and, unbeknownst to him, started a long and strong heritage of cattle ranching in the area. Soon after, the area would see other cattlemen such as the William & McHaney brothers in Hidden Valley, the McKinney Ranch in Morongo Valley, the Barker-Shay Cattle Company north of Yucca Valley and the Talmadge brothers' enormous IS Ranch which spanned across much of the San Bernardino Mountains. Cows and horses didn't get the whole desert to themselves. In 1873, the DeCrevecoeurs, a sheep farming family, settled in Morongo Valley.

Mark "Chuck" Bemis Warren moved to the Yucca Valley area in 1876 and is argued as the man responsible for bringing life to the area. Warren came to San Bernardino in 1860 from his home state of Maine and started work as a freighter, hauling goods from the west coast as far east as Arizona. He married Sylvia Warren in 1866 after meeting her and her family two years earlier near Baker, CA, while transporting goods. They had 11 children in total, Wilson, Margaret, Susan, Minnie, Mary, Walter, Charles, Herbert, Edward, Frances & Lela. Edward, Frances & Lela were born in Morongo Valley.

In 1881, Warren dug a 160' deep well just north of the present day airport in Yucca Valley. He later set up a windmill, constructed a water trough for cattle, built a cabin and then a barn. The site known as "Warren's Well" became a watering hole and rest stop for many early settlers traveling through the area. Warren and his wife later moved down to Morongo Valley after purchasing the DeCrevecoeurs' property, where their home became another way point to many passers by. While the story is slightly debated; many people believe that Warren's three oldest sons lived at and maintained the well up in Yucca Valley. 15 cents was the recorded fee for a team of cattle to drink as much water as they'd like.

Around the same time that new settlers to Morongo Valley and the Warren's Well area had found a great new source of water & community, the native Indians in Twentynine Palms were having similar amenities taken from them. As Southern Pacific Railroad gained the rights to huge portions of desert land they also acquired the water rights and eventually held ownership of an area known as the Oasis of Mara in Twentynine Palms. The Oasis was a seasonal village and gathering grounds of the Serrano & Chemehuevi. Quite a lot of Indians lived at the Oasis of Mara permanently, but, favoring miners and cattlemen over the natives, Southern Pacific denied all tribes access to the water. Without water, many people were forced to leave and by 1888 there were only 40 Indian residents recorded in the area.

The desert is a very beautiful and special place. But, if history is any lesson, the West can also be extremely harsh. Atrocities and hardships aside; both of California's San Bernardino and Riverside Counties started to see a sharp increase in population. So too did the Morongo Basin, as prospectors, homesteaders and ranchers all started calling the High Desert their home. While mining and cattle ranching flourished, the 750,000 acre IS Ranch included a small isolated little slice of western heaven, then known simply as Pipes Country. The Pipes included present day Pioneertown as well as the Sawtooth Mountains, Burns Canyon, Rimrock, Pipes Canyon, Yucca Mesa and Water Canyon. Some of the earliest recorded residents of Pipes Country included:

- In the early 1870's Hezekiah Quick moved to Yucca Valley and Andrew Culbertson moved to Twentynine Palms. Both men were Veterans of the Civil War.
- The Reche family, who moved to the area currently known as Landers, CA, just north of Yucca Valley, in 1887. Their original family homestead is now the site of the world famous Integratron.
- William & Sarah Shay, who were some of the first people to settle on the Yucca Mesa. The Shays were Co-Owners of the Barker-Shay Cattle Company and built the Water Tank at Coyote Well and the Landmark Windmill nearby. They also helped build Barker Dam in Joshua Tree Park and dug a well for human consumption in Twentynine Palms.

- Ernie Sanders, Lionel Sall, as well as Mr. & Mrs. Frank Bull were also some of the earliest settlers on the Yucca Mesa.
- Walter Gehre and his family were some of the first residents of present day Pipes Canyon. Soon after moving to the area, they sold their property to Fred and Barbara Pearce, who turned it into a very successful rest home.
- John Minter was an early resident, but he too sold his property shortly after moving to the Pipes. He sold to William & Camilla Hudson who moved up to the canyon from Warren's Well area.
- Then there was Stanley Bowden, who gained a bit of local fame for having the first documented indoor bathroom in the area.
- Charlie Reche, already an early settler, moved his family into Pipes Canyon from their original homestead in Landers.
- Ben Jutes, John Olson, Caryl Nyberg & Pete Lager were prospectors who were commonly referred to as the "Swedes" and arrived to the Pipes from Mexico in 1918 while searching for diamonds. They established the famous Onyx Mine and soon brought along their partners Lem Parsons, Slim & Evelyn Conklin, Ray & Billie Reynolds, Merle Armitage, George & Louise Crawford, May & Harlow Porter, Dorthy Chapman Rash and Johnny Kee Sr. Along with his family.
- The Kee's settled in the area as far back as the late 1920's. Grant Allen Kee Homesteaded the area just north of present day Pioneertown and was soon joined by his brother, Johnny Kee Sr., one of the Swedes' partners, along with John's wife Addah and their sons, John Jr., Charlie, Corky & Roy.
- In 1945, Daniel & Louise Pekarovich built their ranch in Rimrock, which sits right between the Old Mormon Trail and Pipes Canyon. Three of their six children, Daniel Jr., Mary Ann and Joan, lived there with them. Later on in 1945, they also opened the Rimrock Motel which was the first motel in Pipes Country.
- Tom McIntosh was also an early resident of Rimrock. He was a local real estate agent and later became the first self-appointed Sheriff of Pioneertown.
- Other early settlers to the Rimrock area included Reece & Irene Fox, Ruby & Tom "Pop" Vincent, Dick & Ruth Bosley, Bert & Mabel Norman, Fred Moninger & his wife Beverly, May Small, Jack Duckett, Bert Clow, Red Davidson, Ivan Whiltsie, Martha Foote and Don Carter.
- Bill Kramer was an early settler who moved to the area from Iowa in the 1920's. He had been poisoned by gas in WWI and after his doctor told him that he only had six months left to live, he decided to move to an isolated area and enjoy some solitude. Kramer chose to move to Rattlesnake Gulch, just off of the old Mormon Trail, where he built a small cabin. He had enough friends who would visit him, and bring along supplies when they did, that he never had to leave the property. Kramer kept a pen of homing pigeons at his isolated cabin which could alert his friends if he ever had an emergency.
- Margie Mattoon Hamilton was an early resident to the area just south of Pipes Canyon and was also a key component in the discovery and early history of Pioneertown. Margie worked as a nurse at the Good Samaritan Hospital on Wilshire Boulevard in Los Angeles in the early 1930's. While working there, she cared for a man by the name of Frank Mattoon who had been gassed in an industrial accident while working in Arabia as a diesel engineer for Standard Oil Co. Frank and Margie married as soon as he was released. They moved to Pipes Country mainly so Frank could benefit from the fresh air. Around 1939 they purchased a ranch and by 1940 they had 3,000 Leghorn Chickens that produced 2,8000 eggs a day! Their farm was equipped with an Egg Room, a Candler, a Weigher, an Inspection Area and a Cooler. They sold and delivered eggs to the Bagley Store in the Twentynine

Palms Plaza, to Lilly's Grocery Store in Yucca Valley, to customers in Joshua Tree, Morongo Valley, White Water, Palm Springs, Cathedral City and even Banning. Frank and Margie Mattoon were good friends with Dick Curtis and his wife, Ruth.

Far down the mountains, in 1884, Judge John Guthrie McCallum bought land from the Southern Pacific Railroad and moved from San Francisco to the area that is now Palm Springs. He brought his family there to the desert to help ease his son's Tuberculosis and in turn they became the first non-Indian settlers in the area. The area started to see steady growth and in 1886 a Dr. Welwood Murray built the first hotel in the area: The Palm Springs Hotel. However, it wasn't until 1909 that the opening of the Desert Inn hotel put the Village of Palm Springs on the map as a tourist destination. Shortly after that, the area started to blossom into the bustling city which we know it as today.

While 1909 saw the birth of a new desert community below, it also saw "The West's Last Famous Manhunt" in the lands above. The story of Willie Boy, a 28 year old Paiute-Chemehuevi Indian, has been written about more than almost any other Indian in the West. Much like the initial discovery and early history of Pioneertown, the true story of Willie Boy's history has been embellished over the years and is the source of much debate to this day. Far surpassing Pioneertown's various contradicting tales or differentiating records-Willie Boy's story has so many different versions told of almost every possible detail that it would make for the greatest, longest, Choose Your Own Adventure Book ever! Numerous newspaper articles, books and documentaries were written about Willie. Even a movie about Willie Boy was made in 1969. But they each paint a slightly different picture. To try and explain Willie's whole story here, even in minute detail, would honestly, easily, double the number of pages in this book. So, his story will be summed up extremely tight here, only because of how interesting and incredible it truly is.

Willie was in love with Carlota (also known as Isoleta and Lolita) Boniface, the 16 year old daughter of William "Old Mike" Boniface. Willie & Carlota wanted to be married but Mike and other family members wouldn't allow it due to the fact that they were very distant cousins. The couple tried to run away together but were quickly found by family while the Bonifaces were living in Twentynine Palms. Mike then took his family to camp at the Gilman Ranch in Banning in an attempt to get Carlota away from Willie. On the night of September 26th, 1909, Willie Boy accidently or intentionally killed Mike Boniface at the Gilman Ranch with a rifle. Carlota then fled with Willie by force or by her own free will. The couple then set out on a race across the desert that would make the Mint 400 look like an innocent little children's game. Mike Boniface was very well liked in both the Riverside and San Bernardino Counties and a posse looking to track down Willie was formed very shortly after Boniface's murder was discovered.

The posse was the first of many and included, but was surely not limited to, key trackers and local lawmen such as San Bernardino County Sheriff John Ralphs, Riverside County Sheriff Frank Wilson, Deputy Sheriff Charlie Reche, Ben & Waldemar de Crevecouer, Joe Toutain, Willie Pablo, Joe Nolan, Segundo Chino and John Hyde. On September 30th, posse members found Carlota's dead body in Pipes Country. While still highly debated, the most recently discovered evidence points to a member of the posse as having been the killer and not Willie Boy. In either event, the men failed to capture their target and Willie lead them on a chase across the desert to Twentynine Palms and back to the Pipes Country.

On October 7th, after an 11 day manhunt, a group of five men tracked Willie Boy up Ruby Mountain where they found themselves in a trap. Shooting from a high residing cluster of rocks and using smokeless powder, which further helped to keep his location unknown, Willie got the draw on his pursuers. He swiftly shot at each of them, killing four of their horses and hitting Deputy Sheriff Charlie Reche in the leg. Wounded, horseless and pinned down, the group sent member John Hyde on foot to Warren's Well to retrieve help. When night fell the men were able to retrieve Reche's horse, the only surviving steed, and tied Reche to its saddle before heading to Warren's Well by moonlight. While they retreated towards the main posse, the men heard one last gunshot echo through the desert landscape behind them.

Another five posses were quickly formed and some 75 men continued to roam around the desert in search for the man who had been dubbed "the Mad Dog of Morongo". Stories started to spread and many people started to fear that there would be an Indian uprising in the area. Residents of San Bernardino reported seeing smoke clouds in the mountains and many ranchers and miners from isolated areas began to make their way into the cities seeking safety from potential Indian violence. President William Howard Taft was in the middle of his Western Rail Tour at the time and was due to arrive in Riverside on October 12th. Stories were published, one of particular interest done by E. A. Fowler for the New York Sun, which speculated that an Indian raid, lead by Willie Boy, was organizing with the intention to assassinate the president. All of this later bustle was sadly pointless and unnecessary.

On the morning of October 15th, eight days after Charlie Reche was wounded while in pursuit, posse members found the dead body of Willie Boy atop Ruby Mountain where he had lead his last assault. After the famous shootout with posse members on October 7th, Willie had taken his own life with his last bullet. The men burned his badly decomposed body where they found it. And so marked the end of the West's last famous manhunt and a pivotal chapter in the history of the Morongo Basin. Willie Boy's story is unlike any other in American history, especially when you ponder the more interesting notes. Like the fact that Willie was able to allude men on horseback for over a week by sprinting on foot, reportedly taking 7' and 8' long strides as he blew through the desert like the wind. Or the fact that it is highly probable that, contrary to what many people believe, Willie Boy may have actually escaped and lived to be an old man. One thing that can be said for sure is that Willie had a huge impact on the High Desert and Western history.

After that incident, the Indians living at the Oasis of Mara all began moving to the reservation in Banning and, sadly, the Oasis was completely abandoned by 1913. However, the nearby Dale Township was experiencing quite the opposite situation and was steadily increasing in population. The 1900 Census was the first available Census that included a location in the Morongo Basin; Dale. In the Census it is recorded that there were 44 residents, 13 Chemehuevi and three Serrano Indians living in the Dale District at the time. In 1910, a few more residents who's names would forever be remembered in the stories of local history moved to the Morongo Basin. George Barth, also known as Bill Keys, moved to the Joshua Tree area in 1910. Joseph Heard and Byron Pearce each filed homesteads near Warren's Well the same year.

Morongo Valley's first school, teaching grades 1 - 8, was opened in 1912 and was taught by an 18 year old young lady by the name of Lena Alice Sturdy. In 1914, during the first World War, many residents of the Morongo Basin left the area in order to work where they were needed more. Many more residents left shortly after that when the U.S. Government halted all mining in the area that didn't support the war. But even with a great deal of people finding their way elsewhere, the High Desert was still growing. 1915 saw the first School in Yucca Valley, the area then still commonly referred to simply as Warren's Well. The first teacher was Christine Snelling and the first class was made up of 15 students which included Christine's two younger brothers. The first Emergency School was held up in Pipes Canyon that same year.

People were truly spreading out a bit more evenly all over the High Desert. The 1920 Census showed that the Dale Township had dwindled down to only eight residents while the newly defined Morongo Precinct, now Morongo Valley, had a population of 26. Ten years later, the 1930 Census recorded the newly established Twentynine Palms Township, which encompassed the greater Morongo Basin, as having 258 residents. Travelers through the Morongo Basin started to see more homesteading families and settlers to the area as mining became just one of many ways to make a living in the High Desert. One example would be Mr. Harrell's story. Before 1922, the area that we now call Yucca Valley was casually referred to as "Warren's Well". But that changed after W.A. Harrell moved to the area from Texas.

Harrell settled near the present day intersection of Apache and HWY 62 where he established the Lone Star Ranch. There he sold gasoline, groceries, guns, hardware, livestock and anything else that people might ask for. The Lone Star Ranch even offered a Mail-Order Bride service to residents of the High Desert. From 1922 until 1946 the area we now call Yucca Valley was known on many maps, including AAA maps, as "Lone Star." In 1943 Ed & Hilda Hardesty purchased Lilly's Grocery Store in "Lone Star". A few years later they accepted a contract from the County of San Bernardino to house 30 USPS PO Boxes. Lilly chose the name "Yucca Valley" and the name stuck like a cactus quill.

Up in the mountains above Pipes Canyon, the first dam in Big Bear was built as far back as 1884. But the town didn't see many permanent residents other than trappers & prospectors until a new dam was built in 1912 and a highway bridge installed over it in 1923. During the later 1920's, many High Desert residents saw a number of tourists traveling both to and from the Big Bear area. But tourism truly began to soar once the Joshua Tree National Monument was established in 1936.

Unfortunately for prospectors, mining expenses started to grow too high for many to turn a profit throughout the 1930's. Shortly afterwards, the government halted all mining activity that didn't benefit WWII. The population would have taken a dive if it were not, in part, for the areas many cattle ranchers. Cattle ranching in the Morongo Basin reached its peak in the 1930's. Around this time, the massive IS Ranch once sold over 200,000 pounds of walking burger in a single transaction.

Even with the heavy tolls inflicted upon mining in the area, the population was steadily growing. John Colin Hastie was a Canadian born man who moved to Riverside and then to Twentynine Palms in 1937. Hastie saw a big opportunity in an up and coming area and began providing the first public transportation in the Morongo Basin: The 29 Palms Stage & Express. The 29 Palms Stage & Express offered to deliver anything under ten pounds for ten cents as well as a shuttle service. He drove "Old Betsy", which was a twelve-seat Eckland Streetcar that had been mounted atop a 1928 Chevrolet truck chassis and furnished with a wood-burning stove. Seven days a week, from Twentynine Palms down to Banning and back up, year after year, Hastie hauled passengers, banking transactions, shopping lists, bails of hay and just about anything else that you can think of.

Up above Old Betsy's route, in Landers, an airport was opened at Giant Rock in 1938. Travelers who didn't enjoy a long drive off the paved roads in order to get to Pipes Country or the surrounding villages could now fly right to the High Desert. The new accessibility to the High Desert didn't come a moment too soon. 1938 also saw the implementation and early effects of The Small Tract Act, more commonly referred to as the "Baby Homestead Act". It was enacted mainly in response to a great deal of WWI veterans who were interested and eager to move to the deserts of southern California for its many health benefits. Homesteaders were now allowed to claim tracts as small as five acres.

The general rate for individuals who were interested in homesteading the High Desert included a $5 Filing Fee before the land they wanted was then leased to them at an annual rate of $1 an acre. After leasing the land for three years, the only other requirement was that the homesteader build, at a minimum, a 10' by 12' structure on the property that passed government inspection. After three years of leasing the land and building at least a 1o' by 12' structure, homesteaders were able to then purchase the land for $1o to $2o an acre. The population started to rise faster than ever and was well documented in the 194o Census taken by W. L. Trigg, which recorded 1,o37 residents living in the Morongo Basin.

As more people moved to the High Desert, new roads started to cut through grazing pastures, newly built fences started to divide the landscape and automobiles started replacing horses on the dirt roads. All of this made it very difficult for local cattle ranchers to continue living off the land. Cattle ranchers in the Morongo Basin began to see the troubling effects of a growing population in the 193o's, but the ultimate blow came in 194o when the Taylor Grazing Act was passed and banned all grazing in the Joshua Tree Monument. By 1945, Jim Stocker, a former San Bernardino County Sheriff turned cattle rancher, held the last grazing permit in the Morongo Basin and kept his business in operation for many years. The very last recorded cattle drive through the High Desert was in 1957.

During WWII, from 1942 through 1945, Twentynine Palms was used as a naval auxiliary air station. Afterwards it was turned into the Marine Corps Training Center, Twentynine Palms. Over the years it has undergone numerous changes and is now officially known as the Marine Corps Air Ground Combat Center, Twentynine Palms. After WWII, the Morongo Basin saw a huge boom in homesteading and thousands of little brick and wood structures started to pop up all over the desert. The spectacle gave birth to the name "Jackrabbit Homesteaders", which became the commonly used name for people who took advantage of the Small Track Act's very minimal requirements for homesteading. The huge homesteading boom in the Morongo Basin was so big that at one point in time, Joshua Tree was actually called "The 5-Acre Tract Capital of the World".

By 1945, Pipes Country was a bustling little community with a very bright future and an ever increasing population. The villages that surrounded the Pipes were all bustling as well, with amenities like airports, lodging, public transportation, very easily attainable land and even a National Monument. Although America still stood in the shadow of WWII, the deserts of Southern California were blooming full of life and growth. The American dream lived on.

Chapter 2

The Infamous Dick Curtis

Dick Curtis was born Richard Duddly Dye on May 11th, 19o2, in Newport, Kentucky. His early life is a bit of a mystery, but he was recorded living in California as early as 1910 and working in Hollywood as young as 17. A 1910 census shows that his family lived in Apartment #47, at 7o6 Polk St, in San Francisco, CA. His first known acting role was in 1919 as an extra in the film *The Unpardonable Sin* alongside Blanche Sweet, Mary Alden, Wallace Beery and Bobby Connelly. In total, he made over 25o film and television appearances as an actor. In order to keep afloat during the earlier years of his career, Curtis worked quite a few different jobs between productions. He worked as a dish washer, an insurance salesman, a railroad brakeman and a soda jerk; just to name a few random positions.

He continued working in Hollywood as an extra and bit player through the 192o's before heading east and spending some time working on Broadway. Some of his work there included *Live and Learn* and *Damn Your Honor*. It is assumed that while working in New York, he adopted the name "Richard Curtis" as his stage name. A New York City marriage record shows that on June 11th, 1924, a 22 year old Curtis married then 21 year old Elsie H. Spencer. It is unknown how long they stayed married, however Curtis' son, John Curtis, was born in 1929. Curtis soon left New York and returned to Hollywood sometime around 193o to continue his acting career.

In 1932, while filming the original classic, *King Kong*, Curtis was seriously injured while portraying one of Cal Denham's crewmen. While the incident only left him with a broken ankle and the need for an emergency appendix operation, the initial reports of the accident stated that Curtis had died from the injuries he sustained. On July 7, 1934 the *Hollywood Filmograph* wrote about Curtis' accident while filming *King Kong*. Even though the article headline read "*VERY MUCH ALIVE*" and previously filmed productions that Curtis had worked on continued to debut throughout that year, some people still thought that he had died until he returned to work. But he wouldn't actually return to acting for almost two whole years as a result of those injuries.

At the age of 33, Curtis would marry Ruth M. Sullivan, another 21 year old girl. They were married December 2nd, 1935 in Santa Ana, CA, and they would remain together until Curtis' death almost 17 years later. The marriage license shows that he lived in a house at 1536 N. Western Blvd, Hollywood, CA, during that time. The Good Samaritan Hospital in Los Angeles is just five and a half miles away from that house and was likely where Curtis received extended treatment during his recovery from the *King Kong* accident. Ruth had a friend named Margie who was a nurse at The Good Samaritan Hospital. Margie married a former patient of her's named Frank Mattoon who was a friend of Curtis'. After Frank and Margie Mattoon got married they moved out to Pipes Country.

Throughout the 1930's, Westerns, and more-so the menacing roles of the villains in said Westerns, became Curtis' main niche. He worked alongside Hollywood heavyweights like Kermit Maynard, Tom Mix, Tim McCoy, Johnny Mack Brown, Fred Scott, Bill Elliott and Charles Starrett. Starrett, who starred alongside the infamous Curtis in two dozen films, was said to refer to his constant on-screen run-ins with Curtis as "the never ending fight". It is highly likely that sometime while he was working for Columbia Pictures from 1938 to 1944, Curtis was introduced to The Sons of the Pioneers who were signed on as Starrett's supporting singing group in 1937.

For several years in the late 1930's, while at the the height of his career, Curtis worked in over 40 productions a year. Standing at 6'3", typically looking mean or angry in most of his roles, more often wearing a neat, recognizable mustache and repeatedly playing a villain or henchmen - Curtis became known as "the meanest man in Hollywood". Much to the contrary, all reports of Curtis' private life tend to paint the portrait of a very courteous, creative, fun, happy, polite and professional man. While working for Columbia Pictures, he was able to stretch his acting abilities ever so slightly when he became a frequent adversary to *The Three Stooges* and played villains more comical than menacing.

In 1936 Curtis's daughter, Phyllis, was born. The 1940 Census shows that Curtis and his wife Ruth lived at 6816 Woodrow Wilson Drive, Los Angeles, CA. It also shows that in the year 1939, Curtis worked 49 weeks and earned over $5,000. Although he slowed down some, Curtis kept very busy during the early half of the 1940's, working in almost 60 productions from 1940 through 1945. Almost all of his work from 1938 until 1944 was done exclusively for Columbia Pictures before he started to branch out and work for other studios like Universal Republic. His role as Tartar Chieftain in *The Phantom* marked the last serial he would do for Columbia before working on one of Universal's last serials, *Lost City of the Jungle*, with Russell Hayden. Curtis' career was in full stride. He didn't know it yet; but he was about to create something that would change his life, the lives of many other people and the very history of Hollywood.

If you ask people how Dick Curtis found Pioneertown, you will commonly hear one of two answers: The legends or the facts. It's a sad fact that Curtis died at a young age and took much of Pioneertown's undocumented history with him to the grave. While researching for this book, multiple failed attempts were made in an attempt to find living relatives or close personal friends to interview. Unfortunately, his second wife and children have all passed away, as have many of the other people who were associated with the origins of Pioneertown, CA.

In the absence of Curtis, or anyone else of authority to fill us in on all the facts, the research for this book utilized local research centers, old news papers & publications, San Bernardino & Los Angeles county records, old maps, land title records and business records. After thorough investigation, there are still some paramount questions left unanswered and some very gray areas left up to debate. That all being said, we can say one thing for sure: Dick Curtis is truly the father Pioneertown!

The legend has a few different variations but has stayed pretty consistent since the 1940's. The story starts off with an old lady that Curtis knew in Los Angeles. She was ill and borrowed $25 from Curtis, either to pay a doctor's fee or to purchase medication. When she wasn't able to repay the loan in cash, she gave Curtis a deed to some undeveloped land north of Los Angeles to cover her debt. He later sold that land for $150 and took the money to a Southern Pacific land agent where he said something to the effect of "put this money towards some more sand".

His investment grew for a number of years and he soon found himself with a considerable amount of property in the desert north of the booming town of Palm Springs. His land laid inside what was then called Pipes Country, which encompassed present day Pipes Wash, Pipes Canyon, Gamma Gulch, Yucca Mesa, the Sawtooth Mountains, Pioneertown, Chaparrosa Wash and Water Canyon. He was under the impression that the land was simply worthless sand, unable to support more than cactus and rocks. But he was curious about his investment all the same and decided to check it out for himself. After arriving at Palm Springs, presumably in 1945, Curtis found that the land was only accessible by horseback. But that didn't stop him.

Curtis saddled up and set out through Yucca Valley for a first hand view of his desert land investment. When he found himself on his property he was atop a large plateau of tall swaying grass, surrounded by tall mountains on all sides. He said something to the effect of "this is it" to his horse and immediately knew what he wanted to do. He then headed back to Los Angeles to gather support for what would soon be called Pioneertown. . . Or so the story goes.

What we know as fact and what is most logically assumable about how Curtis actually discovered Pioneertown presents a few significant key arguments to the legends. Southern Pacific Railroad had acquired the land in the 1870's and there are no records of the land being bought or sold before 1946. By 1945 the area soon to be Pioneertown was surrounded by established settlements like Lone Star (Yucca Valley) to the south plus Rimrock and Pipes Canyon to the north. Around the age of 43, Dick Curtis visited Pipes Country and the spot that inspired him to create Pioneertown. The most logical route he would have taken was *not* along the cattle trail through Water Canyon in northern Lone Star, a similar route to that of present day Pioneertown Road, but south from Pipes Canyon.

Dick and his wife Ruth's friends from Los Angeles, Frank and Margie Mattoon, operated the largest egg farm in the High Desert from their property in Pipes Canyon during the 1940's. It is highly probable that Curtis *didn't* ride up into the hills alone when he came across the future location of Pioneertown. He was more likely visiting his friend's farm which was just a few miles to the north. The Mattoons delivered eggs to all the surrounding villages, by horse *and* by car, which means that there was already an established road within three miles of future Pioneertown.

All of this information is thrown askew when facts from Joshua Tree National Parks's past are revealed. In the 1940's, Joshua Tree officials were worried about the vast many acres of non-federal land that still resided inside of the Monument's boundaries. In 1945, Dick Curtis announced that he planned to purchase nearly 3,500 acres of land from the Southern Pacific Railroad, which still owned the majority of the non-federal land in Joshua Tree at that time. The acreage that he planned to purchase was a large portion of the Lost Horse Valley, right in the heart of the JTNM. Curtis made his plans to establish Pioneertown in Lost Horse Valley public, making it perfectly clear that he already had the idea for Pioneertown early in 1945.

In an effort to solidify the JTNM's boundaries, Monument Superintendents James Cole and Frank Givens, along with Nation Park Service Realty Specialists, negotiated a very detailed and complex land swap and purchase with Southern Pacific Railroad. The deal lead to the Monument receiving more than 12,800 acres of SPR land inside of Lost Horse Valley and Dick Curtis acquiring public land in what is now Pioneertown. Perhaps that story about Curtis loaning an old lady money, which later lead to his purchasing land from SPR, was true and the SPR land in question was located in Lost Horse Valley.

However Curtis reached his destination, it is certain that he fell in love with the land that later became Pioneertown and that he already dreamed of constructing a Western themed movie ranch to be built both as a traditional town and a filming location. His idea would serve as a permanent location for shooting westerns, a town for permanent residents and tourists alike, a money saver and a potential money maker - a living breathing movie set right in the heart of a very progressive desert community. Curtis headed back to Los Angeles to formulate his plans for the land's potential.

How he found the land for sure is sadly unknown. But in the 194o's, the surrounding desert cities were a hot spot for tourists, prospectors, adventurers, western enthusiasts and general progressive expansion, as well as a popular vacation area for Hollywood's elite. One thing that is clear for sure, without any shadow of a doubt: however Curtis came across the land that became Pioneertown, he undeniably left his mark on it!

King Kong (1933) Left to right are Dick Curtis, Fay Wray & Bruce Cabot

Dick Curtis' List of Acting Credits:

1919 - The Unpardonable Sin - Uncredited
1926 - Tell It to the Marines - Marine in Barracks (uncredited)
1930 - Shooting Straight - Butch
1930 - The Silver Horde   Fight Spectator - (uncredited)
1930 - Up the River - New Inmate (uncredited)
1931 - Secret Service - Prisoner Buying Goobers (uncredited)
1932 - Girl Crazy - Cowboy Giving Directions (uncredited)
1932 - Hell's House - Cop on the Beat (uncredited)
1932 - The Famous Ferguson Case - O'Toole (uncredited)
1933 - King Kong - Member of Ship's Crew (uncredited)
1933 - The Druggist's Dilemma (Short) - Man in Crowd (uncredited)
1934 - A Successful Failure - Man in Rally Crowd (uncredited)
1934 - King Kelly of the U.S.A. Otto - Palace Guard (uncredited)
1934 - The Silver Streak - Boulder Dam Foreman (uncredited)
1935 - Clive of India - Hoodlum on Dock (uncredited)
1935 - Code of the Mounted - Snakey/Henchman
1935 - Condemned to Live - Villager at Pit Rim (uncredited)
1935 - Just My Luck - Henchman (uncredited)
1935 - Mutiny Ahead - Stevens
1935 - Northern Frontier - Pete/Henchman (uncredited)
1935 - Racing Luck - Dynamite
1935 - Romance in Manhattan - Man at East River (uncredited)
1935 - Skybound - Master of Ceremonies (uncredited)
1935 - The Arizonian - Saloon Patron (uncredited)
1935 - The Miracle Rider - Copelee (uncredited)
1935 - The Nitwits - Cop on Stakeout (uncredited)
1935 - Trails of the Wild - Henchman Roper
1935 - Western Courage - Henchman Bat (uncredited)
1935 - Western Frontier - Pioneer Settler (uncredited)
1935 - Wilderness Mail - Henchman Jacques
1936 - Burning Gold - Swede
1936 - Crashing Thru Danger - Foreman
1936 - Daniel Boone - Vince/Frontiersman (uncredited)
1936 - Federal Agent - Curbside Cabbie (uncredited)
1936 - Ghost Patrol - Henchman Charlie
1936 - Go-Get-'Em, Haines - Mike/Cab Driver (uncredited)
1936 - Phantom Patrol - Henchman Josef
1936 - The Crooked Trail - Kirk/Miner (uncredited)
1936 - The Lion's Den - Henchman Slim Burtis
1936 - The Traitor - Henchman Morgan
1936 - Wild Horse Round-Up - Bill
1936 - Wildcat Trooper - Henri (uncredited)
1937 - A Lawman Is Born - Lefty Drogan
1937 - Bar-Z Bad Men - Brent/Ranch Foreman
1937 - Boothill Brigade - Bull Berke
1937 - Counsel for Crime - Hood (uncredited)
1937 - Guns in the Dark - Brace Stevens
1937 - Headline Crasher - Joe (uncredited)
1937 - Life Begins with Love - Radical (uncredited)
1937 - Moonlight on the Range - Henchman Hank
1937 - Motor Madness - Sailor (uncredited)
1937 - Murder in Greenwich Village - Campbell Security Guard (uncredited)
1937 - One Man Justice - Henchman Hank Skinner
1937 - Outlaws of the Prairie - Dragg
1937 - Paid to Dance - Mike Givens
1937 - The Frame-Up - Slim (uncredited)
1937 - The Gambling Terror - Henchman Dick

1937 - The Game That Kills - Whitey
1937 - The Old Wyoming Trail - Ed Slade
1937 - The Shadow - Carlos
1937 - The Singing Buckaroo - Henchman Odie
1937 - Trail of Vengeance - Henchman Cartwright
1937 - Two Gun Law - Len Edwards
1937 - Valley of Terror - Henchman Buck
1937 - Blake of Scotland Yard - Henchman Nicky
1938 - A Nag in the Bag (Short) - Dan the Bookie (uncredited)
1938 - Adventure in Sahara - Karnoldi
1938 - Blondie - Daily Gazette Reporter (uncredited)
1938 - Call of the Rockies - Matt Stark
1938 - Cattle Raiders - Ed Munro
1938 - City Streets - M. C. Welfare Officer (uncredited)
1938 - Flat Foot Stooges (Short) - Mr. Reardon
1938 - Juvenile Court - Detective Capturing Dutch Adams (uncredited)
1938 - Law of the Plains - Jim Fletcher
1938 - Little Miss - Roughneck (uncredited)
1938 - Penitentiary - Tex (uncredited)
1938 - Rawhide - Butch/Saunders Henchman
1938 - Reformatory - Guard (uncredited)
1938 - Rio Grande - Ed Barker
1938 - Smashing the Spy Ring - Williams (uncredited)
1938 - South of Arizona - Ed Martin
1938 - Squadron of Honor - Craig
1938 - The Colorado Trail - Henchman Slash Driscoll
1938 - The Lady Objects - Jail Guard (uncredited)
1938 - The Little Adventuress - Race Starter (uncredited)
1938 - The Lone Wolf in Paris - Palace Vault Guard (uncredited)
1938 - The Main Event - Sawyer
1938 - The Spider's Web - Malloy (uncredited)
1938 - Time Out for Trouble (Short) - Louie Derringer
1938 - West of Cheyenne - Link Murdock
1938 - West of the Santa Fe - Matt Taylor
1938 - Who Killed Gail Preston? - Henchman Mike
1938 - Women in Prison - Mac
1938 - You Can't Take It with You - Strongarm Man (uncredited)
1939 - All-American Blondes (Short) - (uncredited)
1939 - Behind Prison Gates - Capt. Simmons
1939 - Blind Alley - Trooper with Joe (uncredited)
1939 - Boom Goes the Groom (Short) (uncredited)
1939 - Flying G-Men - Henchman Korman
1939 - Glove Slingers (Short) - Madigan/Kid Benson's Trainer (uncredited)
1939 - Homicide Bureau - Radio Broadcaster (voice, uncredited)
1939 - Let Us Live - Convict on Death Row (uncredited)
1939 - Mandrake, the Magician - Dorgan/Thug
1939 - Missing Daughters - Henchman (uncredited)
1939 - My Son Is a Criminal - Gangster (uncredited)
1939 - My Son Is Guilty - Monk
1939 - North of Shanghai - Creighton
1939 - Now It Can Be Sold (Short) (uncredited)
1939 - Oily to Bed, Oily to Rise (Short) - Clipper/Swindler in Back Seat (uncredited)
1939 - Outpost of the Mounties Wade Beaumont
1939 - Outside These Walls - Flint
1939 - Overland with Kit Carson - Henchman Drake
1939 - Riders of Black River - Blaize Carewe
1939 - Romance of the Redwoods - Gas Station Attendant (uncredited)
1939 - Scandal Sheet - Guard
1939 - Spoilers of the Range - Lobo Savage

1939 - Taming of the West - Rawhide
1939 - The Amazing Mr. Williams - Joe (uncredited)
1939 - The Awful Goof (Short) - Joe Mark
1939 - The Lone Wolf Spy Hunt - Heavy (uncredited)
1939 - The Man They Could Not Hang - Jury Foreman Clifford Kearney
1939 - The Stranger from Texas - Bat Stringer
1939 - The Thundering West - Wolf Munro
1939 - Those High Grey Walls - Convict (uncredited)
1939 - Trouble Finds Andy Clyde (Short) - Policeman
1939 - Two-Fisted Rangers - Henchman Dirk Hogan
1939 - We Want Our Mummy (Short) - Jackson (uncredited)
1939 - Western Caravans - Mort Kohler
1939 - Yes, We Have No Bonanza (Short) - Maxey
1940 - Blazing Six Shooters - Lash Bender
1940 - Blondie on a Budget - Tony/Mechanic (uncredited)
1940 - Boom Town - Hiring Boss (uncredited)
1940 - Bullets for Rustlers - Strang
1940 - Men Without Souls - Duke
1940 - Pioneers of the Frontier - Matt Brawley
1940 - Ragtime Cowboy Joe - Bo Gilman
1940 - Rockin' Thru the Rockies (Short) - Indian Chief (uncredited)
1940 - Terry and the Pirates - Master Fang
1940 - Texas Stagecoach   Shoshone - Larsen
1940 - The Son of Monte Cristo - Guard (uncredited)
1940 - Three Men from Texas - Gardner
1940 - Wyoming   Corky - Henchman (uncredited)
1940 - You Nazty Spy! (Short) - Mr. Ohnay (uncredited)
1941 - Across the Sierras - Mitch Carew
1941 - Arizona Cyclone - Quirt Crenshaw
1941 - Billy the Kid - Kirby Claxton
1941 - Ellery Queen and the Murder Ring - Policeman (uncredited)
1941 - Honky Tonk - Tough Man on Train (uncredited)
1941 - I Was a Prisoner on Devil's Island - Jules
1941 - Mystery Ship - Van Brock
1941 - Sea Raiders - Mate on the 'Astoria' (uncredited)
1941 - So Ends Our Night - Gestapo Stormtrooper (uncredited)
1941 - Stick to Your Guns - Nevada Teale
1941 - The Roundup - Ed Crandall
1942 - City of Silent Men - Frank Muller
1942 - Jackass Mail - Jim Swade
1942 - Men of San Quentin - Butch Mason
1942 - Pardon My Gun - Clint Hayes (uncredited)
1942 - Shut My Big Mouth - Henchman (uncredited)
1942 - Tombstone: The Town Too Tough to Die - Frank McLowery
1942 - Two Yanks in Trinidad - Sea Captain
1942 - Vengeance of the West - Jeff Gorman
1943 - Batman - Agent Croft of Section 50 (uncredited)
1943 - Cowboy in the Clouds - Roy Madison
1943 - Higher Than a Kite (Short) - Gen. Bommel (uncredited)
1943 - I Can Hardly Wait (Short) - Patient (uncredited)
1943 - Jack London - Cannery Foreman (uncredited)
1943 - Riders of the Northwest - Mounted   Victor Renaud (uncredited)
1943 - Salute to the Marines - Cpl. Mosley
1943 - The Cross of Lorraine - Nazi Guard in Village (uncredited)
1943 - The Phantom - Tartar Chieftain (uncredited)
1943 - You Can't Beat the Law - Prison Guard (uncredited)
1944 - Crash Goes the Hash (Short) - Prince Shaam of Ubeedarn
1944 - Gambler's Choice - Mr. Hadley (uncredited)
1944 - Hey, Rookie - Sergeant (uncredited)
1944 - His Hotel Sweet (Short) - Undetermined Role

(uncredited)
1944 - Lady in the Death House - Willis Millen
1944 - Mystery of the River Boat - Craig Cassard
1944 - Spook Town - Sam Benson
1944 - The Black Parachute - German Lieutenant (uncredited)
1944 - Waterfront - Drunken Sailor (uncredited)
1945 - Blonde from Brooklyn - Soldier (uncredited)
1945 - High Powered - Worker (uncredited)
1945 - Off Again, on Again (Short) - Louie Derringer
1945 - Pistol Packin' Nitwits (Short) - Rawhide Pete
1945 - Scared Stiff - Bus Driver (uncredited)
1945 - Scarlet Street - Detective (uncredited)
1945 - Snooper Service (Short) - (uncredited)
1945 - The Bandit of Sherwood Forest - Castle Gate Guard (uncredited)
1945 - The Great John L. - Waldo (uncredited)
1945 - The Last Installment (Short) - Brannigan Bull Henchman (uncredited)
1945 - The Master Key - Reicher (uncredited)
1945 - The Mayor's Husband (Short) - Gangster
1945 - Wagon Wheels Westward - Henchman Tuttle
1946 - Abilene Town - Cap' Ryker
1946 - California Gold Rush - Chopin/the Harmonica Killer
1946 - Get Along Little Zombie (Short) - Joe Mulligan
1946 - Hot Water (Short) - Malloy
1946 - Lawless Breed - Bartley Mellon and Captain Isaac Mellon
1946 - Lost City of the Jungle - Henchman Johnson
1946 - Renegade Girl - Joe Barnes (as Richard Curtis)
1946 - Santa Fe Uprising - Henchman Luke Case
1946 - Song of Arizona - Henchman Bart
1946 - The Scarlet Horseman - Jed (uncredited)
1946 - The Three Troubledoers (Short) - Badlands Blackie
1946 - Traffic in Crime - Jake Schultz
1946 - Wild Beauty - John Andrews
1947 - Bride and Gloom (Short) - Joe Keeler
1947 - Wyoming - Ed Lassiter
1949 - Navajo Trail Raiders - Henchman Brad
1950 - Bad Medicine - Clint Bolton
1950 - Man of the House - Spike
1950 - Matter of Courage - Soapy Farrell
1950 - T.N.T. - Henchman Ed Simms
1950 - The Sheriff of Santa Rosa - Hutch Logan
1950 - A Slip and a Miss (Short) - Neighbor's husband
1950 - Cargo to Capetown - Charlie - Sailor in Bar (uncredited)
1950 - Covered Wagon Raid - Henchman Grif
1950 - Rock Island Trail - Barton/Railroad Agitator (uncredited)
1950 - The Gunfighter - Townsman at Funeral (uncredited)
1950 - The Jackpot - Moving Man (uncredited)
1950 - The Lone Ranger (TV Series) - Clint Bolton / Soapy Farrell / Spike
1950 - The Outriders - Outrider at Dance (uncredited)
1950 - The Sun Sets at Dawn - Guard (uncredited)
1950 - The Vanishing Westerner - Bartender
1950 - Wabash Avenue - Jim/Poker Player (uncredited)
1950-1951 The Gene Autry Show (TV Series) - Johnny McLean/Doc Leary/Sam Foreman/ Ed Simms
1951 - Frame for Trouble - Sam/Foreman
1951 - Gunslinger in Paradise - Noah Geiger
1951 - Harsh Reckoning - Henchman Bob Guthry
1951 - Lady Mayor - Sheriff Graham
1951 - Revenge Trail - Johnny McLean, alias Doc Leary
1951 - Right of Way - Crutch Bellows
1951 - Six Gun Party - Henchman Max
1951 - The Ghost of Poco Loco - Henchman Clint
1951 - Western Fugitive - Sam Dawson

1951 - Whiplash - Rawhide
1951 - Adventures of Wild Bill Hickok (TV Series) - Sheriff Graham
1951 - Chicago Calling - Road Gang Foreman (uncredited)
1951 - Don't Throw That Knife (Short) - Mr. Wycoff
1951 - Government Agents vs Phantom Legion - Regan
1951 - Inside Straight - Marshal (uncredited)
1951 - Lorna Doone - Garth (uncredited)
1951 - Rawhide - Hawley (uncredited)
1951 - Red Ryder (TV Series) - Rawhide
1951 - Roar of the Iron Horse, Rail-Blazer of the Apache Trail - Campo/The Baron's Chief Gunman
1951 - The Range Rider (TV Series) - Sam Dawson / Henchman Max / Crutch Bellows
1951 - The Red Badge of Courage - Veteran (uncredited)
1951 - The Texas Rangers - Prison Guard (uncredited)
1951 - The Tooth Will Out (Short) - Shemp's Last Patient (uncredited)
1951 - Three Arabian Nuts (Short) - Hassan
1951 - Whirlwind - Lon Kramer
1952 - Bronco Buster - Bartender (uncredited)
1952 - Heebie Gee-Gees (Short) - Big Dan
1952 - My Six Convicts - Guard (uncredited)
1952 - Rootin' Tootin' Tenderfeet (Short) - Mr. Luke
1952 - Rose of Cimarron - Clem Dawley

The Three Stooges #131 *Don't Throw That Knife* (1951) Shemp, Larry, Moe & Dick Curtis

Lost City of the Jungle (1946) L. Atwill & Dick Curtis

Rio Grande (1938) Charles Starrett & Dick Curtis

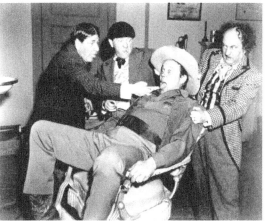

The Three Stooges #134 *The Tooth Will Out* (1951) Shemp, Moe, Larry & Dick Curtis

Chapter 3
Pioneertown Incorporates

World War II officially ended September 2nd of 1945. But America had lived under its dark shadow for quite a long time by that point. It was an era of great efficiency, pride and patriotism. During the war, Americans had rationed extensively. They had been encouraged to farm and hunt their own food and they were basically required to either enlist, work, educate, entertain, donate or do whatever they possibly could to support America's fight. After the war, anything that promoted growth, independence, resourcefulness or living the American dream was highly supported by all.

Curtis was no stranger to the Hollywood scene at that time. By 1945 he had over 180 acting credits to his name. Western themed movies and serials were in full stride then. Half or so of Hollywood's elite wore cowboy hats and boots regularly. While he did have plenty of roles off the dusty trails of the western frontier; Curtis spent a great majority of his time wearing cowboy duds in front of the camera.

Location shooting in Westerns became more popular in the late 1930's and shortly after, one thing that Curtis began to notice about almost every one of his cowboy themed acting jobs was the large budget a production company needed to create sets for filming. In some cases, half mile long false-front filled city blocks and even entire towns might have been constructed in order to film a single movie. This was the norm at the time. But there is always room for improvement.

Exactly when and how Dick Curtis discovered the area that would become Pioneertown are a bit of a mystery, but the basic layout of his grand idea was relatively well documented. He was convinced that the land had the potential to evenly and synergistically benefit production companies, celebrities, current High Desert residents, those interested in moving to the desert and even tourists. Curtis imagined a western themed town, to be constructed with multiple intentions: a film production friendly town, complete with the necessities to support the natural pulse of full-time residents. A living, breathing movie set.

Curtis believed that if the land were developed into a small western themed town which could easily cater to film production companies, then there would always be ample work and business for the residents. Said production companies would simultaneously stand to save a great deal of money by renting a fully furnished and functioning town instead of constructing filming locations. The town would also serve as a great tourist destination which would help to further promote both the local and California State economies.

Furthermore, there was an obvious thrill associated with the idea of erecting a town that could so easily benefit a great number of people while also being directly related to Curtis' particular line of work. The plan that Curtis had conceived was a grand one! One much too large for any single man to bring to life. He was an established actor and lived quite well for those times, but he wasn't wealthy enough to erect a town all on his own. To see his dream come to life, Curtis would need money, partners, promoters, civil engineering experts, permits, a real estate team and help from plenty of other professionals.

Just like its original discovery, Curtis' first promoting of Pioneertown is also a bit of a mystery. In 1945 he had a long list of celebrity friends and colleagues, many of whom were big hitters in the Hollywood scene. The land he hoped to develop offered so much western geological diversity that it could easily be played off as just about any western State in America. It was an isolated area while still remaining close to a very up and coming area, complete with a newly established National Monument and just a short drive from both Palm Springs and Los Angeles. These were all facts which made the concept's potential easy to advertise. Add to that the great savings that the town could potentially offer to film production companies, the possibility of large profits that initial town investors, businesses and residents stood to earn and the opportunities it could offer people both in and out of the Hollywood scene.. All said and done, Curtis' idea was truly as good as gold!

It is unclear who Curtis approached with his idea first, but it didn't take long for him to find the right people to help bring his dream to life. Years before, while working alongside Charles Starrett, Curtis got to know Starrett's musical group, The Sons of The Pioneers, as well as actor Roy Rogers and Rogers' sidekick, Smiley Burnette. While working on *Lost City of the Jungle* in 1945 he grew a closer friendship with Western actor Russell Hayden. It is presumed that Curtis met Frank McDonald through Roy Rogers or Russell Hayden, as they had both previously worked with the veteran Western director on multiple occasions.

Of all the names in Curtis' address book in 1945, Roy Rogers was surely the most famous. A couple years earlier in 1943, Rogers was voted the Number One Western Star At The Box Office at which point Republic Pictures began billing him as the "King of the Cowboys". At one point in the early developmental process of Curtis' dream, it is reported that the title "Rogersville" was actually considered for the town's name. While it would have been a valid marketing approach to attach Rogers' name to the town at the time, one can only assume that the name "Rogersville" was scrapped for multiple reasons.

While Rogers' played an absolutely huge role in the project, he didn't actually discover the area, nor was he responsible for the town's original conception. Dick's impressive acting career aside, the name "Curtisville" wouldn't have brought in a fraction of the attention that Rogers' stardom would have attracted. Furthermore, no one wanted any one person's name to preponderate the spirit that they wanted the town to radiate. The Sons of the Pioneers were quite famous during that time and they attracted a much broader audience while still appealing mainly to Western fans. That is presumably why Curtis and his partners decided to name the project "Pioneertown". The Sons of the Pioneers are still an active music group to this day and were actually one of the USA's earliest Western singing groups.

Curtis' dream for a living breathing movie set in the High Deserts of California had grown into an actual plan. With his friends backing up his concept, inspiring new ideas and helping to formulate the details of their prospect; Pioneertown's groundwork was laid down at a rapid rate. The dream that initially struck Curtis quickly turned infectious to anyone who became involved and soon excitement began to inspire an angst among everyone to see their dreams in person, not just on paper and in their heads. That angst drove Curtis and his partners to finalize their plans post haste.

Pioneertown was surely becoming a reality sooner than later and the excitement among all of those involved was palpable. The early days of its incorporation are a bit hazy and tend to be divided between the legends and the facts. The story that has been told from as far back as 1946 speaks of Curtis seeking out 17 investors who each put up $5oo to fund incorporating Pioneertown. However, to this day, not a single article, biography, record or story, old or new, has ever listed all 17 of the said investors.

In fact, all previous recordings of the events have failed to list off more than five or six of the original investors, if you don't count when they list The Sons of the Pioneers. But even if you added up all the members of The Sons of the Pioneers during 1945 - 1946, along with all the other names listed in the most detailed accounts of Pioneertown's history, you still don't get 17 investors. This is probably due to the fact that the original "investments", if there were indeed any, were handled as private or personal loans. To date, there are only three names on all of Pioneertown's business records filed in the State of California: Dick Curtis, Thomas Carr and Frank E. Gray.

While it isn't substantiated that there were truly 17 original investors who ponied up $5oo to help get Pioneertown incorporated, it is highly believed to have been the case. Alternate possibilities might have been that the "17 original investors" were in fact the people who purchased Pioneertown's first preferred stock options, or, were the first people who committed to buying land in Pioneertown and were then reported as "original investors". In all honesty, it could have literally just meant 17 of Curtis' closest and most famous friends at that time. Dick Curtis' acting career was in full stride back then and it is hard to believe that he would have needed to borrow $8,5oo from 17 people. After thorough, diligent, investigation of Pioneertown advertisements, key celebrity biographies, newspaper archives plus City, State and County public business, land and title records - the names of potential original investors have been narrowed down to a small handful of prime suspects.

Whether they were investors before or after Pioneertown's actual incorporation, these are the people who are most likely to have been Dick Curtis' "original 17 investors". They are listed from top to bottom by those with the most potential to the least:

- Russell "Lucky" Hayden: Western Actor, Producer, Director, Friend of Curtis' and one of the First Land Owners and Developers in Pioneertown
- Roy Rogers: Western Actor, Friend of Curtis', A Founding Member of The Sons of the Pioneers and One of the First Land Owners in Pioneertown
- Dale Evans: Western Actress, Wife of Roy Rogers and One of the First Land Owners in Pioneertown
- Tommy Carr: A Member of The Sons of the Pioneers, Friend of Curtis' and One of the Three People Listed in Pioneertown's California Business Incorporation Documents
- Bob Nolan: A Founding Member of The Sons of the Pioneers, Friend of Curtis' and One of the First Land Owners in Pioneertown
- Lloyd Perryman: A Member of the Sons of the Pioneers, Friend of Curtis' and One of the First Land Owners in Pioneertown
- Shug Fisher: A Member of the Sons of the Pioneers, Friend of Curtis' and One of the First Land Owners in Pioneertown
- Minna Gombell: Movie Actress, Friend of Curtis' and one of the First Land Owners as well as the Only Celebrity to Develop Land in Pioneertown Other Than Russell & Mousie Hayden
- Frank E. Gray: Unknown Investor and One of the Three People Listed in Pioneertown's California Business Incorporation Documents Other Than Curtis
- Frank McDonald: Famous Western Director and Friend of Curtis' who later Worked in Pioneertown Quite a Lot
- Terry Frost: A Member of The Sons of the Pioneers, Named as an Original Pioneertown Investor Independently from The Sons of the Pioneers on Multiple Accounts and Friend of Curtis'
- Bud Abbott: Comedian, Actor, Friend of Curtis' and a Frequent Pioneertown Visitor
- Ken Carson: Western Actor, Friend of Curtis' and a Frequent Pioneertown Visitor
- Louella Parsons: Screenwriter, America's First Movie Columnist, Friend of Curtis' and a Frequent Pioneertown Visitor
- Ralph Dawson: Three Time Academy Award Winning Film Editor, Friend of Curtis' and a Frequent Pioneertown Visitor
- *MAYBE* - Tim Spencer, Karl Farr, Hugh Farr and/or Pat Brady: Other Members of The Sons of the Pioneers During 1945/46, All Friends of Curtis' and All Frequent Pioneertown Visitors
- *MAYBE* - Lillian Porter "Mousie" Hayden: Actress, Wife of Russell "Lucky" Hayden and One of the First Land Owners and Developers in Pioneertown
- *MAYBE* - Lou Costello: Comedian, Actor, Famous Partner of Bud Abbott, Friend of Curtis' and a

Frequent Pioneertown Visitor
- *MAYBE* - Adele Mara: Actress, Friends with both Curtis & Rogers and a Frequent Pioneertown Visitor
- *MAYBE* - Gene Autry: World Famous Western Actor and Friend of Everyone Listed Above (With the possible exception of Frank E. Gray)
- *MAYBE* - Fletcher Jones: An Original Member of the Pioneertown Board of Directors, Land Owner and Developer in Pioneertown
- *MAYBE* - William Murphy: An Original Member of the Pioneertown Board of Directors, Land Owner and Developer in Pioneertown

Dick Curtis set up the company's first office in what was then part of the illustrious Studio City, at 8511 Sunset Blvd, Los Angeles, CA 90046. The building they occupied is now known as the Sterling Sunset Plaza, sister to the historic Sterling Plaza in Beverly Hills. One of 30 P.O. Boxes available in Yucca Valley, Box 29, was set up under the name "Mane Street Pioneertown". Pioneertown's first two land purchases were both from Southern Pacific Railroad sometime in early 1946 after working over contracts for months with the Joshua Tree National Monument and SPR.

The newly purchased land included the 13,000 acres that made up Pioneertown and Rimrock, followed by an additional 4,000 acres of land between the two small villages. The rest of the area Curtis wanted to purchase, an additional 15,000 acres, was federal land owned by the U.S. government at that time. It is said that the federal land contract was a nightmare to finalize, but Curtis was sly as a fox and saw to it that the deal went through as quick as possible. It is fun to note that if Dick Curtis had wound up purchasing land in Lost Horse Valley instead of Pipes Country, the name "Mane Street" would have fit the area like a glove!

In May of 1946, with a total of 17,000 acres of land at the time, Pioneertown hired William E. Grigsby to survey the area and make an appraisal of their investment. His original appraisal of the land was for $394,861.54. While the original investors might not be known for sure, the documents of Pioneertown's incorporation were signed on March 18th and filed in the State of California on March 25th, 1946. Their original authorized capital stock value was $500,000, which was divided into 255,000 shares. 5,000 shares of preferred stock valued at $50 each and 250,000 shares of common stock valued at $1 each. Only nine of the common shares were secured. They were equally divided between Dick Curtis, Thomas Carr and Frank E. Gray, whom each paid $3 for their three secured shares of common stock.

The following month, on April 23rd, they changed their total number of stock shares to 500,000 shares: 250,000 shares of preferred stock valued at $1 each and 250,000 shares of common stock valued at $1 each. Then on May 6th, they changed their authorized capital stock value to $1,500,000, which was then divided into 1,500,000 shares. 250,000 shares of preferred stock valued at $1 each and 1,250,000 shares of common stock valued at $1 each. On September 23rd, 1946, they dropped the "Land" portion of their name and officially became the Pioneertown Corporation.

Pioneertown had a great many supporters, investors, board members and employees. While there is a great deal of recorded Pioneertown Corporation history, it is difficult to piece together the entire crew. This is a list of the confirmed Pioneertown Team Members:
- Dick Curtis: President and General Manager
- Tommy Carr: First Vice President
- Frank McDonald: Second Vice President
- Russell Hayden: Treasurer
- Alexander Bradner: Architect and Planning Commissioner
- Fred Moninger: Architect and Planning Engineer (Assistant to Alexander Bradner)

- Daniel Keohane: Secretary
- Maude Ransom: Assistant Secretary-Treasurer
- Richard M. Wambsgans: Registered Accountant and Auditor
- Fletcher Jones: Member of the Board of Directors
- William Murphy: Member of the Board of Directors
- Charles L. Nichols: Member of the Board of Directors
- William E. Grigsby: Land Surveyor and Appraiser
- Bill Dennis: Land Promoter and Co-Head of Pioneertown Land Corporation
- Gordon Brown: Land Promoter and Co-Head of Pioneertown Land Corporation
- J.B. Webb: General Sales Manager of Pioneertown Land Corporation
- Leonard P. Wikof: President of the Pioneertown Utilities Company
- Johnnie Kee: President of the Pioneertown School Building Board
- Art Daly: Public Relations & Advertising Counselor
- Hazel Strong: Public Relations & Advertising Counselor

There were many, many more people that helped with Pioneertown's early development, however their roles, sadly, have not been determined as of yet. The following unknown board members' names were each mentioned, if not praised and thanked, numerous times in Pioneertown documentation and are listed here in no particular order: Philo J. Harvey, Walt Giles and Curt Bush. It is speculated that even Roy Rogers and Dale Evans might have actually been original Pioneertown Board Members.

Pioneertown Land Co was established early on as a sub-division of the main corporation and also went by the name of Pioneertown Development Co. It was run by Gordon Brown, William Dennis and J.B. Webb and was responsible for land research, sales and early promotions. They got right to work! The areas now known as Pipes Canyon and Rimrock Canyon, as well as Chaparosa Wash and Pioneertown proper, were extensively investigated, thoroughly surveyed, mapped out and subdivided into both commercial and private lots ranging from 1.25 to 1o acres in size.

The heart of Pioneertown was to be Mane Street. Named "Mane", like a horse's mane, both for the fun of it and also to emphasize the outstanding law that no horseless carriages were allowed to drive on Mane Street. The heart of Pioneertown, Mane Street, was to constantly remain as true to an 188o's Western town as possible and was to never be paved. The original street layout, future roads, communities and utility routes, as well as Mane Street itself were all established. The very first private lots (or "Rancho Sites", as they advertised them) that were offered to the general public started for as low as $9oo.

Curtis' dream was truly starting to take shape as Pioneertown Corporation purchased trucks, tractors, engineering equipment and building materials. The Pioneertown Builders Emporium got to work operating a newly constructed rock crusher to help clear the area. This was the very first industrial activity in the area. The Builders Emporium then set up a camp near the site where they soon dug Pioneertown's first well. Hasting's Well, the camp site and the surrounding valley was named Stud Valley by Shorty and Jim Creswell. With the initial steps taken, a celebratory function was certainly called for. However, a great deal of work needed to be laid out and completed before any ceremony could be held, as the area was still quite overgrown and isolated.

The first phase of development encompassed 13,ooo acres of land and included the establishment of the first well site plus general land surfacing and road development in town. Curtis appealed to San Bernardino County for help in the form of a better road leading to Pioneertown, as the current route was a narrow, winding dirt trail, that one could barely consider a two-lane road at most points. The county wasn't interested. So it was up to the original Pioneertown Corporation members to improve the path which slowly crept up the mountains from Yucca Valley and into their new town.

The Old Mormon Trail started in Yucca Valley and worked through Water Canyon before heading up and through Pioneertown. It then followed along through the valley, past Rimrock Canyon, past Burns Canyon and continued all the way up to Big Bear. Road improvements from Yucca Valley, past Pioneertown and all the way to Big Bear were greatly desired by members of towns from both sides of the road. But the very first developmental plans only called for widening, leveling and in some cases, slightly rerouting, the road leading up to Pioneertown from Yucca Valley.

Russell Hayden and his wife, Mousie, were detrimental in the road's early development. They actually drove all the way out to Los Angeles to pick up dynamite when it was needed for cutting through the boulder ridden terrain. It was recorded that tough-as-nails Mousie looked a little pale after Russell had driven them both back up the bumpy dirt road, along with the explosives, which were held up front in the cab with them, resting between her feet.

In addition to easier road access, early plans were also proposed for the erection of an airport to the east of town and a 4o acre recreational lake to the north west. The dreams of a lake were very short lived and would never see any real chance of development for multiple reasons. However, they did make for some really nice initial promotions. But Curtis and the other members of Pioneertown were avid about an airport being developed very early on so they could easily fly guests and potential investors into town. Unfortunately, there was simply no room for it in the first phase's budget. The solution they came up with was simple: Pioneertown Road was laid out so that it paralleled Mane Street one block to the south and so that the last 2,5oo' of road laid down in the first phase of construction ran absolutely straight as an arrow. This allowed for small aircraft to easily land literally one block from Mane Street in Pioneertown.

September 1st, 1946, was announced as the date for the ground breaking ceremony. A week prior, on August 28th, The Desert Views Newspaper printed news of Pioneertown's Grand Opening: "A Free Newspaper, For A Free People In A Free Country". The first phase of construction planned out was for the erection of Mane Street proper and a local office on said street for Pioneertown Land Co to operate out of. The list of Hollywood celebrities who RSVP'd to the event included Roy Rogers, Dale Evans, Russell Hayden, Lillian Porter "Mousie" Hayden, Bud Abbott, Robert Mitchum, Lucille Ball, Yvonne De Carlo, Janis Page, David Bruce, Martha Vickers, John Carroll, Adele Mara, Sally Patten, The Sons of the Pioneers and many, many more.

All the tools and supplies that the Pioneertown Corporation would need to build a legitimate town had been purchased. The basic site and layout, as well as a dirt road that connected it to Yucca Valley, had been mapped out, cleared and leveled. All the State and County permits for more development were acquired. A date was set, invitations for a ceremonial ground breaking event were sent out and word was spreading quick. Virgin ground in the great State of California was about to be broken by the King of Cowboys and the Queen of the West and everyone was invited!

Chapter 4

Breaking First Ground

A Ground Breaking Ceremony was held at Pioneertown on September 1st, 1946. An article highlighting the event was published that day in The San Bernardino County Sun. It read "Movie Celebrities to Launch Development of 'World's Most Unusual City' on Desert Today". In attendance were Dick Curtis, Roy Rogers, Dale Evans, Russell Hayden, Lillian "Mousie" Porter-Hayden, Bud Abbott, Robert Mitchum, Yvonne De Carlo, George Tobias, Janis Page, David Bruce, Martha Vickers, John Carroll, Jack Lunden, Adele Mara, Sally Patten, Gene Lester, The Sons of the Pioneers and members of the San Bernardino County Board of Supervisors; just to name a few.

Cars, carpools, trucks, tractors, horses and even a couple small airplanes delivered guests to the celebration. People even hiked along the four miles of winding dirt road from Yucca Valley to attend. There couldn't have been a better September day to host such an event. The weather was ideal for mid-summer in the desert: a high temperature of 95 degrees, a low of 7o, no humidity and next to no wind. Nearly 2oo people with smiles on their faces and stars in their eyes showed up to a town that hadn't even been built yet. The lack of shade was easily ignored in the presence of celebrities, cold drinks and a barbecue buffet!

The ceremony lasted nearly all day and came to a head in the early afternoon at the grand event: the ground breaking. With the help of Dick Curtis, a giant crowd of supporters and a contractor grade long handled flat shovel - Roy Rogers picked up the first scoop of earth that *was* California Desert as it rose from the ground and became part of Pioneertown as it was laid back down again. The crowd watched from atop the freshly cleared Mane Street as the action took place from inside of the barely framed out Land Office, which was to be the first building completed in town. Pioneertown was happening!

The following months would see the birth of some of the first buildings on Mane Street, starting with the Land Office, which was completed in less than 9o days. Just after that, the temporary Pioneertown Duds & Saddlery building, which was later used as Pioneertown's second official Post Office, was completed adjacent the Land Office and operated by Mr. and Mrs. G. Sando. One structure that was built in haste, a block north of Mane Street and well away from the public, was the Generator Building which housed a massive Caterpillar D311 Diesel Electric Generator that powered all the businesses in town. This was one of Pioneertown's heaviest initial investments, totaling over $2o,ooo in parts and labor.

Ten acres just south of Rimrock were dedicated as a community park named Picnic Park. One of the very first businesses to operate in Pioneertown was the Chuck Wagon, run by Marie Bush and Toodles Senn, which served warm food and cold drinks. The Chuck Wagon first began serving residents and visitors from Pioneertown's Picnic Park but temporarily moved to a location on Mane Street to cater to larger crowds until the completion of the Grubstake Cafe. It is still a little hard to say exactly when each individual building was completed and in what order. But it is certain that Pioneertown's Mane Street saw some very quick and sporadic development.

Every weekend would bring with it a flock of tourists, curious locals and reporters and as each week passed, more and more homes, attractions and establishments began to pop up all across town. It was recorded in the 1948 Pioneertown Corporation Annual Report that an astonishing 3o business buildings were risen in the first year of construction with more still being built. One early addition to Pioneertown was a line of antique gas lamps that ran down the center of Mane Street and added quite the Western ambiance.

Jake Price constructed rodeo grounds that he named The OK Corral on the west end of Mane Street. The OK Corral included a large 1oo' x 4oo' ring, additional rodeo corrals, pins and an area to set up seating. The OK Corral would soon see the addition of wood bleachers and even multiple two story lookouts. Just to the east, across the road named after the veteran Western actor Tom Mix, sprung up Maggie's Feed Barn and White's Hardware, which soon changed to White's Grocery.

Maggie's Feed Barn was an all-in-one horse and livestock supply store that was owned by Maggie, Lloyd and Floyd McDonald and was run by Shorty Creswell and Bryan Johnson. It was recorded that they served over 25o beef sandwiches at its grand opening in 1947. White's, wanting to add a little extra Western themed flair to their establishment, choose to use an "8" instead of a "9" when they painted the face of the building. It facetiously read: "Est. 1847". Further east, Mrs. Elwood Hutcheson established Nell's Ice Cream Palace, which was managed by Mrs. "Mac" MacKinnon and was an obvious favorite of the younger weekend tourists. Adjacent was the Chuckwagon Café which served hot coffee and traditional home cooked meals.

Across Mane Street, on the corner across from the OK Corral, George and Pee Wee Toal opened the the Frosted Pantry, which was a frozen foods delicatessen that served residents with ice, frozen meats and other cold treats. The Frosted Pantry also used a Jeep to deliver goods to residents of Pioneertown. Directly next door was Marble's Electric Shop. Fred Marble's Electric Shop did indeed have a handful of customers as the generator house served electric to the town and many home sites also ran their own generators. Further east along Mane Street was the Barber Shop & Beauty Corral, home of Cecil the barber. Next door to the Beauty Corral was the wonderfully fragrant Barbeque Corral which was famous for serving barbecue all day long. The Corral was reported to have been so busy at times that they had piles of gnawed up rib bones in the back stacked so high that they needed to have trucks come haul them all away.

Back on the north side of Mane Street, next to the Chuckwagon Café, was the Kitchen and Bathrooms for the Pioneertown Campground, which offered camping sites just to the north of town. Next door to the Campground Services was the Pioneer Gem Trader which was owned by "A" and "E" Davenport. The Davenports offered cut and polished stones for costume jewelry and "E" was also a Land Dealer. The Gem Trader would soon be renamed the Tole Mine and later, the Wooden Indian due to the large wooden Indian that stood on its front porch. The Wooden Indian, which officially opened on June 18th, 1948, was a shop where one could purchase magazines, newspapers, orange juice, pop corn, candy or a cigar and later served as the Post Office for over a year. Further east, Harry and Nell Althoff opened Althoof's Furniture Store which was run by their son, Jim Sullivan. The Furniture Store provided Pioneertown with custom handmade wood furniture and repairs along with discount household items and other home construction services.

Following along and crossing back over Mane Street, you would come across the Red Dog Saloon, which was the second business to officially open in Pioneertown. The Red Dog became an instant highlight in the High Desert. The saloon was adorned with a spectacular wooden bar which was relocated from the historic Oatman, AZ. The Red Dog Saloon was built by contractor Bill Wolfe, his brother Rick Wolfe and their friends for a total of about $6,5oo. Owners, Al Lipps and Don Kokx, were said to have personally flown directly to Pioneertown in a private airplane in order to pick out the spot for their saloon. They landed on Pioneertown Road, checked out the town, chose the spot they liked, signed paperwork at the Land Office and took off back into the sky.

Beer was free on opening day and their grand opening party was said to have gone until the late hours of the following morning. The Red Dog Saloon acted as a community gathering spot during holidays, big events and town meetings and was a hot-spot for both locals and visitors alike. It gained some immediate fame as it was the site of the first working shower on Mane Street. In its first few weeks of operation, that shower was actually used by everyone involved with building the town and working on the roads, all free of charge. Further fame followed when dancer and local celebrity Dazzlin' Dallas Morley began performing there. In his youth, radio host Don Imus painted Morley's face on the barroom floor. Val Jones and "Cactus Jim" tended the bar.

Just east of the Red Dog was the Grubstake Restaurant, dubbed the "Men's Hotel", which offered a calmer, more diner-type restaurant atmosphere. Next door to the Grubstake was the Pioneertown Gazette and printing shop, run by a man named Roy Brown. Brown published the first newspapers in town by painstakingly using a vintage iron publishing press. The Gazette is easily recognizable due to the tall old Joshua Tree that grows through its front porch. Like many of the structures on Mane Street, it was built with filming in mind. In addition to the beautiful tree atop its porch, at one point in time there was even a faux staircase that could easily attach to the side of the Gazette to give it the appearance that it was a two story house. The first edition of the Pioneertown Gazette cost "ONE OUNCE OF GOLD DUST OR FIVE CENTS - U.S. GOV'T MONEY", or $2 for an annual subscription.

On the other side of Mane Street, across from the Gazette, a large concrete platform was laid down which was to be the foundation for a movie theater and auditorium. The land directly behind the concrete platform was zoned to be the Pioneertown Public Pool. Neither the theater or the pool was ever built. But people began taking advantage of the flat surface the concrete platform offered by using it for dancing and outdoor events and it was soon called the Outdoor Dancing Floor. In 1948 Johnnie Kee constructed a large rock watering trough in the center of Mane Street between the Gazette and the Land Office for all the thirsty horses on Mane Street.

Trigger Bill's, a vintage .22 caliber shooting gallery for all ages, opened on April 3rd, 1948, two lots east of the Gazette and across from the concrete platform. The artistic and hand made 1930's target machinery was brought up to Pioneertown from an older shooting gallery in Ocean Bear, CA. The Silver Dollar was a six thousand square foot building in between Trigger Bill's and the Gazette that opened in June of 1948. The Silver Dollar was a venue for large dance parties, including the Friday Night Dances where the "Blue Notes" Orchestra always played. It also housed multiple types of legalized gambling such as "Quizo", a variation of Bingo, which was played every Saturday and Sunday. The Silver Dollar's interior was designed to be easily collapsed in order to provide production companies with a large indoor filming space whenever they needed it.

Tommy Thompson, a professional shipbuilder, began constructing a bowling alley with his wife, Lillian Thompson, in 1947. Lillian was commonly in full old-timey-lady costume while out and about in Pioneertown. She went by the name "Cactus Kate" while in character. It was very common to see Cactus Kate in just about every performance the town put on for visitors. The Thompson's work on the bowling alley was finished in 1949 and they had even included a station in the back to use as a Post Office for Pioneertown.

The Thompson's daughter, Alice White-Creswell, ran that station for a year until she served as Postmaster in Pioneertown's first official Post Office. Roy Rogers rolled the very first ball, a strike, at the grand opening celebration for the knotty pine paneled Pioneer Bowl. Rogers was the only man allowed on the lanes while wearing his cowboy boots which were said to be custom tailored boots, complete with bowling soles. He faced off against Tommy Thompson and won the first game with a score of 211, which remained the high score for over a week.

Pioneer Bowl had six lanes, pinball and arcade games, they held bowling leagues, offered Duckpin Bowling as an optional alternative to traditional American bowling and hired local kids to work as pin-setters, as they had no machine to do return them automatically. Artist Wallace Roland Starx painted the inside of the bowling alley with pictures of Pioneertown's history and local figures. Across Mane Street from the bowling alley was Pioneertown Photos which was operated by Harold Church who sold cameras and offered complete photo services to the town. Harry Schaad opened the Nickelodeon, which was actually a children's arcade, next door to Pioneertown Photos. Because they both planned to open the same week and were directly next to each other, Church and Schaad had a joint grand opening celebration

Further east a bit, back on the south side of Mane Street, Mrs. Pearl Seidl established The Likker Barn, which was home to Pioneertown Liquor and sold the first alcohol in town. They sold whiskies, beer, wine, brandies and gin. Mrs. Seidl ran the quote "No Injuns Allowed - BY GOV'T ORDER" along with her promotions for the Likker Barn. Directly next door was Carol Burgess Gift Shop which was built to look like an old Marshal's Office. Even further east was the Klip & Kurl Beauty Shop, who at one time, while in the prime of their business, stressed that customers needed to make appointments as long as two weeks in advance.

Then, clearly marking the east end of Mane Street, there was the Golden Stallion. A grand building constructed of used railroad ties. It could accommodate nearly 1oo people in the main dining hall which was adorned with a pair of life sized horses painted in gold leaf atop its pale blue walls. Henry Jew, Frank Gee and Marilyn Moon invested a total of $75,000 to build and open the restaurant. The Golden Stallion served both American and Chinese dishes and was actually rather famous around the High Desert cities after its grand opening on April 16th, 1948. Some even went as far as to say that they "served the best Chinese food in over a hundred miles". Behind the restaurant, half a block south, was an adobe building built by George Sinclair in 1948.

The north side of the adobe building which faced Mane Street served as an old time Pony Express Station while the south side which faced Pioneertown Road served as a gas and car-service station. Sinclair sold Signal Oil products and gasoline as well as Lee Tires. Red and Al ran the pump station which hosted two visible gasoline pumps. On the other side of the Golden Stallion, across Mane Street to the north, was the Old Pioneer Trail Lodge which was built by Cliff and Glnny Priest. It was managed originally by Lilly Thompson and then Mrs. Marvel Lind. They rented by the day, week or month and the daily rates were $6 for a double or $8 to sleep three adults. The large rectangular buildings were also constructed out of old railroad ties. The Old Pioneer Trail Lodge served as the local motel and became very well frequented by both celebrities and tourists alike, as it offered the only indoor sleeping quarters in town.

The first cross street running north-south to cross Pioneertown Road when entering the town was named Curtis Road, after Pioneertown's founder, Dick Curtis. Continuing west down Pioneertown road, the following crossroad was named after Dale Evans, who purchased land to the south of Mane Street. The next, William S Hart Road, was named in honor of the famous Western actor. Hart was not only an American silent film actor, but also an accomplished screenwriter, director and producer who had made quite an influential impact on almost all of the celebrities who were behind Pioneertown's creation. Sadly, he passed away just a few months before Pioneertown's ground breaking ceremony.

A block west of William S Hart Road was the road named after Roy Rogers, who had purchased property south of Mane Street and two blocks west of Dale Evans' property. The couple would be soon be married on New Years Eve, December 31st, 1947. As a married couple they would later co-own land south of Mane Street in Pioneertown. The next street to the west was named after the late veteran Western actor Tom Mix, who starred in almost 3oo silent films. The last north-south running street to divide Pioneertown was named after the star of both Broadway stage and Hollywood film, Minna Gombell. Gombell purchased land to the south west of Mane Street and was sadly the only Hollywood celebrity other than Russell and Mousie Hayden who both developed the land that they had purchased and lived on it.

In 1947 Pioneertown saw just as much personal promotion as production. The Los Angeles Times published articles in January and in February, both of which highlighted and promoted Pioneertown. Then, on March 25th, the Desert Sun ran a full-page ad which advertised new land for sale and invited people to join Dale Evans, Roy Rogers and The Sons of the Pioneers as Land Owners at Pioneertown: "Where the Old West Lives Again". The Desert Sun ran an additional article on the same day that announced the completion of the dirt road connecting Pioneertown and Yucca Valley. The southern half of the old cattle route that went all the way up to Big Bear had seen some significant improvements.

Tim Spenser wrote the song "Out in Pioneertown" which was recorded by The Sons of the Pioneers along with Milton Estes & the Musical Millers in 1947. It was an obvious homage to the new town as Pioneertown was offered a 5o% cut of its interests. It became the official theme-song of the town as it quickly turned into the most highly requested song for The Sons of the Pioneers to sing while performing for friends and fans along Mane Street. Visitors in the early days of Pioneertown were often treated to random celebrity appearances and spontaneous performances by famous musicians, quite often The Sons of the Pioneers, on Mane Street.

The new community started to blossom and as it did, the residents were treated to a number of activities that brought everyone together on Mane Street. Pioneertown's first Mass was held outdoors on July 26th, 1947. Father John L. Lima M.M., an old friend of Dick and Ruth Curtis from Bedford, MS, used a covered wagon as an altar for the celebration. The following month, on August 15th, Curtis held a grand sized surprise party for his wife, Ruth, at the Grubstake Cafe. Over 1oo people attended her party.

In August of 1947, the members of Pioneertown Corporation, 9o% of stockholders present or represented, gathered at the Red Dog Saloon for the first official Board Meeting. It can surly be understood why so many Board Members hosted a smile for the duration of the meeting. Topics that were discussed included, but obviously weren't limited to, general updates on the progress of the town's construction, the success of land sales to date, the current and future filming in town, Pioneertown Road updates, plans for heavy promotions and the issue of renaming the corporation.

All of the Board Directors were reelected for another year at that meeting. A month later, on September 23rd, the organization that had generally been known as "Pioneertown" changed their official title to "Pioneertown Corporation". Their first fiscal year had ended with a deficit of $2,3o3.28 but only a month into the following year, Pioneertown Corporation had a net profit of $8,884.86. As of May 31st, 1947, they showed a corporate net worth of $436,817.71, including all assets and liabilities. At that time, the common $1 shares were valued at $1.12 each.

It didn't take very long for Pioneertown to find itself in front of the camera. The first filming in town was done by Inter-American Productions during the spring and summer of 1947. A short documentary series from the Jerry Fairbanks Company, in association with Paramount Pictures, titled *Unusual Occupations* and directed by Robert Carlisle, was then filmed at Pioneertown in December of 1947. Carlisle, an editor, director and producer, who would later become well known for his work as the sound editor on the television series *Lassie*, highlighted the town in *Unusual Occupations: Modern Pioneers*.

The special featured Dick Curtis, The Sons of the Pioneers, Roy Rogers, Rogers' daughter Cheryl and his trusty horse Trigger, all enjoying themselves at Pioneertown. Released later in 1948 after a few legal hassles, the short glimpse into the early beginnings of Pioneertown life was shown in movie theaters nation wide, at Southern California County Fairs and to potential investors when they visited Pioneertown Corporation sales offices. Shortly after, *The Valiant Hombre*, released in 1948, was shot both on Mane Street and in the surrounding town and mountains. It told the story, well, one of *many* stories, of the infamous Cisco Kid.

The Cisco Kid was a fictional Western character created by O. Henry in his 1907 short story *The Caballero's Way*. Movies based on the many adventures of the Cisco Kid began in 1914 and ran steadily until 1950, when the kid found his way onto Television. Pioneertown's first major production came when producer Philip N. Krasne decided to film *The Valiant Hombre* there in 1948. He brought along stars Duncan Renaldo and Leo Carrillo, as well as John Litel, Barbara Billingley, John James, Stanley Andrews and many more. Philip Krasne, Duncan Renaldo and Leo Carrillo, in particular, would become very familiar to Pioneertown in the years to come.

To help further promote the town, and simply to have a fun time, Pioneertown Corporation entered into the forth annual Palm Springs Western Week Parade. On Saturday, October 18th, 1947, 60 residents of Pioneertown and members of the Rawhide Riders, a local riding group founded by John Hamilton, rode 40 horses and three horse drawn vehicles 46 miles down to the Western Week Field Club in Palm Springs. One of the horse drawn vehicles was a fully stocked chuckwagon which served dinner to the participants before they all camped out for the night. On the following Sunday, the 19th of October, they rode in the big parade before riding all the way back up to Pioneertown.

Later, also in October of 1947, Pioneertown hosted a three day event to help raise funds for the new school house. They called it the Korny Karnival. Starting on Halloween Day, Friday, October the 31st, the town was home to horse riding shows and competitions, a Western Fashion Parade, western clowns, carnival games and rides, dancing shows and competitions, happy campers, goulies, ghosts and an all-day barbecue! Admission was free and all of the proceeds from the event went towards the Pioneertown school budget.

Land in Pioneertown started selling quite fast. Homes to the north and south of town were being built just as fast as, or faster than, buildings on Mane Street. Aside from the appeal of living and working alongside Hollywood celebrities, one of many reasons for the increase of sales was due to the work of an old-timer and local prospector, Charles V. McClure, of Yucca Valley. McClure had been prospecting the area near Rimrock known as Rattlesnake Canyon until all mining was suspended due to WWII. But after the suspension was lifted and prospecting returned to the area, gold and mineral claims started popping back up all over the desert. Shortly after that, word spread about the discovery of a five mile long vein of gold that, in part, stretched through the north western tip of Rimrock in Pioneertown.

Even though the validity of the gold vein wasn't substantiated, most interested parties quickly began adopting the theory that the gold which McClure had discovered in Rattlesnake Canyon was proof positive that the vein existed. Quite a few non patented gold claims and even a few patented claims were filed through the Rimrock area and along the Old Mormon Trail. This might be the reason why Roy Rogers and a couple of the Sons of the Pioneers joined Dick Curtis in purchasing land at the far north west corner of Rimrock.

The first couple of years to follow Pioneertown's ground breaking ceremony brought with them an absolutely amazing level of interest, activity and development. Over 200 people called Pioneertown "home" on a year round basis and many more people owned land in the town by 1948. All 13,000 acres of the first phase of development were nearly sold or being developed in haste, if not already completed and occupied. Right out of the gates and already in full stride, Pioneertown had absolutely no plans to slow down as it quickly grew larger and more famous.

Chapter 5

First Bumps in the Road

Pioneertown's land sales had exploded. They sold over 3oo home sites in the first three weeks of incorporation! Some of the first residents to purchase land in Pioneertown were Claude Guinan, Rene and Mabel Mallette, Harry and Lil Althoff as well as Bruce and Jean Burns. In 1948 the Burns became the largest land owners in the area after they purchased a half section, or 32o acres, off of Skyline Ranch Road. It just so happened that most of the other first recorded homesite owners in Pioneertown included a number of Hollywood's most prominent reporters, columnists and radio personalities. Requests for information skyrocketed once America knew that these additional celebrities were land owners in Pioneertown. People like Louella Parsons, Hedda Hopper, Jimmy Fidler, Erkine Johnson, Jimmy Starr, Art Baker and BeeBe Kline all became associated with Pioneertown as they openly promoted the living breathing movie set in the High Deserts of southern California.

Louella Parsons, also known as the "Queen of Hollywood", was the first gossip columnist in the United States. At the peak of her career her columns were read by over twenty million people in 4oo newspapers worldwide. Hedda Hopper, of *Hedda Hopper's Hollywood* for the Los Angeles Times, was Parsons' bitter rival. Jimmy Fidler, another rival of Parsons', was a radio and television personality as well as a syndicated columnist with his *Jimmy Fidler in Hollywood* column which was printed in 187 different publications. Erkine Johnson was a columnist, a radio figure and an actor who was famous for both his column *Hollywood Notes* and his TV Series *Erkine Johnson's Hollywood Reel*. Jimmy Starr was a screenwriter and Hollywood columnist who wrote the novel, *The Corpse Came C.O.D.*, which was made into a movie that actually featured Starr along with Parsons, Hopper, Fidler and Johnson.

Art Baker, of the LA radio station KFI, was a famous radio, film and television celebrity who was active and busy in Hollywood for nearly 4o years. BeeBe Kline was a representative of Paramount Pictures' publicity department and actually owned land out in Joshua Tree. Kline became a highlight in Pioneertown when she started writing a special column for the Gazette called *The Stud Valley News*. Her column told the tales of the eclectic men and women who made up the small "colony" that was Pioneertown's Studd Valley Trailer Park.

Minna Gombell was another celebrity-name associated with Pioneertown that helped to drive early land sales. Gombell was an actress who appeared alongside names like Laurel & Hardy, William Powell, Myrna Loy, Esther Williams, Bing Crosby, Maurice Chevalier, Ida Lupino, Humphrey Bogart, Clark Gable and Spencer Tracy in over 1oo films and Broadway plays, including a leading role in the 1939 classic *The Hunchback of Notre Dame*. In 1930 she came to California from New York when the play she was acting in, *Nancy's Private Affairs*, moved to the El Capitain Theater in Hollywood. Gombell and her business partner, De Churchill, were both very interested in Pioneertown from the start and purchased home sites very early on. Churchill designed a house and Gombell personally oversaw the entire building process at her homesite which sat at the south end of the street named in her honor.

Throughout 1947, radio, newspaper and promotional film advertising campaigns for Pioneertown's land sales and business opportunities were in full throttle. Art Daly and Hazel Strong, of the public relations and advertising firm Daly-Strong in Los Angeles, were appointed as the Public Relations & Advertising Counselors to the Pioneertown Corporation. Land Brokers for the Pioneertown Land Company like Charles M. Baker, Nicholas "Nick" Treosti, Don Julio Eisenbruch- "The Happy Gringo", Tom McIntosh and "Mac" MacKinnon heavily promoted the town's potential. Kurt Bush was a Land Broker who catered specifically to visitors from Big Bear. Promoters would bring in potential land buyers by whatever means necessary.

Interested parties were personally driven from Los Angeles, bused in from other major cities and in some cases they were even flown directly to the High Desert by promoters with access to private airplanes. It was joked that Bill Dennis and Gordon Brown, key land promoters for Pioneertown Land Corporation, became travel agents, due to the incredible number of potential land buyers from all across the country that they personally brought into town. Mr. Frank Kara of Seattle, WA, designed a Pioneertown Bumper Sticker that was an extra treasure added to informational packets sent out to interested parties. All of the requested informational packets and brochures on Pioneertown were mailed out free of charge.

In 1947 the Pioneertown Corporation had business and promotional offices at 85o1 Sunset Blvd, 8511 Sunset Blvd, 4o16 Wilshire Boulevard and at 135o North Highland Avenue in Los Angeles, at 24028 Jensen Drive in Canoga Park and at numerous other locations in Burbank, Van Nuys and Studio City. That year, Pioneertown Land Co received a post card from the Post Master of Pioneer, California, Mary E. Whitford. It read: "I heard your broadcast last night about Pioneertown. Please send me more information on the town. Do they have a post office? We get a lot of mail miss-sent up here--and I wondered where the place was. It sounds most interesting."

More and more professionals began offering their services as more and more home sites were sold. Pioneertown Freighters, run by Jack Duckett and Francis Livingston, offered the use of 4oo horses to help the people of Pioneertown haul their goods and materials into town. Pioneertown Motor Corporation was run out of the Gazette and had an advertising deal with JEEP Motors. They offered discounted rates on vehicles that were specifically capable of making the drive up to Pioneertown. In the early days of Pioneertown's establishment, the nearest source of building supplies was all the way down in Banning. In response, The Builder's Emporium of Pioneertown in Studd Valley, run by Lew, Geo and Ollie, began offering just about anything that a contractor or handyman could need.

Wm. Rogers of Rock Gas began delivering propane gas to residents of Pioneertown. Flora B. Stone became known as "The Girl Sign Painter" and was advertised as "tops in painting business signs at Pioneertown". Pioneertown Plumbers was operated by McCluer Senn, a resident plumber who advertised "your plumbing done this way or that away. But always the right way." The Kee family established the Diamond Kee Ranch which offered resort style lodging in addition to horse riding and boarding facilities. Wayne Mills, a man who offered horse shoeing services to residents of Yucca Valley, Morongo Valley and Twentynine Palms, began making bi-weekly appointments to Pioneertown.

The Halloween Korny Karnival in 1947 brought in a great deal of funding for a much needed school. As the number of students began to rise, the residents of Pioneertown got to work building a one room school house completely with donated funds, materials and labor. The brick building sat on the west end of town, across Pioneertown Road from the the O.K. Corral and would serve children from kindergarten through the ninth grade. The first school teachers were Mrs. Pearl Jones and Mrs. Clyde Biddle. Pioneertown's first class started with 18 local students in 1947 and quickly grew to 29 before the end of the school year. By that time, Pioneertown rivaled nearby villages in population and businesses. When residents and business owners finished all the building they could do themselves, a company named SPS Construction took over the majority of the work left in town.

The County of San Bernardino assumed the obligation of maintaining the four and a half miles of Pioneertown Road that connected Pioneertown to neighboring Yucca Valley in 1948. After asking the County for help for two years while Pioneertown residents blasted boulders apart with dynamite, hauled off truckloads of rocks, cut and then maintained a clean route for automobiles to get up the hill - the County decided to take over the rest of the job. The Thompsons hosted a party in their unfinished bowling alley on Mane Street for all the residents of Pioneertown to rejoice. The celebration, which was said to have lasted over 16 hours, included free beer and barbecue with live music and lots of dancing.

As the population grew, a number of clubs formed in town, including the Jeep Club, the Rawhide Riding Club, the Pioneertown Corporation Organization and the Pioneertown Businessmen's Association. The Jeep Club was a club of 4-wheel-drive loving residents who enjoyed taking their vehicles far off the beaten path. The club was mainly inspired by Dick Curtis' extreme Jeep expedition to Big Bear via the Old Mormon Trail and at one time they held a sponsorship by Willys-Overland Motors, a key producer of Jeeps, which had only become available to the public after their success as the primary light 4-wheel-drive vehicle of the United States Army & the Allies during WWII.

The Rawhide Riding Club was a youth group of local horse riding enthusiasts who gathered to play games, ride trails, rope steer and basically do anything else one could do with a horse. Roy Rogers had originally planned to construct a "Cowboy College" where he, and of course Trigger, would teach the young pioneers of the future how to ride and care for horses, as well as shoot, rope and live in the great outdoors. The college never came to be. But a man named John Hamilton, along with Rogers and Dick Curtis, the sponsor and president, organized the Rawhide Riding Club in its place. At the time, on any given day, horses outnumbered residents in Pioneertown and the new city was a very highlighted stop on the California State Riding Trail from Los Angeles to the Joshua Tree National Monument.

Charter members included Royal Low, Harry Schaad, Hilton Johnson, Harry Newton, Morris Remillard, Roger Whiltsie, Edward Moon, Duane Lipps, John "Dusty" Coots, Danny Pekarovich, Roy Kee, Charles Kee, George Sinclair, David Duarte, George White, Richard Bosley & Joe Tunstall. After connecting with The Arrowhead Area Council #o48 of the Boy Scouts of America in 1947, a council which covered the greater San Bernardino County at the time, it is believed that the Rawhide Riding Club became the first Mounted Boy Scout Troop in the United States. The Rawhides won the "Most Typical of the Desert" Award while riding alongside the "Queen of Pioneertown", Beverly Moninger, at the Palm Springs Circus Parade in 1948 . That same year, Heart throb Jane Russell attended a show in Pioneertown that was put on by the Rawhides for a 4th of July celebration.

The Pioneertown Corporation Organization was a group formed to address matters between board members, share holders, land owners, residents and business owners. This organization was unlike official board member meetings in that no actual financial information was discussed and was unlike the Businessman's Association in that members were not restricted only to those who ran establishments in town. The Pioneertown Businessman's Association was formed in the early months of 1947 to help unite and organize all of the new business establishments on Mane Street. Cecil Sly, of SPS Corporation, was elected as the Pioneertown Businessman's Association's first president and Al Lipps, co-owner of the Red Dog Saloon, took over the position in 1948. Original members included Val Jones of the Red Dog Saloon, Ronald Young of Pioneer Bowl, Marge and Ray White of the Golden Stallion, Cactus Kate of the Pioneer Townhouse, Nell and Harry Althoff of Althoof's Furniture and Honey Fellers, Pioneertown Realtor.

In February of 1948, Dr. R. E. Guenther, D.C., set up a temporary office at the Klip 'n Kurl on the east side of Mane Street and began offering the first medical services, chiropractic care, in Pioneertown. Later that year and just down Mane, Mrs. Pearl Seidl sold the Likker Barn to Mrs. Katherine Newton who opened the Gold Nugget Coffee Shop. The Gold Nugget didn't see very many years in operation and afterwards, the barn was then used on and off by the Pioneertown Development Co. and as the Pioneertown Visitor's Headquarters. Honey Fellers, easily the most well known local Realtor, worked out of the Likker Barn from the time it was a coffee shop until it was used by the Pioneertown Development Co.

Frank and Margie Mattoon's chicken farm was still producing thousands of eggs a day in 1948. Margie's daughter, Lois Elaine, had ridden a horse to school her whole life. When she began High School, which was all the way out in Twentynine Palms, her parents got her a little Plymouth Truck for the long trek. She then helped her parents out by delivering eggs along her route to school. Sadly, Frank Mattoon died in 1948. Margie stayed at the chicken farm and kept it in operation. She grew close to John Hamilton, the founder of the Rawhide Riding Club, and it didn't take long before they were married.

John Hamilton was a retired police officer from Bakersfield who had found Pioneertown when he moved to Yucca Valley to live with his brother, Rex. John was a lover of all things equestrian. Always happy to rent his horses to production companies in town; John Hamilton even found himself riding horses on camera in quite a few films. Lois was also known to ride on camera from time to time and did a little trick riding with The Sons of the Pioneers whenever they were in town. Margie wasn't quite as fond of the camera and typically gave them a wide berth whenever they were rolling.

It was obvious that there were going to be a bunch of productions coming through town that wanted to use Pioneertown residents as extras in their films. But a small forgotten requirement kept the majority of residents and visitors behind the camera during earlier productions. In order to appear on camera for television or a movie, one needed a Screen Actors Guild card or Screen Extras Guild card. Ralph Kingston and Bill "Frenchy" French were two of the first Pioneertown residents who traveled down to Hollywood and got their SAG and SEG cards. Both Kingston and French appeared in a handful of films and multiple television shows that were filmed in Pioneertown. The pair even worked up in Big Bear and later in Chatsworth for Gene Autry's Flying A Productions.

Pioneertown's second annual Board Meeting came in August of 1948. It was announced that John Kee would be President of the Pioneertown School Building Board. A new project of particular interest to Rimrock residents was announced: The Diversion Dam in Burns Canyon, which was to store and supply water for Rimrock, was an $18,ooo project engineered by Ralph O' Neil of Glendale, CA, that was scheduled to begin in late October of 1948. News of Dick Curtis' visit to San Francisco earlier that year was also discussed. Curtis had been negotiating with the U.S. Government for over a year and a half to purchase the land adjacent to Pioneertown.

During his trip to San Francisco they finally came to an agreement and the Pioneertown

Corporation was able to purchase the 15,000 acres between the Pioneertown village and Rimrock. After acquiring the additional land, 5,000 acres south west of the initial Pioneertown development were immediately subdivided into ranchos. The new subdivision was called the Outlaw Flats and 1.25 acre lots were listed at $1,2oo - $1,6oo. 1oo of the best lots were set aside for a special promotion that was only available to stock holders. Any stock holder with over 6oo shares was allowed to purchase one of these prime locations for only $675 and were even able to finance them with only $275 down and 18 monthly payments of $22.22.

Pioneertown Corporation's net value as of February 29th, 1948, including all assets and liabilities, was $1,o59,874.o9; up over $6oo,ooo from their net value of $436.817.71 one year earlier on May 31st, 1947. Their common $1 stock shares were valued at $3.36 each; up $2.24 from the year before. The Pioneertown Corporation then offered another 75,ooo shares of common stock for $2.25 a piece. The funds derived from the sale would go towards purchasing more land, improving the roads and extending the roads and utilities into the new Outlaw Flats development. Unfortunately for everyone involved, not all of the topics discussed at the second annual Board Meeting were pleasant.

A feud between Dick Curtis and Pioneertown Land Corporation Co-Heads and land promoters Bill Dennis and Gordon Brown had been brewing. Curtis wanted to focus on establishing more of a residential community with a Western themed Hollywood twist while Dennis and Brown aimed to focus more towards commercial sales and creating more of a business organization with some Western themed residential investments. There had been a slight drop in land sales prior to the Board Meeting and it was also announced that there was actually less well water available than early estimates had predicted and San Bernardino County had already refused to pipe water into town. These factors just added fuel to the fire burning between Curtis and the Pioneertown Land Corporation.

Nothing between the feuding parties actually came to a head at the Board Meeting and it is said that residents of Pioneertown were both equally divided and brutally passionate about the feud. But after no residential subdivision plans were made for the remaining 1o,ooo acres of newly acquired land by the Pioneertown Land Development Team and their focus openly and abruptly shifted away from the sale of homes, Dick Curtis hung up his hat and stood down from his position as the President of the Pioneertown Corporation. He was replaced as President by Russell Hayden who's position on the Board of Directors was replaced by engineer R. W. O'Neil in July of 1948. While he no longer held a position on the Board of Directors, Curtis remained a land owner and the largest stockholder in the Pioneertown Corporation. He continued to stay heavily involved with the productions and activities in town which kept a steady population of over 2oo year-round residents.

The development of new homesites in Pioneertown discontinued, but promotions for the remaining ranchos were still in full force. On August 28th of 1948, Thrifty Drug Co. of Los Angeles, CA, put on a "Pioneer Day Sale" which included a grand prize 1.25 acre ranch site in Pioneertown's new subdivision. Another prize included an all expenses paid weekend to Pioneertown for eight people. Over half a million copies of Thrifty's Pioneer Day's shopping advertisement were printed and distributed to residents of Los Angeles County. That same year the Pioneertown Gazette distributed 15,000 copies of it's first issue to visitors of the Los Angeles County Fair in Pomona.

In the late 194o's there was a boom in the turkey ranching business in the High Desert. In 1949, it was recorded that there were 19 large farms with almost 5o,ooo turkeys just in Joshua Tree alone. The turkey ranching would have continued to boom in the area had it not been for the winter of 1948 - 1949. December was wet and cold. But, starting the first week of January and continuing for five straight days, a heavy snow started to fall over the desert. The worst winter storm recorded in over 6o years then proceeded to reshape the High Desert into a winter-wonderland. Residents of Pioneertown had to bundle up tight while businesses up and down Mane Street closed that week and for many days afterwards. When the storm finally passed, there had been an amazing 19.3 inches of snowfall in Twentynine Palms, 27 inches in Joshua Tree and a truly breathtaking 44 inches from Yucca Valley, through Pioneertown all the way up to Big Bear.

It took a good while for Pioneertown and the rest of the desert to thaw out. By the end of February, 1949, three million copies of the song "Out in Pioneertown" had been pressed by recording manufacturers. That same month, Pioneertown was cited as the birthplace of a new coffee vending machine: The Coffee-Teria. There were a handful of Browden Corporation stockholders who lived in Pioneertown that pushed the corporation to debut their new coffee machine in the Western themed town. The new contraption was a non-electric liquid coffee vending machine that for ten cents would dispense a freshly brewed cup of Maxwell House coffee with fresh cream and cubed sugar for anyone who preferred it. The hot coffee vending machines were very well received when they arrived in the cold and recently winter scared desert town.

While shooting a scene for *The Cowboy and the Indian*, filmed in March of 1949, Gene Autry's stunt horse, Champion's double, was spooked by gunfire and managed to free its reigns. The horse, still wearing Gene's $5,000 saddle and bridle, took off into the desert in a flash and wasn't seen again for over 24 hours. Teams of crew members and residents endlessly searched the desert and even Autry's airplane was sent up to see if it could locate the horse from the air. After all else had failed, it was John Jr. and Charles Kee, just 17 and 13 years old at the time, who were able to return the horse to Gene.

With their younger brothers, Corky and Roy, also helping out, the Kee brothers tracked the horse for five straight hours before locating him half way to Pipes Canyon. Gene Autry rewarded the boys with a check for $100 and their story and pictures wound up in the local newspapers that week. Shortly after that, Roy Kee, the youngest of the Kees brothers, caught the attention of both Gene Autry and Russell Hayden because of his excellent riding skills. Roy Kee rode for Gene Autry's show, doubling for actor Billy Gray, as he raced from the sheriff's office to find the man who killed his father.

While filming Columbia Pictures' *Cody of the Pony Express* in 1949, Producer Sam Katzman and Director Spencer Gordon Bennet took full advantage of Pioneertown. They turned the Pioneer Townhouse into a cavalry fort by erecting a tall log gate in front of the motel and removing the "Townhouse" to give the appearance that it was a completely fenced in fort. When watching *Cody of the Pony Express*, later released in April of 1950, you can clearly see the motel, complete with its cavalry fort gate, in the very first scene of the movie. Once the production was finished, the logs that were used to create the tall gate were pulled up and left in town, for future production companies to use. Some of those long wooden logs still line the parking lot at the east side of Mane Street to this day.

On February 18th, 1949, Dorothy Sall gave birth to "Danny Boy" Sall at the Thomas H. Ince Memorial Hospital in Twentynine Palms. Named after his father, Daniel Sall, Danny weighed seven pounds and five ounces and was credited as the first infant resident of Pioneertown. The following week, on February 27th, Mary Ann Pekarovich, of the Pekarovich family who owned the Rimrock Hotel and a senior at the Twentynine Palms High School, was crowned Miss Twentynine Palms. Mary Ann went on to represent Pioneertown at the historic National Orange Show in San Bernardino, CA. The show was held in the first permanent National Orange Show Exhibition Hall which opened in 1925. It was an almost 100,000 square foot building, said to be one of the largest and finest exposition buildings in the nation, that was sadly destroyed in a fire just months later.

The Pekarovich family installed a generator on their property the year before and started running electric lighting and refrigeration at the Rimrock Motel in 1948. Initial plans with the California Electric Power Company called for a $25,000 advance before they would begin working to bring power-lines into Pioneertown. The Pioneertown Corporation then began lots of work on the roads to make it an easier job for the CEPC. Trigger Bill and Johnnie Kee did a good deal of the dynamite blasting that cut through boulders to straighten out the roads while they were being improved. After having spent over $2o,ooo in general land improvements which were planned out prior to the electric situation, but which also happened to significantly lower the work load for the electric company, a new deal was worked up which brought power lines into Pioneertown at no cost to the Pioneertown Corporation.

Power lines reached Pioneertown and the electricity was turned on in 1949. The familiar hum of Pioneertown's diesel generator chugging along in the distance was soon silenced forever. Tommy and Lillian Thompson were the first residents to get electricity directly to their house just north of Mane Street. Pioneertown village received power first, followed by Outlaw Flats, Rimrock and then Pipes Canyon shortly thereafter. After the road leading into Pioneertown, Outlaw Flats and then Rimrock was improved, they decided to push along a little further. Russell Hayden, the new President of the Pioneertown Corporation, accurately believed that improving the old Mormon Trail up to Big Bear would be a great means of increasing interest in Pioneertown while also opening up new activities to residents of both towns.

Bill Kramer, the old man who had moved out to Rattlesnake Canyon in 1922, grew more and more suspicious of what sounded like enormous explosions in the distance which seemed to echo through the canyons like man made thunder. As the blasting of dynamite to clear boulders along the old trail continued, visitors to Kramer's cabin informed him of the Western themed boomtown that had popped up almost over night. Kramer had spent the better part of three decades in solitude on the isolated mountain range when he found society starting to creep up and into his world.

After building up a little courage and gathering enough supplies for a long day's journey, Bill Kramer left his cabin in the Spring of 1949 and walked down through Rimrock and into Pioneertown. Entering from the west side, Kramer walked down Mane Street in awe of what had been happening in the valleys below his mountain cabin. Just as awestruck were the residents of Pioneertown who had no idea who Kramer was. They couldn't tell if he was an exceptional actor playing an impressive role or the vivid apparition of a departed pioneer from centuries past. After explaining his story to the townsfolk, Bill Kramer became a bit of a local celebrity, but out of respect, he was given his privacy and left alone to his cabin, just as he enjoyed it.

In 1949, Pioneertown was also introduced to Dazzlin' Dallas Morley. Morley had divorced at a young age and got her name due to the spangles that she liked to wear while performing. She had taught herself how to play the piano by ear and enjoyed singing as well. On a weekend trip to Twentynine Palms with a friend, they randomly decided to turn off the main highway and drive a few miles up the steep hill to Pioneertown. While in town at the Red Dog Saloon, Morley started to play the piano and sing a few songs for everyone. The crowd at the saloon loved her and Morley didn't just love the crowd; she loved the Red Dog Saloon and Pioneertown itself.

When her friend was ready to return home to Hollywood, Dallas gave him the the key to her apartment. She told him that she needed him to bring her stuff up in a week or as soon as he could and then bluntly announced that she wasn't leaving. Morley was hooked on Pioneertown and likewise, Pioneertown was hooked on Dazzlin' Dallas Morley. The San Bernardino County Mounted Posse would ride their horses up to Pioneertown and directly into the Red Dog Saloon on an annual visit. Their routine was simple: Ride to Pioneertown, Ride into the saloon, hitch the horses at bar, order the horses a pitcher of beer, order themselves a beer.. and then watch Dazzlin' Dallas!

On July 26th, 1949, Mrs. Ole Skare, Co-owner of the Barbecue Corral on Mane Street, was bitten by a rattlesnake at her cabin to the north east of town. She was able to find help fast enough to survive without any serious injury, but her encounter marked the first snake bite recorded in Pioneertown. Val Jones, former bar tender of the Red Dog Saloon, purchased the business along with his wife, Pearl Jones, in 195o. Later that year the Post Office was moved from the area in the back of

Pioneer Bowl across the street and into the ten by twelve foot building that had previously housed Pioneertown Duds & Saddlery. The first official Postmaster of Pioneertown was Alice White Creswell. In 1951 Hester Downing Guinan was hired on as a replacement clerk and in 1955, when Alice retired, Hester became the second Postmaster of Pioneertown.

After land sales slowed down, they never really picked back up again. Many people in town feared that Pioneertown would go under completely without Dick Curtis at the reigns. Pioneertown would have hit rock bottom had filming not picked up so fast. *The Gay Amigo, The Darling Caballero, The Cowboy and the Indians, Satan's Cradle* and *Riders in the Sky* were all filmed in Pioneertown and released just in 1949 alone. New faces to Pioneertown's list of many famous friends now included the singing cowboy, Gene Autry as well as Pat Buttram, Sheila Ryan, Bob Livingston, Tom London, Gloria Henry, Mary Beth Hughes, Jo-Carroll Dennison, Don Beddoe, James Millican, Hugh O'Brian, Harry Harvey, Jane Adams, Dickie Moore, Peggy Stewart, Ross Elliott, Ben Corbett, George J. Lewis, William Fawcett, Lew Ayres, Teresa Wright, Victor Jory, Jimmy Hunt, Barry Kelley, William Bakewell and Jacqueline White; just to name a few in no particular order.

While the vast majority of visitors, famous or not, grew to love Pioneertown almost instantly, it clearly didn't rub everyone the right way. While filming *The Capture* for RKO Pictures late in 1949, Lew Ayres stayed in the Pioneer Townhouse. At that time, there was a sign on the side of the road as you were driving into town that read "Live Here & Live Longer". Ayres, after filming his scenes and lodging in town for over a week, was reported to have written ".. It Only Seems Longer" on the bottom of the sign which had greeted visitors as they entered Pioneertown. Ayres' story was truly an exception. One story quite opposite to his, is that of Juan Herminio Cintrón García, who visited Pioneertown in October of 195o.

At that time, García was a Legion Chief of Puerto Rico who was credited as the first G.I. to become a Department Commander and also did so by winning with a unanimous vote. He operated two Markets in Ponce, PR, which was a Municipality of Puerto Rico, before he became the mayor of Ponce, PR, for four years. Juan had traveled along with 14 delegates to the Legion Convention in Los Angeles, CA. He had heard about the nearby Pioneertown from a personal friend of his who owned land in the original development. Juan Herminio Cintrón García was a very big fan of Western cinema and admittedly fell in love with Pioneertown when he visited after the Legion Convention. Before he had to leave, García noted that he would never forget the friendly faces, the wonderful charm or the opportunity to see Western productions being filmed in person.

Pioneertown had seen some ups and some downs. Founder Dick Curtis was no longer President of the corporation, but it had been left in good hands and Curtis was still a very active member of the community all the same. While land sales had slowed down considerably by 195o with the population of Pioneertown having only surpassed 3oo full-time residents, more movie and television productions were being filmed in town than at any other time in Pioneertown's history. Mane Street, then filled from end to end with businesses and attractions, was full of life and still gleaming with potential in the early 195o's.

Chapter 6

Three Amigos Saved Pioneertown

Pioneertown was already in a pinch by 1948. Land sales might have been a little slow before, but they almost came to a complete halt shortly after Dick Curtis stood down as President. Pioneertown Land Corporation Co-heads William Dennis and Gordon Brown, much to Curtis' protest, had steered Pioneertown's aim away from residential development and more towards business development. The problem then was the simple fact that Dennis and Brown weren't hardly as Hollywood-savvy as Dick Curtis was. As land sales were tanking, the corporation was aiming to profit from a large boost in business from Hollywood production companies that they didn't really know how to attract.

There were three men who came to the aid of Pioneertown at that point in time. Each of them had their own motives, goals and agendas. They hardly knew each other when they became involved with the little town. But they all became good friends by the time that they had each left their marks on Pioneertown. Without the hard work of these three gentlemen, it is very likely that Dick Curtis' dream would have simply died off by the end of the 194o's. Listed in the order by which they became involved with the corporation, these are the three amigos who saved Pioneertown:

Russell "Lucky" Hayden

Russell Hayden was born James Michael Lucid on June 11th, 1911, in Chico, CA. In 1943, his mother, Minnie Harvey Lucid, filed an affidavit for the correction of his original birth certificate. His name and birth date were both changed to Russell Hayden Lucid, born June 10th, 1911. While it is unclear exactly why this was done, it might have been due in part to his enlistment in the U.S. Navy during WWII, where he served from December 27th, 1943, until October 24th, 1945. Hayden started his Hollywood career behind the cameras on the Paramount Studios lot during the early 1930's. Not exactly interested in acting at the time, he worked as a general laborer, a laboratory technician, as an assistant cameraman and as a film cutter before he was promoted to the position of business manager for film producer Harry "Pop" Sherman's production company.

In 1935, Sherman signed actor James Ellison to portray "Johnny Nelson" in Paramount's *Hopalong Cassidy* series; a series that ended more than a decade later and included 66 films. Ellison appeared as the sidekick character, Johnny, in eight of the *Cassidy* films before he left the series in 1937 to pursue leading roles. "Pop" Sherman then offered Hayden $1,000 per film to replace James Ellison in the *Hopalong Cassidy* series where he would play the character "Lucky Jenkins". Russell Hayden jumped on the deal and went on to act in 27 consecutive *Cassidy* films from 1937 through 1941. Afterwards, he was forever known, by both friends and fans alike, as Russell "Lucky" Hayden.

"Pop" also used Russell Hayden in four of Paramount's Zane Grey films before Hayden partnered with Columbia Pictures where he starred with actor Charles Starrett in eight films. Hayden then starred in two films for Universal Pictures before serving in the U.S. Navy for two years during WWII. Hayden returned to Universal once the war was over and began working on the 13 episode series *The Lost City of the Jungle*, where he starred alongside none other than the infamous Dick Curtis. While he became heavily involved with Pioneertown's incorporation and early establishment, he also continued acting, working for Republic Pictures and Lippert Pictures and then again with Columbia.

His last starring role was in the television series *Cowboy G-Men* in 1953, before he started working behind the camera again, then as a producer. Russell Hayden's first wife was actress Jane Clayton, who would later land the role of the first mother on the television show *Lassie*. Russell met Jan while filming the *Hopalong Cassidy* adventure *In Old Mexico* in 1938. They were married shortly after, from 1938 until 1943 and had a daughter they named Sandra. Hayden's second wife was actress Lillian "Mousie" Porter, who he married on July 4th of 1946. Mousie got her name when Darrel F. Zanuck, a fat cat at Fox, said "You're a cute little mouse." Just like Russell, both Mousie and Sandra Hayden's names are peppered throughout the history of Pioneertown.

Hayden started Quintet Productions in the mid 1950's and was quickly able to sell the television series *Judge Roy Bean* into syndication. By 1955, Russell Hayden had built a small but faithful reproduction of Langtry, TX, on his property in Pioneertown, which he named Hayden Ranch. There he produced and directed all 39 episodes of the *Judge Roy Bean* series. Much like Pioneertown's Mane Street, Hayden Ranch offered plenty of amenities to production companies in addition to an ideal shooting location, such as equipment storage areas, crew lodging, film developing facilities and a readily available supply of Western themed extras, ready to act in their projects. Aside from all of his work with the corporation and the community itself, the addition of Hayden Ranch to Pioneertown couldn't have come at a better time as the increase in local production work helped to counter the decline in land sales.

Unfortunately, tragedy struck the Haydens in 1956 when Russel's 16 year old daughter, Sandra, died very unexpectedly. Sandra "DeDe" Jane Hayden, born July 11th, 194o, was the daughter of Russell and his first wife, Jan Clayton. DeDe, who spent much of her youth in Pioneertown, appeared in some of the Judge Roy Bean episodes and actually started worked along with her father as a dialog director at a very young age. In addition to the Hayden Ranch, she also lived with her mother in Hollywood. On the evening of September 22nd, 1956, DeDe left her mother's house and headed for the Hayden Ranch, but chose to wear her contact lenses instead of her glasses. Her family believes that was the catalyst for the tragedy that came shortly after.

Less than 2o minutes from her mother's house, Sandra ran a stop sign at the intersection of Whitsett Ave and Riverside Dr in North Hollywood. Her car collided with 19 year old driver Lloyd A. Frerer Jr. of Sherman Oaks and she died at the scene. After her death, Hayden was crushed. Russell and Mousie moved to Scottsdale, AZ, for a few years while Russell produced *26 Men*. For a time, the thought of Pioneertown only stirred up a great depression for Hayden. But after a few years, Russell and Mousie returned to the Hayden Ranch.

When Karen "PeeWee" Pekarovich, of the Rimrock Motel Pekarovichs, lost her leg to cancer and was expecting more complications on the way, it struck a chord with the Haydens. They were good friends with the Pekarovich family and Karen reminded them of Sandra. Wanting to do something positive in Sandra's name, Russell and Mousie started the Sandra Hayden Memorial Foundation in 1977. The foundation would host an annual July Barbecue Benefit to raise funds for those in need. Barbara Hardesty was the first President of the board and Mousie was always the board Secretary. The first Benefit Barbecue raised $5,19o for Karen Pekarovich, the first benefactor of the Sandra Hayden Memorial Fund. The Haydens hosted a number of attractions in addition to good barbecue, such as hole-in-one golf competitions against the Sawtooth Mountains, gun shows and live music.

Later recipients of the SHMF were Lloyd Vaughn Smith, a 1o year old left in a coma after being run over by a motorcycle; Joe Noone and Paul McCormick, two Joshua Tree men who suffered serious heart attacks; Billy Royal, a sick youngster from Yucca Valley; Doreen Kelly, a Yucca Valley student with leukemia; Vicki Wilson, a mother of three suffering from cancer; Dazzlin' Dallas Morley, who needed to have three separate operations in one year; David Henry, a Yucca Valley father of two suffering from cancer; and John Cirio, a Vietnam War Veteran who suffered from a deadly kidney disease. Circo was the recipient of the record breaking $6,247.87, gathered in 1985 when almost 4,ooo people attended. Circo was also the last recipient of the SHMF, as the foundation ended in 1985, fours years after Hayden's death.

Of the three men listed in this chapter, Russell Hayden was the only one who attended Pioneertown's ground breaking ceremony. Hayden was the first Treasurer of the Pioneertown Corporation and then took over the role of President when founder Dick Curtis stood down late in 1948. He, along with his wife Mousie, were elemental in the early development of Pioneertown Road and the efforts to establish a road along the Pioneer Pass and up to Big Bear. He was also the only person highlighted in this chapter who not only purchased residential property in Pioneertown, but also built a home in town and stayed an active member in the community until his very last days.

Philip N. Krasne

     Philip Ned Krasne was born May 6th, 1905, in Norfolk, NE, and was the youngest of three brothers. His parents, Herman J. Krasne and Rose Bernstein, were immigrants from Bialystok, Poland, who worked in the clothing industry. The Krasnes owned a People's Department Store in Council Bluffs, IA, where Philip graduated from Abraham Lincoln High School at a very young age. Philip then attended the University of Michigan where he, again, graduated at a very young age, in 1927. The University of Michigan awarded Krasne with first honors in the Chicago Alumni Medal and the Paul Gray Testimonial for excellence in oratory in 1925, which included a $1oo cash prize and a bronze medal. Krasne then traveled to California where he received his LLB degree from the University of Southern California School of Law and was admitted to the bar in 1929.

     Philip Krasne worked as an attorney all over Southern California for almost a decade before he found his way into entertainment law in 1936. Krasne counseled for Edward Alperson's Grand National Pictures in Hollywood, CA. Grand National was one of a handful of Poverty Row production companies. "Poverty Row production company" was a Hollywood term which was used to indicate a B movie studio. He earned the official title of "producer" in 1938 when he was promoted to Vice-President in charge of production at Grand National Film Distributing. Grand National acquired the rights to *Angels With Dirty Faces* and a contract with actor James Cagney in the late 193o's while Cagney was battling with his home studio, Warner Bros, who had breached their contract with him. Cagney filmed *Great Guy* for Grand National, but, fearing that he would be further typecast as a gangster, he refused to work on the film *Angels With Dirty Faces* and opted instead to star in *Something to Sing About*.

Krasne was counseling for Grand National Pictures while they filmed *Something to Sing About* in the summer of 1937. By the time it was released that September, the final production costs had gone considerably above the film's original budget, totaling around $900,000. The production company had seen some unsuccessful projects and after *Something to Sing About* released to a poor box office performance and only generally favorable reviews, Grand National Pictures quickly crumbled. The rights to the unfilmed *Angels with Dirty Faces* was sold to Warner Bros and after reaching a new agreement with Cagney, the film was shot and released. It is fun to note that while it was recorded as one of his personal favorites, had Cagney not chosen to film *Something to Sing About*, Hollywood History, the story of Philip N. Krasne and ultimately, Pioneertown, might have all turned out quite differently! Grand National Picture's studios were purchased by the Producers Releasing Corporation, better known simply as "PRC". While attaining the studios, PRC also hired on Philip N. Krasne as a legal counselor.

One of Krasne's friends and fraternity brothers was Fred Ziv, a king of American radio and television syndication and owner of the Fredrick W. Ziv Company. At some point while Krasne was working for PRC, Ziv mentioned to him that he wanted to find something that he could produce with an unforgettable sound signature or a trademark phrase. Something like *The Lone Ranger's* easily recognizable trademark phrase, "Hi-Yo, Silver, Away!" In the early 1940's Krasne found a property owned by Doubleday Publishers with great potential: O. Henry's character, *The Cisco Kid*. After working over different catch phrases to go along with the property, Krasne came up with what would soon become the The Kid's signature tag line, "He-ey, Cis-co!... He-ey, Pan-cho!"

The Cisco Kid had spawned numerous films by the time that Krasne came across it. The motion picture rights were being used by Twentieth Century Fox for a series of motion pictures when Krasne began to push Doubleday to sell him the radio rights. O. Henry's original description of the Cisco Kid character in his short story *The Caballero's Way*, first published in 1907, was brief at best, but depicted a sociopathic cold blooded killer with a short temper who aided in his lover's murder. As well, the first depiction of the Cisco Kid was probably not a Mexican himself, as he was actually quoted as having murdered "mostly Mexicans" in the first sentence of O. Henry's story. While the character had eventually been portrayed in a more positive light throughout the years, Krasne wanted a different, stronger character. He aimed to mold the Kid into a great hero of the west.

Although Krasne only wanted the bare rights to the character, Doubleday Publishers' attorney, Leonard Meiburg, battled with him for the better part of a year, demanding that the character's radio rights would only be turned over if Doubleday was paid for every episode Krasne intended to make. Krasne made it clear from the beginning that he wanted more than just the radio rights to *The Cisco Kid*. In addition to radio, he wanted the motion picture rights as well as rights to the newly forming medium of television. However, the contract that Doubleday Publishers had with Twentieth Century Fox made that impossible for Krasne. It prohibited Doubleday from releasing the film and television rights to anyone else until 20 years after Fox had finished producing *Cisco Kid* titles. Philip N. Krasne did not let that stop him. *The Cisco Kid* had been a great success for Twentieth Century Fox, but was considered a second feature, or "B-movie" series. Productions of that caliper were distributed for a set fee and were only able to make a set profit. So, as the franchise grew in popularity, so too did the production budgets, until a point where there was next to no profit margin left for Twentieth Century.

In 1941, Twentieth Century Fox released *Ride on Vaquero*, which received decent reviews in the States but poor reviews from Mexico, who abhorred the costume that the Kid wore in Fox's films. Mexico's main complaint was that many people believed the Kid dressed more like a ballet dancer than a caballero. America was deep into WWII at that time and was trying to promote their Good

Neighbor policy with Mexico. That put pressure on Fox to make the Kid look more appealing to Mexican review. Between the minimal profit margins and the new political pressure, it was clear that *The Cisco Kid* series had run its course with Twentieth Century. Spyros Skouras, then the president of Twentieth Century Fox, heard that Krasne dearly wanted the *Cisco Kid* rights.

Acting only out of the kindness of his own hart, Skouras decided not to restrict Doubleday Publishing from releasing the Kid's rights. On May 6th, 1942, Philip N. Krasne's 37th birthday, Spyros Skouras called Krasne to give him the good news. After a very long legal debate with Doubleday Publishers, an agreement was finally made which allowed Krasne and Ziv put *The Cisco Kid* on the radio, October 2nd, 1942. The weekly, then thrice weekly, nationally syndicated series eventually included over 600 episodes and originally starred Jackson Beck as The Kid and Louis Sorin as his trusty sidekick, Poncho. Krasne worked very hard to give Ziv exactly what he'd asked for, and in the process, he had even coined one of the most famous radio introductions in history: "Here's adventure! Here's romance! Here's O. Henry's famous Robin Hood of the old west- The Cisco Kid!"

With *The Cisco Kid* on the radio, Krasne then aimed to put him back on the big screen. He addressed the poor reviews of the Kid's appearance by hiring a consultant from the Mexican embassy to oversee a revamping of the Kid's wardrobe. The Kid was re-dressed in a less stylish and more rural costume that everyone unanimously saw as more of an authentic caballero's wardrobe. With the wardrobe changes in place, the Mexican government was happy. In early 1945, Krasne teamed up with the Monogram Pictures Corporation, another Poverty Row company, and director John P. McCarthy to began production of his first Cisco Kid film. *The Cisco Kid Returns*, starring Duncan Renaldo as the Kid and Martin Garralaga as Poncho, was released on April 3rd, 1945. Duncan Renaldo went on to star as the Kid in two more films for Krasne that year, *In Old New Mexico* and *South of the Rio Grande*.

Krasne filmed at Monogram Ranch in Newhall, CA, as well as Mission San Fernando Rey de España in Mission Hills, CA. His first three films received good reviews but did not turn a big profit. There was one more obstacle that Krasne had to overcome if he wanted to continue producing *Cisco Kid* titles: production costs. Labor costs had been suppressed during the war and were rising annually as unions grew more powerful. In addition, filming in the Los Angeles County incurred the production team multiple time restraints and increased transportation expenses. Krasne took some time to try and find a solution to his increasing production expenses. In his absence, Monogram Pictures continued to produce six *The Cisco Kid* titles from 1946 through 1947, which starred Gilbert Roland in the lead role. They too received decent reviews but did not bring in much of a profit.

It was around this time, in 1947, that Philip N. Krasne heard about what Dick Curtis and his friends were doing at Pioneertown. When Krasne arrived in Pioneertown there were less than a handful of buildings completed on Mane Street and there had yet to be anything filmed in town. But, even in the absence of a completed Mane Street, Krasne saw its potential. The isolated location was an ideal area that was free of smog, automobile and airplane noise. It also hosted food and lodging accommodations for his crew members and the means to board horses to boot. Krasne was sold. He purchased 40 acres of land near Russell Hayden's property and the filming rights for all 32,000 acres of Pioneertown. *The Valiant Hombre*, the first film to be produced in Pioneertown, was released December 15th, 1948. Duncan Renaldo returned to star as the Kid for Krasne and was accompanied by Leo Carrillo as Pancho. The famous duo would later reprise their roles in four more films and over 150 television episodes, all of which were filmed in Pioneertown.

Krasne produced a total of five *Cisco Kid* films in Pioneertown, which included *The Valiant Hombre* in 1948, *The Gay Amigo*, *The Daring Caballero* and *Satan's Cradle* in 1949, followed by *The Girl From San Lorenzo* in 1950. In 1949, Krasne and Fred Ziv began producing of *The Cisco Kid* television series through Ziv Television Programs. The weekly show consisted of 30 minute episodes and first aired on September 5th, 1950. It focused on the adventures of two desperadoes who were wanted for unspecified crimes, but who maintained Robin Hood like celebrity and were known simply as the Cisco Kid and Pancho. Duncan Renaldo and Leo Carrillo starred in all six seasons which included 156 episodes, all shot at Pioneertown in just over four years.

Philip N. Krasne produced nearly 4o episodes a year and would shoot as many as six episodes at the same time, while filming in Pioneertown. Krasne was the man responsible for insulating, soundproofing and retrofitting the Silver Dollar gambling and dance hall into Pioneertown's historic Sound Studio on Mane Street, which he then used to film the vast majority of *The Cisco Kid's* interior shots. Before Krasne came to Pioneertown, the Silver Dollar was used for indoor filming, but wasn't exactly insulated or soundproof and had very poor acoustics.

While the vast majority of America watched television in black and white, Krasne knew that the day of color television was just around the corner. So he chose to film the entire series in color, which was then automatically reprinted in black and white for public broadcasting. Although about 99% of viewers weren't able to see it in color until the 196o's, Krasne's choice lead *The Cisco Kid* to become the first television series to ever be filmed entirely in color. The first season was shot in 35mm. Standard procedure at the time then called for the 35mm prints to be reprinted in 16mm before broadcasting. This practice resulted in an audible wobble on the show's soundtrack which didn't sit very well with Krasne. In his attempt to remedy the situation, Krasne, curious why shooting wasn't just done in 16mm in the first place, was informed that there was no 16mm editing equipment available. That *really* didn't sit well with Krasne, who then instructed his team to modify moviolas and other editing equipment for 16mm film.

The work that Krasne's production team completed not only fixed the show's soundtrack, but it also decreased the budget by removing the demand for the film to be reprinted from 35mm to 16mm after shooting. But there was more. The true icing on the cake was the fact that Krasne's production team was then able to escape union rules as filming in 16mm was considered amateur at the time and was therefore not policed by Hollywood unions. After totaling up the profits saved from filming in Pioneertown and from filming in 16mm, Krasne and Ziv realized that their new television series was akin to their radio series of the same name, in that it was a viable product for syndication. When Ziv Television Programs began selling the broadcasting rights for *The Cisco Kid* series to Television markets all over the world, it became the first television series to ever be syndicated.

Krasne later sold his interest in the Cisco franchise to Fred Ziv. With the money that he made, Krasne formed two companies with former RKO and Universal Pictures producer, Jack J. Gross. Gross-Krasne Productions was a television production company and United Television Programs was their distribution company. The team purchased the California Studios, now the Raleigh Studios, to house their productions. Very shortly after Gross-Krasne was established, Lew Wasserman, of MCA and Universal Studios, contacted Krasne to say that he wanted to buy them out. Krasne didn't really care to sell his newly organized enterprise and candidly told Wasserman that he would sell for one million dollars. Lew Wasserman backed down. But half a year later, Krasne received another call from Wasserman. By the time that phone call was over, Krasne had become a millionaire.

In addition to making Hollywood history, Philip N. Krasne was an early land owner in Pioneertown who helped form the Pioneer Studio Locations. He retrofitted the Sound Studio on Mane Street and brought the first film productions to Pioneertown. Krasne was a pioneer of both radio and television production, who's diligent work ethic and ingenuity not only helped to put Pioneertown on the map, but also helped to make it the historical Hollywood Western resource that it is today. Of the three amigos highlighted in this chapter, it is easy to see why Philip N. Krasne was cited as "the man who saved Pioneertown."

Gene Autry

     Gene Autry, "The Singing Cowboy", was born Orvon Grover Autry on September 29th, 1907, in Grayson County, TX. Autry began singing in the local church choir at the young age of five and his mother taught him how to play the guitar when he was twelve. He purchased his first guitar from a Sears, Roebuck & Co. catalog for eight dollars. In order to help support his family, he dropped out of High School in 1925 and worked as a telegrapher for the St. Louis-San Francisco Railway. While working there, especially while working through the late hours of a night-shift, Autry would play his guitar and sing to help pass the time.

     In 1927, famous actor and vaudeville performer Will Rogers heard Autry playing at the telegraph office in Chelsea, OK, and suggested that the young guitarist go to New York and get a job on the radio. Less than a year later, in the autumn of 1928, Autry auditioned for Nathaniel Shilkret, director of Light Music for Victor Records in New York. Shilkret informed Autry that he sounded like two other artists which Victor Records had just signed and suggested that Gene get a job singing on the radio to gain more experience.

     While he didn't gain a recording contract that day, Autry left with a letter of introduction from Shilkret. Somewhere around this time, Orvon Autry began using the name Gene Autry. When he had asked the elder crooner Gene Austin what he thought of the name "Orvon Autry", Austin suggested that Orvon go by the name "Gene Autry" instead. By the end of 1928, Gene Autry was singing on Tulsa's radio station KVOO-FM as "Oklahoma's Yodeling Cowboy". The following year he signed a recording contract with Columbia Records and began working in Chicago on the WLS-AM radio show *National Barn Dance*.

     In 1932, Autry co-wrote his first big hit, *That Silver-Haired Daddy of Mine*, a duet with friend and songwriter Jimmy Long. He also married his first wife, Jimmy Long's niece, Ina Mae Spivey, the same year. In 1933 Gene Autry found himself in a pinch when he lost his accordion player. He was unable to locate a replacement and while spreading the word for help, he was told about a young man named Smiley, in Tuscola, IL, who played multiple instruments on the WDZ airwaves. Shortly afterwards, singer and songwriter Smiley Burnette became a member of the *National Barn Dance* radio show as well as a close friend of Autry's.

Gene and Smiley were discovered by film producer Nat Levine the following year. They made their film debut in 1934 as part of a singing cowboy quartet for Mascot Pictures' *In Old Sante Fe*. Then, in 1935, Levine cast them both in *The Phantom Empire*, a twelve-part serial in which Autry played the starring role. There Gene met another very close friend, for many years to come: the original, Champion the Wonder Horse. Champion was one of several horses that Gene rode in *The Phantom Empire* and had previously been owned by Western actor Tom Mix. Gene purchased Champion for $75.

In 1939, Gene then purchased a 1,2oo acre ranch in Berwyn, OK, which he named the Flying A Ranch. The *Gene Autry Flying "A" Ranch Rodeo* show began the following year. Though he was born in Texas, he was moved to Oklahoma at a very young age and began his radio career in the same state. In honor of all that Gene had done in Oklahoma, the town of Berwyn, OK, was renamed "Gene Autry", OK, on November 16th, 1941. Like Russell Hayden, Autry wanted to serve his country during World War II.

On July 26th, 1942, by request of the Pentagon, during a live broadcast of his *Melody Ranch* radio show, Gene Autry was inducted into the U.S. Army Air Forces as a Technical Sergeant. Part of his regular duties in the Army Air Forces included keeping up his regular radio program. One week after Gene was sworn into the military, the *Gene Autry Melody Ranch* radio show officially became the *Sgt. Gene Autry* radio show. The program continued airing music, comedy and action stories, but now included a heavy patriotic theme, which continued until August of 1943 when Autry was given new orders. In June of 1944, he earned his service pilot wings and was promoted to Flight Officer before he was assigned to the 91st Ferrying Squadron of the 555th Army Air Base Unit, Air Transport Command at Love Field. Autry served with this unit as a pilot on cargo type aircraft until October of 1945. Gene transferred to Special Services at the end of the war where he took a USO troupe to the South Pacific until he was honorably discharged from service in 1946. During the war, Gene Autry was awarded the American Campaign Medal, the Asiatic-Pacific Campaign Medal and the WWII Victory Medal.

When Autry returned to filming after the war he didn't have a solid sidekick; something every lead cowboy needed. The man who previously filled the role, Smiley Burnette, had continued working for Republic Pictures through WWII and after starring with actors like Sunset Carson, Bob Livingston and Roy Rogers, his contract was over on June 3oth, 1944. Burnette then began working for Columbia Pictures alongside Charles Starr on the *Durango Kid*, replacing actor Dub Taylor when he left the series. With Smiley already working elsewhere, Gene turned to actor Pat Buttram to fill his sidekick role.

Buttram had come to Hollywood in the early 194o's and worked as a sidekick to Roy Rogers. But, as Rogers had two friends who already took turns filling that role, Buttram was quickly dropped. Gene and Pat's first film together was *The Strawberry Roan*, directed by John English and filmed in Santa Clarita, CA, before it was released in 1948. English was under contract with Republic Pictures from 1935 until the studio went under in 1959. He directed many of Gene Autry's films during his time with Republic Pictures and then went on to direct for Autry's Flying A Studios afterwards. Pat Buttram would go on to co-star in more than 4o films and in over 1oo television episodes with Autry.

In 195o, Buttram sustained heavy injuries while filming a Gene Autry television show in Pioneertown. Smiley Burnette substituted for Buttram in the following episode, *Whirlwind*. Then, when the *Durango Kid* series ended two years later, Smiley teamed back up with the Singing Cowboy for Autry's final six films. Gene Autry was also very well known for his many Christmas holiday recordings, including *Santa Claus is Coming to Town, Frosty the Snowman,* his biggest hit *Rudolph the*

Red-Nosed Reindeer and his personal composition, *Here Comes Santa Claus*. He wrote *Here Comes Santa Claus* after he was the Grand Marshal of the 1946 Santa Claus Lane Parade, now the Hollywood Christmas Parade. Autry's choice for the song's title came very easily, as he remembered everyone at that parade excitedly repeating "Here comes Santa Claus!" His 1947 recording of the song became an instant holiday classic.

While it is unclear exactly when Dick Curtis introduced Gene Autry to Pioneertown, it is certain that Autry became a very intricate part of Pioneertown before Curtis left the corporation in 1948. Gene was not an original investor in the Pioneertown Corporation. However, early on, in the town's time of need, when land sales were slow but the potential was still high, Autry convinced director John English to film at Dick Curtis' new movie colony. Autry would go on to star in a great number of productions that were filmed in Pioneertown, which, in turn, helped the town become what it is today. His work in the late 1940's and early 1950's came at a point in time when Pioneertown needed business really bad.

In 1949, Gene Autry was detrimental in the erection of the Yucca Valley Airport. An avid pilot, Autry had already flown to Pioneertown on multiple occasions by that time and knew how much money and time could be saved by flying, rather than driving, to the High Desert. After Gene announced that he would fly the entire cast and crew in for the filming of *The Cowboy & the Indians*, should Yucca Valley establish an airport, it was laid out post haste by Jule Boldizsar and his family. Boldizsar had already established both automobile and aircraft services at the site of Yucca Valley's Sky Corral and knew that a landing strip was well overdue. Autry, true to his word, had the entire production team, along with stars Sheila Ryan, Frank Richards, Hank Patterson, Jay Silverheels, Claudia Drake and Charles Stevens, flown directly to the newly established Sky Corral in Yucca Valley before taking a short drive up to Pioneertown. Champion, however, opted to travel by land in his custom trailer.

Gene continued to work in town through the late 1950's, which helped to keep Pioneertown's blood flowing strong. Gene Autry titles that were filmed early in Pioneertown included *The Cowboy and the Indians* and *Riders in the Sky* in 1949, *Beyond the Purple Hills* and *Indian Territory* in 1950, *Whirlwind* and *Silver Canyon* in 1951, *Barbed Wire* in 1952, *Winning of the West*, *On Top of Old Smoky* and *Last of the Pony Riders* in 1953. *Last of the Pony Riders*, released in November of 1953, was Autry's last big screen role. Autry also produced all 91 episodes of *The Gene Autry Show* as well as all 81 episodes of the *Annie Oakley* show in Pioneertown.

Over the years, Autry would venture into a number of different lines of work. He was the original owner of Challenge Records, who released *Tequila* by the Champs in 1958. That song helped to start the rock-and-roll craze of the late 1950's and early 1960's. He became one of the most popular sports team owners in history when he purchased the Southern California Baseball team The Angels. Autry was a true fan of the sport and spent a great deal of time and money promoting the team. He attended his last Angels game just ten days before he died. An avid collector of Old West memorabilia, Gene established the Autry Museum at Griffith Park in Los Angeles, which is still a popular Western showcase to this day.

Gene Autry made some 640 recordings in his time, over half of which he personally wrote or co-wrote. He sold over 100 million copies of his records and has over a dozen gold and platinum records. Autry is the only person to have received five stars on the Hollywood Walk of Fame. He received a Film Star for his huge catalog of titles, a Music Star for his immense recording catalog, a Television Star for his 91 episodes of *The Gene Autry Show*, a Radio Star for his 16 seasons of *Melody Ranch* and a Live Performance Star for his many decades of entertaining crowds of happy fans.

Chapter 7

Big Dreams Bereft of Water

Gene worked steadily in Pioneertown throughout the 1950's, both as an actor and as a producer. While in town, he would stay at the Pioneer Townhouse, in room #1o. While staying there, he would also rent out the room next door, where Gene and his friends enjoyed coctails and played poker. Room #9 quickly wound up with the nickname "Club 9". Later, while filming *Jeopardy* in 1953, Barbara Stanwyck stayed in room #13 which soon earned that room the title of "the Barbara Stanwyck Room". While filming *The Annie Oakley Show* for Gene Autry, actress Gail Davis continued Autry's tradition of staying in room #1o. Each individual room ended up as host to a wealth of history as the years went on. One room to gain such fame without the aid of a major production in Pioneertown was room #11. Room #11 was the closest room to the outdoor public payphone, the only public payphone in Pioneertown.

Through the 1950's, a second wave of Pioneertown Corporation Board Members became active as other members were replaced over the years. New key members to this second wave of the corporation were Harry Altoff of Pioneertown's Althoof Furniture, Vice-President; Martel Ferris, Secretary-Treasurer; John Martel, Board Secretary and Legal Counsel for the Pioneertown Corporation; and of course, Russell Hayden, President and avid promoter of Pioneertown.

During a shoot for the episode *Mule Train* for *The Gene Autry Show* in 1950, actor Pat Buttram was injured on set. Actress Sheila Ryan accidentally connected with Buttram's head while staging a scene where she was suppose to clock his character with a handgun. Buttram received a handful of stitches in his head and shook it off. But an accident in Pioneertown shortly after, on September 11th, 1950, shocked residents and film crew members to their core.

While filming for an episode titled *The Peacemaker*, again for *The Gene Autry Show*, a prop cannon exploded when its breech failed, sending shrapnel flying in every direction. Autry's longtime friend and partner, actor Pat Buttram, was critically injured as shrapnel from the explosion gashed open his chest and stomach. Sound Boom Man, James Loomis, was also seriously injured when he was sliced open at his abdomen. Additionally, Johnny Brousseau, Gene Autry's Driver, received serious injuries to his kneecap.

Buttram lost a lot of blood and everyone at the scene presumed that he wouldn't survive the injuries. It is reported that Gene Autry, still half in shock himself, worked diligently to keep his old friend conscious by holding his hand and speaking firm, kind words of encouragement. Autry then hurriedly called the Twentynine Palms operator who transferred him through to Dr. Sally Ince. Gene Autry sent his private plane from the airport in Yucca Valley directly to Dr. Sally Ince in Twentynine Palms while an ambulance also headed up to Pioneertown.

By those days, Pioneertown Road saw a steady flow of daily traffic which made it impossible for aircraft to land on it. A large strip of land north east of Curtis Road had been cleared and leveled in order to make up a cheap and adequate landing strip for Pioneertown. Crew members and anyone else at the scene helped to illuminate the makeshift landing strip by car light so that Autry's plane could deliver Dr. Ince directly to the scene of the accident.

Dr. Ince immediately identified a punctured lung and noted that Buttram's cuts were so incredibly deep that she could literally see his lungs as he struggled to breath. Buttram, along with Dr. Ince and Autry, were transported to the Ince Memorial Hospital in Twentynine Palms as fast as possible. After arriving at the hospital, doctors located additional wounds to his leg, including a severed artery, which couldn't be seen sooner for the amount of blood Buttram had lost from his chest and stomach. It was reported that when Buttram arrived at the hospital his boots were filled to the brim with blood. He lost so much blood, in fact, that he needed a total of four blood transfusions before he later stabilized.

That first day and for many days to follow, every member of Gene's Flying A company visited the hospital trying to donate blood. Buttram wouldn't return to work for three months. During his recovery, Gene Autry paid for all of Buttram's personal expenses, as well as any expenses that his insurance didn't cover and kept him on full salary. Newspapers that year falsely reported that Autry had been thrown from the building during the explosion and was lucky to have escaped death. That would have been quite a neat trick, as Gene Autry wasn't even inside the building during the explosion. The newspapers did get it right a year and a half later when they reported that a fully recovered Pat Buttram and actress Sheila Ryan were married on December 26th, 1952.

Yucca Valley flourished in the 1950's. April 5th - 8th of 1951 was the first official Annual Grubstake Days, held in Yucca Valley, as a celebration of the town's great history. The event included a parade, tours of the Joshua Tree National Monument, barbecue and desert fun for all. By the time that Yucca Valley honored the many pioneers who made this land what it is today with Grubstake Days, most of the gold deposits in the High Desert had already been found and the majority of the gold mining activity in the area had died out. But there was still a great deal of wealth in the ground in the form of many other valuable minerals. The Humbug Mine for example, north west of Pioneertown, produced quite a few tons of Uranium ore in the 1950's.

On January 3rd, 1952, Pioneertown suffered another severe blow when Dick Curtis, the founder and indeed the man truly responsible for Pioneertown, died of lung cancer at the young age of 49. He was survived by his wive, Ruth Sullivan, his son John and his daughter Phyllis who had him buried at the Holy Cross Cemetery in Culver City. After stepping down from President of the Pioneertown Corporation, Curtis had started to act heavily once again. From 1950 until his death, early in 1952, Dick Curtis was featured in nearly 50 productions. Curtis was a big fan of *The Three Stooges* and appeared in a dozen titles with the comedy group. Sadly, Curtis died just 15 days before the actor Jerome Lester Horwitz. Horwitz, better known by his stage name, Curly Howard, died at the young age of 48 after suffering a pair of major strokes.

A year later, on June 30th of 1953, Pioneertown was hit with another major blow. The debt for a loan that the Pioneertown Corporation had taken back in 1946 in the amount of $60,000, after interest, had risen to over $80,000. The money was loaned to the Pioneertown Corporation by board members Fletcher Jones, William Murphy and Charles Nichols. The corporation had to default on the loan or they would be in debt forever. They announced that Pioneertown was not going to be able to keep afloat and that the Pioneertown Corporation, which included complete control over Mane Street, was going on the auction block at the end of the year. The date of the public auction was set for December 17th, 1953.

The first date in December was postponed until Wednesday, December the 3oth, after Philip Krasne's resident production company, Pioneer Studio Location, filed a restraining order, which stated that they needed more time to finish settling their business affairs in Pioneertown. Because the new date fell right before the New Year holiday, it was again postponed until January 17th of 1954. As Pioneertown held its breath in the anticipation, it seemed like a cruel joke when the first January date was postponed another week. Finally, on January 22nd, 1954, the Pioneertown Corporation went up for auction at the San Bernardino County Court House.

Original Pioneertown Corporation board members Fletcher Jones of Los Angeles and William Murphy of Culver City won the auction with a high bid of $8o,4oo. They assumed possession and control of Downtown Pioneertown and the 2o,ooo acres of additional land that surrounded it. Jones and Murphy didn't announce any new plans for Pioneertown, however the original corporation disbanded. By 1957, Krasne had left and taken Cisco and Poncho along with him. Gene Autry also left Pioneertown and took his Flying A Productions to Melody Ranch in Newhall, CA, which he had purchased in 1952.

For a long time, Pioneertown sat in wait as the desert around it changed and progressed. The name "Landers" first appeared on survey maps in 1954. That same year, in Landers, George Van Tassel began working on a project that he called "The Integratron". September of 1956 brought the tragic death of Sandra Jane Hayden, Russell Hayden's daughter. Russell and Mousie Hayden, heartbroken by their loss, then left for Arizona shortly afterwards. The Old Woman Springs Highway was paved in 1957. Major changes in the High Desert, like the introduction of paved Highways and the many automobile driving tourists that soon followed, lead to the very last cattle run through Yucca Valley which was recorded in 1957.

The moral in Pioneertown was a bit low, but the nearly 2oo residents kept their chins up and their eyes to the future. The Bravados, the first official gun fighting performance group in Pioneertown, began reenacting stories of the old West on Mane Street in 1958. Pioneertown was then the scene of the 11th Annual State Ride and Convention in 1959. John Hamilton, Charter President of the Equestrian Trails Corral 46, ETI State Director for Pioneertown and founder of the Dusty Trail Riders and Rawhide Riders, was elemental in bringing the annual event to Pioneertown.

Hamilton had a traditional horse ride that he took each year around his birthday where he rode an hour for every year he was alive. At the age of 62, John Hamilton won the Marathon Ride in 1959, which was set up as a benefit for the High Desert Memorial Hospital Building Fund Drive. He won the Marathon Ride by riding through Yucca Valley for 62 hours and six minutes, setting a world record at the time. There were no officials to record the world record however, as no one had expected the ride to be such an incredibly long one. Hamilton only stopped very quickly every four hours to trade horses, use the restroom if needed and replenish his water.

At 8:2oAM on December 27th, 1959, a fire caused $2,5oo in damages to the Red Dog Saloon. It was a dark foreshadowing for how the following decade would pan out. The beginning of the 196o's found Pioneertown starting to act like a wallflower in the never ending party that is the High Desert. In 196o, Frank Sinatra and his Rat Pack vacationed at their friend Jimmy Van Neusan's house in Yucca Valley, but did not visit Pioneertown on their trip. But not all was dull in Pioneertown. On October 12th, 1961, the first telephones were installed in town. Hester Guinan, then Post Master of Pioneertown, received the first of 23 telephones scheduled for installation. The first telephone call out of Pioneertown was from Hester to to Hilda Hardesty, the Post Master of Yucca Valley.

Once again, the High Desert saw another major production that, again, for one reason or another, chose not to shoot in Pioneertown. Director and producer Stanley Kramer filmed the famous comedy *It's A Mad, Mad, Mad, Mad World* all throughout California in 1963. A great deal of scenes were filmed in the High Desert and one particularly funny scene was shot along Old Woman Springs Highway right near the Pipes Canyon intersection. But not even Kramer's 3+ hour extended cut of the famous comedy included a single scene from Pioneertown.

In 1964, a shopping-center developer, community developer and car dealership owner from Cleveland named Benton Lefton purchased the Pioneertown Corporation and announced his plan to turn the area into an all inclusive desert resort town which he called "The California Golden Empire". Lefton was a very successful home builder in the mid-west, but when the two previous owners, Fletcher Jones and William Murphy, handed possession of Pioneertown over to Benton Lefton, the very last of the original Pioneertown family blood line was cut for good. Lefton hired a Hollywood Western Set Designer named Will Hanson, William Snelling of Land Trends Inc. and a famous land planner named Ferdinand Iwasko to help him develop his Golden Empire. Lefton also appointed J. C. Van Horne as a Resident Manager of the organization.

Snelling conducted a feasibility study and Iwasko prepared the master plan before Jennings Engineering Co. staked out the building sites, graded the roads and confirmed the master plan. Benton Lefton first set up his Land Office in the old White's Hardware building before moving to the old Service Station and Pony Express shortly after. In October of 1964, a 12 page brochure which detailed the Golden Empire's big plans was published and made available to the public. The brochure read "A 3o square mile development planned to afford a better living to young and old." Sadly, less than one year later, on March 1st, 1965, the Pioneertown Corporation, already long disbanded, was permanently suspended from the California State Franchise Tax Board.

Lefton's proposed $4oo,ooo,ooo development was set to be built in stages and take a total of ten years to complete. The first stage was to include 5oo 2 acre lots; 5oo larger 2-22 acre lots; about 3,000 acres dedicated to ranchos and summer camps; 1,ooo acres of condos, apartments and townhouses; 1,ooo acres of shopping centers and entertainment; 1,ooo acres of industrial and commercial sites; as well as 1,ooo acres dedicated to more recreation and religion. Mane Street, to an extent, was to remain the same, but was set for a drastic overhaul which would have seen the addition of more shopping, arcades, theaters, more rodeo grounds, more campgrounds and an abundance of public parking.

To everyone's amazement, Benton Lefton was able to sell more than half of the lots that made up the First Phase in less than 9o days. It was shorty after this accomplishment that Benton Lefton optimistically estimated that there would be an access of 35,ooo residents living in Pioneertown by 1975. As the sales continued, there was a slight increase in the tourism and residents kept Mane Street alive with true pioneer spirit. It was around that time that a sign on the side of the road while driving up to Pioneertown once stood. The sign read: "Pioneertown - Population: Genial".

The residents and business owners of Pioneertown are a prime example of what true grit is made of. As the world was changing around them, when times were bleak and their futures were unsure, they stayed strong. A man named Charlie Hanie self-appointed himself as the Sheriff of Pioneertown during the Golden Empire days and patrolled Mane Street keeping the peace and more importantly, ensuring that business owners in town kept to the old West theme. A new business owner to Pioneertown in the early Golden Empire days was actor and *Queen For A Day* game show host Jack Bailey, who purchased the Golden Stallion and the Pioneer Townhouse. While under Bailey's ownership, the Townhouse went by the name of the Golden Stallion Lodge.

Lefton quickly began submitting plans for land development in Pioneertown to San Bernardino County. On June 25th of 1965, the Golden Empire's proposal for a Dump Site on the outskirts of town was denied. The following month, the Jackass Mail was established in Pioneertown by Marie Amos who set up operations in the old Nickelodeon on Mane Street. Jackass Mail reporters were Howard Clark, Honey Fellers, Ida Jones, Dick Kelly, Esther Latham and Darlene Robbins. The Jackass Mail offered a monthly publication much like the original Pioneertown Gazette, but with a bit of an eccentric twist and some extra traditional Western flair. Later that winter, a flash flood in Rattlesnake Canyon destroyed three Jeeps, damaged another two and left eighteen people stranded in the rain until they were rescued by emergency workers.

In February of 1966, the Pioneer Loop Association was formed in an attempt to get State and Federal funding for beautification and maintenance of the 15o mile loop. Said funding would have included the paving of the Pioneer Pass which would have allowed for much easier access to Big Bear and many other points of interest. On March 1oth of the following month, the Golden Empire's proposal for an airport in Pioneertown was approved by San Bernardino County. However, their proposal for an RV Park was denied shortly afterwards. The Golden Empire's inspection of the land for these proposals lead them to publicly disclose that they only considered 2o,ooo acres of Pioneertown economically feasible for further development.

April of 1966 was a very hard month for all of Pioneertown. On Monday, April 4th, the Likker Barn caught fire, but was saved before there was major damage to the building. The cause was discovered to be faulty wiring. Later that week, at 2:55AM on Good Friday, April 8th, the Red Dog Saloon caught fire and burned to the ground in less than 12 hours. Fire fighters had the fire contained within a few hours, but could only prevent it from spreading. It was nearly impossible to extinguish the flames as the building was constructed out of old railroad ties which were heavy with combustible oils. The cause of the Red Dog's fire was discovered to have started at the kitchen stove and there were no signs of arson.

Just two days later, on April 1oth, Easter Sunday, the Golden Stallion, also built of old railroad ties, caught fire and burned to the ground. An employee who was sleeping inside the private quarters in the back of the building was injured, but managed to escape through a window. That fire was determined to have been caused by a cigarette. In just one week, three buildings on Mane Street had caught on fire and two of the most historic and active establishments in Pioneertown had burned to their foundations. The town was truly devastated. Construction of a new, larger Red Dog Saloon was quickly underway and it reopened the following year. However, the Golden Stallion, once the largest restaurant in Pioneertown, was never rebuilt. Later in 1966, more unexpected destruction fell upon Pioneertown as a big winter storm rattled through the High Desert and caused an estimated $34,ooo in damages.

The population of Yucca Valley had begun to thrive around the mid 196o's and exceeded 32,000 residents in 1966. That year, a developer of Yucca Valley's Western Hills named Art Miller began personally busing potential home buyers up to the High Desert. He was personally responsible for bringing an estimated 3o,ooo new residents to the High Desert area in the late 196o's. But even the boom in desert real estate didn't bring production companies back to Pioneertown as many hoped it would. In 1968, writer and director Abraham Polonsky filmed the movie *Tell Them Willie Boy Was Here* in Landers and other areas in the Morongo Basin where Willie lead his famous chase. Yet again, filming was done right in town, but the production did not choose to use Pioneertown.

In 1969, Doreen Thompson joined the Pioneertown Post Office staff as a replacement clerk. Just six years later, in 1975, Thompson replaced Guinan as the Post Master of Pioneertown. Some of the biggest land owners in the area were Pioneertown residents Bruce and Jean Burns who owned a half section, or 32o acres, off of Skyline Ranch Road, just to the east of Pioneertown. In 1972, Mr. & Mrs. Burns deeded 265 acres to the University of California for preservation, research and class field trips. The site is now named the Burns Pinon Ridge Reserve and is a truly valued asset of the University of California.

The ornate circular stone watering trough that used to sit in the middle of Mane Street was illegally moved in the early 197o's by a former Pioneertown resident named Stoney. Stoney, known as a heavy drinker, was a very frequent patron of both the Bowling Alley and the Red Dog Saloon. One night Stoney crashed his car into the stone trough while driving down Mane Street. Due to the Golden Empire's poor management, Dick Curtis' original wish that no automobiles be allowed on Mane Street had been ignored and cars drove freely through town at that time. Stoney was so mad at the trough for damaging his car that he persuaded a friend of his who owned a tractor to come by the next morning. Stoney and his accomplice almost destroyed the historic stone watering trough while pushing it to the north side of Mane Street that day. To this very day, it still remains where the pair left it, but the damage that it sustained now prevents it from retaining water.

By this time, the County of San Bernardino had worked out a deal to pipe a small water system into Pioneertown at the property owner's expense. The utility would need to be owned and maintained by Pioneertown as the county had no intention of managing it. So Pioneertown residents took on the responsibility themselves and set up operations inside the Pioneer Bowl, allowing customers to pay their water bill at the bowling alley. Access to the water system was not cheap and a handful of residents opted to continue using well water. As the Golden Empire struggled to stay afloat through the 1970's, Lefton was hardly able to afford the water system being brought to his own Land Office at the old Service Station and ended up liquidating materials around Pioneertown to fund his water access.

A pair of long time fans of Pioneertown named John and Frances Aleba purchased a handful of the buildings along Mane Street from the Golden Empire in 1972. One of the buildings they purchased was Lefton's old headquarters, the Service Station on the south east corner of town. John and Frances then turned it into The Cantina, where they offered a Tex-Mex menu and a full bar. They quickly attracted a large following, including a great many bikers from across the nation, who referred to The Cantina as a "Biker's Burrito Bar". Later that year, the Golden Empire's submission for an 80 Acre Camping Site was approved by the county in September of 1972.

Sadly, Minna Gombell died on April 14th of the following year, in Santa Monica, CA, from a reported heart attack. Gombell kept her Pioneertown residence until her death in 1973 and visited the property as often as she could in her later years. The following year, Russell Hayden was the Grand Marshal of the 1974 Grubstake Days Parade in Yucca Valley. Later that same year, Russell and Mousie Hayden were both Grand Marshals of the Turtle Days Parade in Joshua Tree. Though it was reopened shortly after the fire which claimed the original building in 1966, the Red Dog Saloon closed their doors for good in 1974. While one set of doors closed, another set opened shortly afterwards when Hans and Esther Gubler opened the Orchard Nursery in Landers at the site of the old Reche family homestead in 1975, the same year the Vietnam War came to an end. After nearly 30 years of entertaining the entirety of Pioneertown, famed resident celebrity Dazzlin' Dallas Morley retired in 1977.

By 1979, it was finally publicly announced that there was not enough water to sustain more growth in the area. Water wells in Pioneertown had been established and then quickly tapped over and over in an attempt to sustain the current residents. San Bernardino County put a restriction on the installation of new water meters and the digging of new wells. A plan to construct one huge communal well in Water Canyon that would then pump water up the hill to provide for Pioneertown was planned out. The proposed fee for property owners was to be $75 per acre for connection to the new water system. In a poll of the local land owners, 190 of 345 land owners responded to a survey and 71% of them voted in favor of the new well. Unfortunately for residents and for Benton Lefton, the plan fell through a short while later. That marked the start of Pioneertown's serious water troubles and the end of Lefton's California Golden Empire, which went bankrupt shortly afterwards.

A Blues singer by the name of Buzz Gamble moved to Pioneertown in the very late 1970's. He lived in town until his death, nearly thirty years later in 2004. Gamble became a local celebrity in Pioneertown and was commonly found either eating, drinking or playing at the Cantina. In the years to follow, Gamble actually spent quite a lot of time renovating the bar inside the Cantina. Celebrity singer Nancy Wilson also became a resident of Pioneertown when she moved to Pipes Canyon in 1980. Wilson soon established the Coldwater Springs Campground for children on her large ranch in Pipes Canyon. 1980 was a particularly harsh year for original Pioneertown resident Margie Mattoon Hamilton. Margie's second husband, John Hamilton, died just two weeks before her daughter, Lois, was tragically killed in a car accident.

In October of 1980, a proposal for a 2o acre RV Park was not approved by the San Bernardino County. Much like the Golden Empire's previous attempt to establish an RV Park, the county did not see there being enough water, nor means of waste disposal, for such a large park in the area. In 1982 Pioneertown saw the arrival of Harriet and her husband, Pappy. Harriet's parents, John and Frances Aleba, had purchased a handful of buildings in Pioneertown in the 197o's and had turned the old service station into the Cantina restaurant and biker bar. Frances Aleba then gave The Cantina to Harriet and Pappy when she was ready to retire in October of 1982. They named it the Pioneertown Palace, but the place soon became known around town as "Pappy & Harriet's" as the happy couple worked hard to change it into a nice family style restaurant with quality food and great music.

Pioneertown lost a great supporter and original founder on June 9th, 1981, when Russell Hayden died from viral pneumonia at the Desert Hospital in Palm Springs. Hayden passed just three days shy of what would have been his 69th birthday. Mousie Hayden, though saddened by her loss, continued to live at the Hayden Ranch and continued to run the Sandra Hayden Memorial Foundation. Half a year after Hayden's death, on November 3oth, 1981, Benton Lefton also passed away. Emergency work was conducted on the existing water system in Pioneertown in 1981. The work ended up costing land owners who used the water system a total of $125 per acre which they were charged the following August.

Just one year later, in August of 1982, 328 Pioneertown land owners were then charged an additional $243 for further development of the water system. Emergency work was again performed to ensure that residents had safe water available. This time land owners received a bill that surely made quite a lot of jaws in Pioneertown drop. The third charge for work done to the water system in as many years, sent out in May of 1983, was for $6oo-$1789 per property. Owners were granted the option to make payments for this final additional charge to their monthly water bills.

The early 1980's weren't all bad. The Morongo Basin Historical Society was established in April of 1982 and the Scarlett Lady arrived at the Hayden Ranch in 1983. The Scarlet Lady was built by Baron Michael Von Redl who came to America in his early twenties during the 19th Century. His partner, Willis S. Kilmer "The Swamp Root King", introduced Von Redl to private railroading while entertaining the Baron in his own car, the "Remlik", or Kilmer backwards. Von Redl was hooked on the idea and commissioned three cars built from the Pullman Standard Company. The first car was an office with indirect lighting, a safe and all the amenities one would need to conduct business. The second was a sleeping car complete with a fireplace, multiple wardrobes and even a bathtub. The third, The Scarlet Lady, was a a saloon car that featured a bar, was adorned with tasseled red velvet upholstery, intricately carved wood decoration, silken curtains and even an observation platform in the back.

Unfortunately to railroad historians around the world, the Scarlet Lady is the sole survivor of those three railroad cars. The Baron would later follow an actress into Mexico and vanish into time. The poor Scarlet Lady was torn from her two sister-cars, trashed and found herself in a railroad junk yard in Williams, AZ. Thankfully if was at this junk yard where two railroad buffs discovered her before she was dismantled and scrapped. They commissioned the famed art director Martin Obzina to restore her before she became a prominent feature in a classy restaurant near Los Angeles. In 1983, Allen Ward was responsible for getting the restaurant owners to part with her. The Scarlett

Lady was then on loan to the Sandra Hayden Memorial Foundation. Ward had all 180,000 pounds of her, including a section of her own track, hauled to the Hayden Ranch where they built a small wooden station platform, complete with wrought iron benches and antique lamps in front of her.

After a handful of people had owned Pioneertown's motel for short stints of time, residents Ernie and Carol Kester bought the Pioneertown Motel in 1984. Both members of the Morongo Basin Historical Society, the Kesters quickly became very prominent figures and local historians in Pioneertown. Much like the rest of the town, the Pioneertown Motel was in a bit of disarray when the Kesters purchased it. Though the Motel might have been a little worse off than the majority of the other structures in Pioneertown at the time.

The Kesters found odd problems quite abundant while renovating the Motel. Some of the most interesting oddities they encountered after purchasing the Pioneertown Motel included having to immediately deal with the fact that only two rooms were furnished with mattresses. Furthermore, one of them was occupied by a long time tenant named Alabama who had been raising goats in his room. Over the years, the Kesters put a lot of time and hard work into beautifying the Pioneertown Motel and preserving its abundant history.

On February 1st, 1984, the County of San Bernardino approved and funded the purchase and installation of an 800 square foot building to house the Pioneertown Volunteer County Fire Brigade's Fire Truck. The County's approval couldn't have come at a better time as just months later, on the afternoon of May 15th, a wild fire which may have been started by a campfire burned over 2,000 acres just four miles to the west of Pioneertown.

A proposal to split San Bernardino County, the largest county in the Continental United States, into two separate counties, was announced in October of 1986. The proposal mainly focused on a new county, to be named "Joshua Tree County" or "Mojave County", which was to be focused around the Morongo Basin. While there were mixed reviews, the vast majority of residents in the San Bernardino County were opposed to the idea and the proposed project failed by 1988. A very cold storm blew through the High Desert in the winter of 1989 - 1990. The chilly wind speeds were recorded as high as 92 miles in the Morongo Basin. That winter marked the start of a new decade and the beginning of a new era of both residents and business owners in Pioneertown.

Chapter 8
Pioneertown's Big Brother: Big Bear

In 1845, Justice of the Peace for the Inland Territory that is present day Riverside County, Benjamin Davis Wilson, was charged with the task of locating and pursuing the infamous Chief Walkara. At one point Wilson commanded a posse of 44 men on his search, 22 of which he sent up through the Cajon Pass and 22 men which he personally lead up Santa Ana canyon towards Yuhaviat in an attempt to surround the renegade Indian cattle rustlers in Lucerne Valley. Yuhaviat had once been a settlement of the Serrano people for many thousands of years; its name was the Serrano word for "Pine Place". However, as homesteaders, trappers and prospectors started to populate the area in the early 18oo's, the soil didn't yield good crops, very little gold was discovered and grizzly bears posed a constant threat to residents, earning the small settlement the unofficial title of "Starvation Flats".

When Wilson and his men arrived in the area they found a few settlers and some peaceful Serrano people in a high altitude watershed which was rich with tall pine trees and large grizzly bears. Wilson divided his men into 11 pairs and sent each team out in search of meat for their journey. When each of his 11 teams returned with a grizzly bear, he decided to name the area "Bear Valley" and the alkali lake to the east "Big Bear Lake". Wilson was unsuccessful in his search for Chief Walkara but the manhunt that he lead through Bear Valley sparked big changes in the area.

The first mining claim in Bear Valley was filed in 1858 by a man named John Cool. Cool claimed 16o acres and established the Bear Lake Silver Mine but did not see much success. The people in Bear Valley, mainly residents of Starvation Flats, eventually hired a gold prospector named William Francis Holcomb to rid the area of the aggressive bears in the early 186o's. Holcomb was known as "the best sharpshooter west of the Mississippi" and his skill with a rifle earned him the lengthy name William Francis "Grizzly Bill" Holcomb.

Holcomb, along with his partner Jack Martin, had come to Bear Valley in 1859 searching for gold. They joined up with Joe Colewell and his party of six other gold miners at Starvation Flats late that fall. After they discovered a nice deposit of placer gold, Martin traveled to Los Angeles to pick up his family and a great deal of supplies. It is said that while traveling through San Bernardino, Martin stirred up a little excitement when he showed off some of the gold they had found. He then received a lot of attention in Los Angeles when he paid for all of his supplies with gold dust. Around that time, early in 186o, William Holcomb noticed a valley north of Bear Valley that caught his curiosity. After falling two bears on his first attempt to explore the new valley, Holcomb's party was held up for a day while they stripped and transported the animals.

The following day Holcomb shot another grizzly bear and, along with his friend Ben Choteau, tracked the injured animal to a creek in the unexplored valley. It was at this creek where they easily spotted placer gold in a quartz ledge. Holcomb quickly filed five gold claims and established a handful of mines near the initial discovery. Within months that area became known as Holcomb Valley and attracted prospectors from all around the world. William Holcomb had sparked the largest gold rush in Southern California.

In June of 1861, Jed Van Dusen, the town's blacksmith, built the first road into Holcomb Valley. Using $15oo in contributions from the locals, he completed a route which connected to the newly established Cajon Pass Toll Road near present day Hesperia. During the 4th of July celebrations in 1861, Van Dusen's wife fashioned an American flag from a miner's shirt and a dance hall girl's skirt. Holcomb hadn't wanted the town to be named after himself; so they instead named it after the Van Dusen's daughter, Belle, who was also the first child born in the town. By November of that year the population of Belleville was nearing 2ooo. But during the November elections, the town lost the opportunity of becoming the county seat by only two votes.

The winter of 1861 - 1862 was the harshest winter ever recorded in California history. Rain and snow started falling on Christmas Eve and didn't stop for 28 straight days. By February, the area was adorned with over 15 feet of snow. After the first couple of very hard years, the town thrived for a brief while before the gold then dried up and all the miners left. By the early 187o's the boomtown of Belleville dwindled down to a ghost town. However, in November of 1873, Barney and Charley Carter discovered gold nuggets near the east side of Bear Valley at their Rainbow claim. Elias Jackson "Lucky" Baldwin soon bought their claims and then began construction of a $25o,ooo 4o stamp mill at his nearby Gold Mountain Mine and started the second gold rush in Bear Valley.

That winter, Sam Baird and four carpenters completed the first work on a small town site that was established on the flats just below the Gold Mountain Mine. The small town would go by numerous names over time, but was originally called Bairdstown after Sam Baird. In 1874 a new shelf road around the south end of Jacoby Canyon was completed in haste by Chinese laborers. The same hard workers then constructed a wooden flume along the mountain side which brought water south from Van Dusen Canyon five miles to Baldwin's stamp mill. At 3:3oPM on March 8th, 1875, the Baldwin stamp ore mill was started up in front of almost 2oo attendants and from that day on, the pounding of the stamps could be heard all across Bear Valley. The first ore they ran was estimated to be worth $7o a ton.

Some 5o homes and stores were rushed to completion at Bairdstown to support the increasing number of miners, mill workers and their families. Unfortunately, the untimely and controversial closing of the Bank of California in August of 1875 lead E. J. Baldwin to close the Gold Mountain Mine. By 1876, the boom was well over and so much of the town's population had left that by November's election, only eight voters cast their ballots in the area. To add insult to injury, Baldwin suffered an additional $8o,ooo loss when his stamp mill mysteriously caught fire and burned to the ground on August 11th, 1878.

The first commercial cattle ranching in Bear Valley was done by a man named Gus Knight, Sr. in 1879. Knight was the first of many cattle ranchers who would find a home in the high altitudes of the San Bernardino Mountains. In 188o the Assistant State Engineer, Fred Perris, persuaded by State Assemblyman Dr. Ben Barton, completed a survey for the State of California. His survey was part of the State's attempt to establish potential sites for high altitude irrigation reservoirs. Perris reported, "Bear Valley is one of the best sites for a water storage reservoir in southern California."

1882 saw the arrival of James Smart, who homesteaded 16o acres to the south of present day Big Bear Lake for cattle ranching. At that time, the nearest city where one could have professional iron cast was Los Angeles. It is said that while Smart was trekking home through the mountains with a brand new *JS* branding iron, the tip of the *J* was accidentally broken off. Smart decided not to return to the big city for a replacement and began branding his cattle with the *IS* brand, which would go on to be one of the most well known brands in the history of cattle ranching in southern California.

Frank Elwood Brown, a civil engineer, and E. G. Judson established the city of Redlands, CA in the early 1880's. Brown traveled through Bear Valley in May of 1883. When he arrived at the west end of Bear Valley, Brown deduced that the site would be the perfect location for a large reservoir that could supply water to the citrus farms down in Redlands. Brown immediately began taking steps towards getting a dam built and was quite successful. He designed the dam himself and raised enough money to purchase the lake site and establish the Bear Valley Land and Water Co. That newly formed corporation's members decided to name the lake they were creating "Big Bear Lake" and rename the old alkali lake, which was originally given the same title by Benjamin Davis Wilson, to "Baldwin Lake" after E. J. "Lucky" Baldwin's rich history in the area.

Construction of the over 3oo' long and over 5o' high dam, which held 25,ooo acre feet of water, was completed before the winter storm of 1884. The Redlands water distribution system then received the first water from the Bear Valley Reservoir on July 1oth, 1885. It took Frank E. Brown just over two years to turn his dream of a water reservoir for Redlands in a reality. 1888 then saw the first resort accommodations available at the newly developed Big Bear Lake. Gus Knight, Jr. and John Metcalf, Jr. opened the Bear Valley Hotel, which could host 3o guests. In 189o, Knight purchased 28o acres of State School land between Baldwin Lake and Sugar Loaf Mountain.

In 1891, the Bear Valley Wagon Road Company was contracted to build a new road from the north shore of Big Bear Lake, known then as Grout and presently as Fawnskin, to connect with the Danaher's City Creek Road near present day Running Springs. The Bear Valley Wagon Road, present day Forest Service Road 2N13 and also known as Snowslide Road, was completed in 1892. That was a very big year for Bear Valley. On May 15th of 1892, the first of many Wilshire Stages left from Redlands headed up to Bear Valley. The tri-weekly trips to Knight and Metcalf's Bear Valley Hotel cost $7 and took almost two straight days. In addition to the new road and the new stage line to the area, 1892 also saw the addition of the first telephone line at Big Bear Lake, which connected the Bear Valley Dam with the San Bernardino Valley.

George Rathbun and Will Talmadge also went into partnership with James Smart on the IS Ranch in 1892. That partnership would go on to change the history of local cattle ranching, which was expanding steadily in the area at that time. A bigger change came when President Benjamin Harrison established the San Bernardino Forest Reserve on February 25th, 1893. It encompassed 737,28o acres, including Bear Valley, which was heavily grazed by cattle ranchers. In addition to the IS Ranch's cattle; at that time the Knights had 175 head south of Baldwin Lake and Metcalfs were grazing 1oo head at Bear Valley. Luckily for those concerned, no administrative officers or rangers were appointed.

Mining activity surrounded Big Bear Lake in the 189o's. Valley Gold company worked out of Holcomb Valley, the Blackhawk Mine and the Rose Mine to the east. Around 1892, "Lucky" Baldwin's son-in-law, Bud Doble, took over operations of the Gold Mountain Mine. For a brief time, the town of Bairdstown was then called "Doble". The second go wasn't very successful and Doble abandoned operations at the Gold Mountain Mine by 1895. But the mine wouldn't stay inactive for very long. All of the activity in Bear Valley really put a lot of stress on all the roads leading in. In 1899, Gus Knight helped to incorporate the Bear Valley and Redlands Toll Road Company. They then built another road to Big Bear Lake from the south, which followed along the old miner's trail from the 186o's and started off at the head waters of the Santa Ana River.

Captain De Lamars, a very successful mine owner and operator in the United States and Canada, took over the Gold Mountain Mine around 19oo. A new, state of the art, 4o stamp mill at Gold Mountain was then built by 4o carpenters and millwrights. Poles were also setup from all the way down in Victor for a new telegraph line that went directly to the mine. The Gold Mountain Mine Stamp Mill was successfully processing ore by the summer of 19oo and was soon running two shifts and crushing over 1oo tons of ore a day. Doble was home to nearly 2oo people and received a new post office on July 27th, 19oo. On Christmas Eve of 19oo, a mysterious fire destroyed the knight hotel at Bear Valley while it was closed for the winter.

In 19o1 L. M. Holt proposed to the City of Redlands that several water companies be consolidated and that a higher dam should be built in Bear Valley to fulfill the need for more water. Much like the water at Bear Valley, there was a lot of improvement left for the four toll roads that lead into the San Bernardino Mountains. The toll roads were poorly maintained and very costly for the estimated 80,ooo annual visitors to the high altitude retreat. Around 19o3 the name "Big Bear Lake" became commonly used to help distinguish the area from the newly developing Little Bear Lake, now present day Lake Arrowhead. Captain De Lamar didn't have the best of luck at Gold Mountain and quit operations around that time.

After the public all but demanded free access to the mountains, San Bernardino County took over the Arrowhead Toll Road in 19o5 and allowed free access. However, they restricted the use of automobiles on the road. That same year, the Forest Service built a log Ranger Station on the north shore of Big Bear Lake at the site of a strong natural spring. In 19o6 Gus Knight, Sr. died and his 6oo cattle and 25 horses were sold to Bill Shay.

The first circular automobile trip through the San Bernardino Mountains was completed on August 27th, 19o8, by John A. Heyser and two other men in a white steam car. The trio left San Bernardino at 8AM and headed up Santa Ana Canyon, past Big Bear Lake, they took the Crest Road to Pinecrest and then passed down through Waterman Canyon and back towards San Bernardino before arriving back to their starting point at 9:17PM. The trip took a total of 13 hours and 17 minutes. The story was reported in newspapers across southern California. The next year, 19o9, saw a lot of changes to the mountains surrounding Big Bear Lake. The County supervisors received a petition asking them to allow automobiles to use the Waterman Canyon road. A test that saw seven cars climb the canyon was completed without incident and from then on, automobiles were granted access to the road on certain days and hours.

On June 26th, 19o9, John "Fritz" Fisher and his friends drove two Model T Ford Runabouts from Redlands to Big Bear Lake using the indirect desert roads. The 1o5 mile trip took 14 hours and 4o minutes. Partially in response to a rapid increase of visitors to the area and partly because the funding was available, the Forest Service connected all of their numerous locations throughout the San Bernardino Mountains with a network of telephone lines in 19o9. Sadly, E. J. "Lucky" Baldwin passed away that year. Thomas H. Oxnam purchased the Gold Mountain Mine and the stamp mill from the Baldwin estate.

In 191o, John S. Eastwood won the contract to build a new and higher dam at Big Bear Lake to replace the one built in 1882. The new dam was built nearly 25o feet downstream of the original rock dam and was over 7o feet tall. Eastwood designed the dam using a new concept at the time which called for multiple thin walled concrete arches for strength instead of simply using a great deal of mass. In August of 1891, W. C. Butler had started working on a replacement dam that was 15o feet below the original rock dam, but the project was never completed. Eastwood would see success where Butler failed, as his dam was completed by 1911 and held nearly triple the amount of water in Big Bear Lake. Upon the dams completion, J. S. Eastwood had successfully created the largest man-made lake in the world at that time.

1911 was the year that the blossoming motion picture industry discovered the San Bernardino Mountains. The first professional production to ever film in the area was debatably *Romance of the Bar O* by the Essanay Company, which was finished on March 9th of 1911. They were soon followed by the Bison Motion Picture Company who arrived on July 1oth. The company hauled five large wagons, six canoes, 26 horses, eight expert riders and 28 actors and actresses up into the San Bernardino Mountains for two months. During their stay they often completed a one reel picture each day.

In 1911, four wealthy men from Redlands purchased the old Pine Lake Hotel and its 44 cabins, originally Knight & Metcalf's Bear Valley Hotel, before changing the name of the resort to Pine Knot Lodge shortly thereafter. The Forest Service established a trail system to help aid in the fighting of future forest fires around that time. One trail they made good use of was the Old Mormon Trail, which still saw a great deal of activity from cattle ranchers in those days.

In 1912, a young man named Kirk Phillips started the Mountain Auto Line to Big Bear Lake with his new white truck. He had seen a white truck with a bench seat transporting people on 5th Avenue in New York and thought that the same concept would work well in the poorly accessible San Bernardino Mountains. He was right! His white trucks, which began transporting freight and as many as 15 passengers at a time, is debated as being the world's second bus line.

The term *stage* was used interchangeably with the term *bus* up through the 1940's. In addition to Phillips' services, Brooks and Shay opened a second auto stage line. Gus Knight was instructed by the County to rebuild the Bear Valley Wagon Road for automobile use in 1913. The County also began construction on a road to Big Bear through Mill Creek using prison labor. Later that year, World Champion Boxer James J. Jeffries purchased the first lot at Gus Knight Jr.'s new subdivision in Bear Valley.

By the summer of 1913, Kirk Phillip's Mountain Auto Line had nine white stages bringing hundreds if not thousands of tourists to Big Bear Lake over the unfinished Mill Creek Road each month. The Pine Knot Lodge, managed by Fritz Fisher, added 20 cabins and made significant interior improvements to the existing cabins. Around this time, the entire village adopted the name "Pine Knot". Clifford Lynn and Ed Moyer set up a sawmill on Big Bear Lake in 1913 and made good use of the extreme changes in the area. Some of Lynn & Moyer's first logs were from trees that were killed by the newly filled lake. 1913 also saw further extension of the IS Ranch when John and Frank Talmadge, Jr. bought the Metcalf Ranch along with its 1,200 cattle and went into partnership with their brother Will.

Shay and Barker purchased 3,500 acres of pasture land beside Baldwin Lake and 600 head of cattle for $30,000 from the estate of the late E. J. "Lucky" Baldwin in 1914. Kirk Phillips, the founder of the Mountain Auto Line died at the young age of 35 in 1914. His partners, Perry and Max Green, assumed operation of the thriving company. Another case of inheritance took place the same year when Charles Oxnam took over control of the Gold Mountain Mill from his ill father before remodeling and restarting operations as the site.

The circular trip through the mountains and past Big Bear Lake could be easily completed by 1914. To help promote the newly completed Crest Highway, County Supervisors gave a tour to members of the press in September of 1914. The "101 Mile Rim of the World Drive" through the San Bernardino Mountains was dedicated on July 17 - 18th, 1915. A huge crowd, including over 100 news reporters, were in attendance for the dedication. The drive received so much attention that operations were taken over by the California State Highway Department just a few years later. The area was receiving plenty of attention then, including plenty of attention from film producers. Some of the productions that were filmed in the area around that time were Cecil B. DeMille's *Call of the North*, D. W. Griffith's *The Clansman* and the Kalem Movie Company's *Mona the Mountain Maid*.

1915 also saw a good deal of trouble in Bear Valley. That winter was harsh and brought some of the deepest snow recorded in years. The hard freeze early that year left Big Bear Lake covered with ice over a foot thick. Then, in September, a fire at the Pine Knot Lodge destroyed the dining room, kitchen and office. The Pine Knot Lodge began rebuilding immediately. Weather conditions were quite extreme again by the end of 1915 and eventually lead to blizzards through the

Winter of 1916. Conditions were so bad that at one point the trek down to Victorville took almost eight hours through the snow. Later, the Santa Ana River road was washed away, the Clark Grade was covered by a large landslide and the Edison Company was forced to hire over 1oo men to open their powerhouse road.

The powerful and rugged White Stages of the Mountain Auto Line were able to begin services up to Big Bear via the terribly muddy Crest Road by May 13th of 1916. They now had 15 White Stages and 22 men on their payroll. Brooks and Shay were forced to shut down their transportation services that year as the roads leading into Bear Valley were closed so often due to the weather that it was simply unprofitable to operate. The weather didn't completely halt the cattle ranching in the area, as Shay and Barker purchased 32o acres from the Talmadge IS Ranch that year. Development was also able to continue through the harsh weather. Anticipating the growth that Big Bear Lake would be attracting, the Bear Valley Development Company began subdividing the land around Big Bear Lake and in October of 1916, the Pine Knot Post Office was opened inside of the Pine Knot store.

During the winter of 1917, the Pine Knot Lodge and a handful of San Bernardino auto dealers offered a prize cup to the first car that could make it up into Bear Valley after March 1st. 25 cars were said to have competed in the "race" and it took an astonishing 25 days for the winner to finish, as they all had been stuck in the deep snow. 1917 saw the start of many big changes around Big Bear Lake. Gus Knight purchased the Oxnam Estate lands around Baldwin Lake and constructed a clubhouse and blinds for duck hunters on the north shore of the lake. The Bartlett brothers built a café, service station and store in the heart of Pine Knot. B. G. Holmes bought the six Blair log cabins on the south side of Pine Knot and changed the name to Indian Lodge. Margaret Betterley purchased land from Gus Knight to the east of Pine Knot and established Camp Eureka.

In July of 1917, Albert Brush began the $1oo,ooo construction of the Big Bear Tavern near the IS Ranch to the west of Pine Knot. Brush's building still exists today and is presently the Presbyterian Conference Grounds. William Cline and Clinton Miller purchased 7oo acres around Grout and started subdividing the land for ranch sites. They changed the name from Grout to Fawnskin and built a large hotel and commercial building which they called the Fawn Lodge. The Fawn Lodge was the site of a post office which opened in May of the following year. A man named James G. Hulme reopened the Gold Mountain Mine and repaired the buildings and machinery. Hulme began crushing 1oo tons of ore per day and ran the mill 24 hours a day, seven days a week.

A pilot named Waldo Waterman landed a World War I Thomas Scout Fighter aircraft in a meadow on the old Shay Ranch in 1919. Waterman was recorded as the first person to fly an airplane into Big Bear and would surely not be the last. Later in September, the first school in Bear Valley opened at Lowe's Camp. John and Mayme Lowe, who's three children were some of the first enrolled, donated the log cabin where Miss Vera McPherson taught. The population in Bear Valley was growing quickly and by 192o there were over 6oo cabins in the area. For the first time ever recorded, over 1oo people remained at the lake throughout the entire winter. Later that year, the Big Bear Chamber of Commerce was established in the bustling valley.

In 192o the Motor Transit Company of Los Angeles bought the Mountain Auto Line and kept Max Green on as the manager. The Forest Service worked half of that year laying out a proposed route through Deep Creek to Big Bear Lake. Pine Knot saw the $2o,ooo completion of the Grizzly Theater which opened to patrons in 192o, but required that early attendants bring their own chairs as the freight service transporting the theater's seats had been delayed. Charles Tayles and W. L. Rideout bought property on the south edge of Big Bear Lake from the estate of Judge J. G. North and started the North Bay Camp and Boat Landing. North Bay being on the south shores of the lake proved to be too confusing, so Tayles and Rideout changed the name to Boulder Bay.

The winter of 1921 was another cold, hard one that left all the roads to Big Bear Lake closed for weeks and in some cases months at a time. Many children in Bear Valley became ill that winter and attempts to get them down the hill took two or more days by sled. In at least one documented fatal case, the winter season proved too harsh for a young girl, Lucy Knickerbocker, who died from a ruptured appendix on the trek down to the nearest medical services.

When winter passed, the Motor Transit Company had 24 new trucks and buses to start bringing in visitors. The new vehicles came just in time for the building boom in Big Bear. 80 new homes were added in 1921 alone and by that year there were 24 resorts and camps around Big Bear Lake. That year saw the Gold Mountain Mine light up from power that they received from a $35,000, 24 mile long, power transmission line from Victorville. An electric engine then replaced the previously used steam engine and cut the mill's overall operating costs. 1921 also saw E. C. Jesserun's purchase of 40 acres to the west of Baldwin Lake. Jesserun's site would soon be developed into the Pan Hot Springs Inn where both indoor and outdoor swimming pools were heated by a natural underground hot spring.

Construction of a shelf road above Bear Creek called "The Arctic Circle" was completed on October 6th, 1923. The new road was well overdue, as an unprecedented 40,000 people visited the San Bernardino Mountains over Labor Day that year. Around that time, Robert T. Moore started the first fox farm in Bear Valley, just east of Pine Knot Village, called Borestone Ranch and the Talmadge brothers purchased 1,130 acres of Bear Valley pasture land from the Shay and Barker Ranch. 1924 saw the first road oiled in the heart of the village. Big Bear Boulevard was oiled from Pine Knot to reduce the dust problem that had come about with the major influx of visitors in the area. The Motor Transit Company also constructed a $25,000 freight and passenger depot on Pine Knot Avenue. In 1924, Coy and Lex Brown's Poligue Canyon Sawmill produced over a million feet of lumber to meet the high demand for construction materials around Big Bear Lake.

Also constructed in 1924 was a concrete bridge that was laid across the Big Bear dam at a cost of $30,000. 60 men were said to have completed the bridge which connected the Rim of the World Highway to the newer south shore road that lead into Pine Knot Village. Other means of traveling to Big Bear Lake weren't so successful. In 1924, Waldo Waterman took off with four passengers in the first commercial flight out of Bear Valley. While returning home, the aircraft ran into some trouble and was forced to make a crash landing in Lucerne. There were no injuries, but the passengers were then forced to drive back to the top of the mountains. By 1925 there were over 200 resorts in the San Bernardino Mountains. That year, a man named Harry Kiener formed a corporation with plans to develop the ranch lands at the east end of Big Bear Valley and started their development by constructing the Peter Pan Woodland Club. The following year, the residents of Fawnskin built a two room schoolhouse for the raising number of children on the north side of the lake.

The winter of 1927 was another harsh and destructive one. The Deep Creek Cut-Off Highway to Big Bear Lake was only open for one week during the entire winter season due to heavy snowfall. Residents and visitors alike couldn't take much more of the poor road conditions. In July of 1927, the State authorized $676,000 in improvements to the Rim of the World Highway. The State Department of Highways Maintenance Station at Fawnskin received their first Snow King Rotary Plow and had it assembled before the following winter. During the summer of 1927, Big Bear celebrated its history by hosting a parade on Pine Knot Blvd. It is debated that this may have been the very beginning of the Old Miner Days annual event that is still celebrated in Big Bear to this day.

In an attempt to gain publicity and business for the bus company, Walter Krukman, General Traffic Agent for the Motor Transit Company, organized a Winter Sports Carnival at Big Bear Lake during the winter of 1928. A competition ski jump supported by the Viking Ski Club of Los Angeles was also constructed that winter. In 1928, The first tests of black-top paving were conducted in the San Bernardino Mountains between the Big Bear Dam and Running Springs. An airport was also established and laid down just to the east of Big Bear Lake in 1928. The Talmadge brothers continued adding to their IS Ranch in 1928 when they bought the remaining 7oo head of Shay and Barker cattle along with 4o acres of grazing land down in the desert. Meanwhile, the Bartlett brothers began constructing a dam on 218 acres of land that they purchased from the IS Ranch to the south of Big Bear Lake.

The Bartletts planned to create a lake and the largest resort in Big Bear Valley, but they never completed their plans. They were successful in creating the lake, which is present day Cedar Lake. The 193o's saw the fast rise of fox farming in Big Bear Valley. R. T. Moore of Maine was credited with setting up Big Bear's first fox farm in the late 2o's on his 84 acres, which included present day Fox Farm Road. Big Bear offered a perfect climate for raising foxes. In the 192o's and 193o's, fur was in high demand and the sought after fox pelts farmed in Big Bear were sold all around the world.

In 1933, the State's Fish and Game Department decided to bring bears back to southern California. The general thought was that outdoor adventurers and tourists would enjoy getting to see them after the California grizzly bear had been hunted to extinction in the early 19oo's. So, they rounded up 27 black bears in Yosemite and relocated them to southern California. Six of those bears came to Big Bear Valley and all the black bears currently living in Big Bear are descendants of those original six. The relocation efforts were a success, with one small catch: The bears that the Department of Fish and Game took from Yosemite were the ones that Yosemite didn't want, as they had been deemed to be troublemakers or aggressive. Legend has it that the black bears which populate Big Bear today have a gene which makes them prone to mischief.

The Big Bear Valley Park, Recreation and Parkway District was formed in 1934, due to the efforts of a man named Clifford R. Lynn. In 1938, the Park District raised enough tax funds to build a toboggan run on a mountain side to the south of the lake, generally reffered to as "Lynn Hill". They also constructed a sling lift which could drag ten people at a time to the top of the hill. These winter facilities were constructed to stimulate winter activity. They hit it off big and persuaded more lodges and businesses in Big Bear to stay open all year long. During an election that was held in 1938, the community of Pine Knot officially changed its name to "Big Bear Lake".

In 1947, the transfer to a winter resort town was all but solidified when a man named Tommy Tyndall arrived in Big Bear and began offering skiing lessons. In 1952, Tyndall created the Snow Summit Ski Corporation and built the largest ski development in the San Bernardino Mountains: a mile long double chairlift which carried visitors clear to the top of the mountain. Winter activities continued to thrive throughout the 196o's and 197o's. Snowboarding became a very popular competitive sport in Big Bear during the late 198o's and is still commonly enjoyed there to this day.

Caltech constructed the Big Bear Solar Observatory on the north shore of Big Bear Lake in the summer of 1968. 197o saw the start of the annual Oktoberfest celebration that is home of "The Highest Biergarten in the United States (in elevation)". The City of Big Bear Lake was incorporated on November 28th, 198o. Through the years there have been hundreds of productions filmed in Big Bear. Some 114 films were shot in Big Bear during the 193o's and 194o's alone. Some famous titles include: *Birth of a Nation* (1915), *Heidi* (1937), *Gone With the Wind* (1939), *Shane* (1953), *HR Pufnstuf* (1969-7o), *War Games* (1983) and *Better Off Dead* (1985).

Much like Pioneertown, Big Bear started off as an unused resource in the San Bernardino Mountains. The name "Pioneertown" was derived from a song by The Sons of the Pioneers. But when Tim Spencer wrote that song, he was writing not only about the Pioneers who made Pioneertown, but also about the very type of people who made Big Bear what it is today. Similarly, both cities saw some of the harshest winters ever recorded in the earliest days of their establishment. They both hit hard times and were near the verge of going under in their earlier days, both more than once, as time went on. They are both surrounded by rich Native American, gold prospecting, land homesteading and cattle ranching history. Both Big Bear and Pioneertown were used heavily by the film and entertainment industries and are year-round tourist towns. One other considerable thing to note which they share in common is the fact that the Old Mormon Trail runs right past both of them.

From the center of Mane Street in Pioneertown to the heart of Big Bear Lake Village is less than 25 miles, as the crow flies. Traveling via the CA-247/CA-18 is just over 65 miles and takes just about 1.5 hours. Driving via the CA-62/I-1o/CA-21o/CA-33o/CA-18 is just about 1oo miles and takes about 2 hours. By way of the Pioneer Pass it is about 35 miles and takes about 1.5 - 2 hours, depending on the road conditions and the vehicle that you drive. Dick Curtis and everyone else in Pioneertown knew just how close Big Bear was. Plenty of people traveled to the lake from Pioneertown via the east or west highway routes and anyone lucky enough to pilot their own aircraft could easily fly up to the top of the mountains in the afternoon, enjoy themselves and then fly back down before the sun set that evening. Those who were good enough on horseback and knew the route well enough could get up the Old Mormon Trail to Big Bear in a days ride.

One August morning in 1947, at 9:3oAM, four Jeeps carrying a group of ten men and two dogs left from Pioneertown headed for Big Bear. They were lead by Dick Curtis via the Old Mormon Trail on the first publicly documented car ride across the trail from Pioneertown to Big Bear. They drove up Burns Canyon about 12 miles before the road disappeared into the forest. They stopped, had lunch and then took some scouting trips on foot before they decided to leave three of their vehicles and safely take the rest of the trip in just one Jeep.

Dick Curtis was at the wheel and the rest of the crew broke the trail ahead of the Jeep as it slowly crept along. Around this point they estimated the average grades to be between 5 & 35 degrees. However, they weren't actually on the trail anymore; they were just heading north west, towards Big Bear. The group started to loose hope and almost turned around to head back home when they ran extremely low on water. But just about the time that they truly contemplated returning, their hope was restored when they spotted the old road that connected the Rose Mine to Big Bear.

The only problem at that point was that the Rose Mine and the road they needed to get to was about 2oo yards up a 35 degree slope. After lots of hard work, the group was able to safely guide the Jeep up the mountain and onto the road. At that point, all ten men and two dogs piled into and stacked onto the single Jeep and slowly headed down to the Grizzly Newspaper office in Big Bear. The exhausted but excited group of Pioneertown representatives were greeted by a welcoming party when they finally arrived in Big Bear at 6PM that evening.

There had been quite a lot of hype about the first Jeep expedition up to Big Bear, well before it was reported in the Pioneertown Gazette that month. After the road from Yucca Valley to Pioneertown was improved by the Pioneertown Corporation, they continued improving it all the way past Pipes Canyon and into Rimrock. But a great number of people wanted road improvements to continue all the way along the Old Mormon Trail and up into Big Bear. The route that Curtis and his group of explorers had taken wasn't exactly a beaten path.

San Bernardino County had already refused to help with the road leading up to Pioneertown and there was no chance that they would fund furthering the road up to Big Bear at that time. So, if residents wanted to see the project through, it needed to be privately funded. During the winter of 1947 - 1948, supporters of the road improvements responded by establishing a simple plan for volunteers to gather donations, get together and help physically cut an adequate road themselves; much like the locals did when they originally improved Pioneertown Road. The idea was originally credited to Mr. & Mrs. W. H. Schmidt of Yucca Valley. But it very quickly gained tremendous public support from residents as high as Big Bear and as low as Palm Springs.

The group's efforts went under the unofficial title of the "Big Bear-Pioneertown Road Project" and was headed by the Schmidts' along with the aid of hundreds of volunteers, donations, promoters and supporters. By March of 1948, workers had already started cutting out a small road from Burns Canyon up to the Rose Mine. A road similar in size and condition to the one that they were cutting already connected the Rose Mine to Big Bear and the plan was to simply make it possible for automobiles to safely get there from Pioneertown.

Some of the hardest work had already been done before Pioneertown's arrival to the scene. The Original route of the Old Mormon Trail went from the Onyx Mine down to Pipes Canyon via a ton of dangerous switchbacks. When the United States Forest Service set up a handful of fire trails in the early 19oo's, they had rerouted the trail along a much straighter path that lead through Rattlesnake Canyon from the Rose Mine and then down to Burns Canyon. Roy Brown and Joe La Borde, Pioneertown Gazette Publishers, aided promotions by running ads in the Gazette which informed people of the project and asked for volunteers and donations. In an April, 1948, edition of the Pioneertown Gazette, the projects accounts were made public. They read:

A Summary of Pioneertown Corporation's Contributions as of 4.17.48:

> Surveyors Salaries $11o5
> Operation, Repairs and Expenses of Caterpillar, Ripper and Grader $1125
> Salary Paid to Operator of Corporation Equipment $539.2o
> Depreciation of equipment $143.5o
> Cash Donations $25o   (TOTAL $3162.7o)

A Summary of Other Contributions Received as of 4.16.1948:

> Pioneertown Corporation $15o
> Twentynine Palms Area $26o
> J. A. Bennell of JT $5o
> Yucca Valley Chamber of Commerce $28o
> Yucca Valley Lions Club $135
> Pioneertown Business Men's Association $537
> Rattle Snake Gulch people $415
> Individual subscriptions from Newspaper Appeal $25   (TOTAL $1852)

Expenditures Up Till 4.16.1948:

> $2338.73   Deficit $486.73
> Expenditures Breakdown - Food for Crew $555.74; Gasoline & Oil $766.49; Gunpowder, Tools, Supplies and Other Equipment $1o16.5

Labor Contributions, In Days, by 4.16.1948:

> Ray Hopman/62, WE Schmidt/38, WH Schmidt/56, McClure/11, Parker/5, Kolb & Helber/1, G. & F. Wilkening/1, Hudman/25, Downing/6 and Arndt/4

Equipment Donations:

> Ray Hopman donated a 65hp. Bulldozer for 61 days; W. E. Schmidt donated a truck for 44 days, the Pioneertown Corporation donated a Roadblade for 16 days and a D-8 Bulldozer for 39 days.

The last of the work on the pilot road up to Big Bear was completed by one of the project's biggest contributors, Ray Hopman, in June of 1948. Pioneertown Corporation then announced that the pilot road was opened for Jeep travel. The first car reported to make the trip from Big Bear to Pioneertown was a Hot-Rod carrying four teenagers. Many others followed very shortly afterwards. While there was still a need for a legitimate road linking the two towns, the simple trail that the volunteers had created proved to be both adequate and popular. A handful of different associations were responsible for improving parts of the road from then on. In 1951, the Valle de las Vistas Club of Twentynine Palms spent plenty of time and money trying to improve the road below the Rose Mine. But there was still a lot of planning and funding needed before any major, much desired work, could be done.

In June of 1955, a Caravan to Big Bear composed of 58 cars, more than 232 people and some 2o horses headed out from Pioneertown to Baldwin Lake via the new pilot road. The lead car had a sign on it that read "We Want A Road To Big Bear" and the cars that followed carried banners for numerous villages that were involved with the push, including Desert Hot Springs, Morongo Valley, Palm Wells, Yucca Valley, Pioneertown, Joshua Tree, Sunfair and Twentynine Palms. The caravan was directed by associated Chambers of Commerce of the Morongo Basin members Ted Richardson of Twentynine Palms and President, Marty Dodson of Joshua Tree and Secretary as well as Jules Boldizar of Yucca Valley and Chairman.

In addition to the hundreds of High Desert residents promoting the idea of a new road, guests of the caravan also included Walt Campbell, the Assistant County Highway Commissioner, representing Commissioner M. A. Nicholas; Lt. Doc Martin of the Twentynine Palms Sheriff's Substation, representing Sheriff Frank Bland; Mr. & Mrs. S. S. Stanley of San Bernardino and Twentynine Palms; Mr. & Mrs. Jesse Ferguson representing the Valle de las Vistas Club of Twentynine Palms as well as P. Hadley, Vice president of the Desert Hot Springs Chamber of Commerce.

The huge group of caravan members all met up at the Red Dog Saloon at 9AM. It was the third day of a heat wave in the desert and temperatures, even in Pioneertown and Yucca Valley, were averaging over 11o degrees. The cars were directed on their way from the Red Dog Saloon by Lt. Doc Martin who spaced them about 2oo feet apart. Only a few cars and Jeeps were known to have had trouble getting up the pilot road during the Caravan. Luckily, Clay Tunstall of the Hi-Way Garage in Yucca Valley had donated his tow truck and personal services for the event.

Upon arriving in Big Bear, the caravan was met by a group composed of Capt. Kendall Stone of Big Bear, Big Bear City Chamber of Commerce President Saff Minder and Secretary-Manager Dave Lents, the "Petticoat Patrol" which was a group of expert equestrians accompanied by their leader, Guide Dee Johnson and dozens of cars filled with excited Big Bear residents. The caravan was lead through the city to the Coldbrook Picnic Grounds where Ted Richardson addressed the group. Richardson announced that there would be a combined 22 miles of grading and straightening needed in order to make the road safe for general use. Welcome addresses were also made by J. B. Quale, the official host for Big Bear as well as Saff Minder and Dave Lents of the Big Bear City Chamber of Commerce.

Though the plan to get a road from Big Bear to Pioneertown was greatly accepted by all, there was still quite a lot of funding needed to get the ball rolling. While the "road" that they were trying to complete already had multiple names like the Old Mormon Trail and "Big Bear-Pioneertown Road", an idea to rename the road was sparked and so to was the "Name the Road Contest" which started late in 1958. People from all around the world were asked to send in their suggestions for what the road should be called and a deadline for entries was set for November 1st. Once they realized how much attention the contest attracted, they extended the deadline to November 13th.

11 prizes were donated to the contest which were to be awarded to the winner. The prizes included a Western Rodeo Shirt designed by Nudie's of North Hollywood and donated by A. E. "Art" Miller of the Western Hills Estates in Yucca Valley, a $1o Portrait courtesy of Bonser Studio, Two Chicken Dinners by Jim and Frannie Brown's Cafe, a Hair Cut from Odie Ray's shop, Two Steak Dinners donated by Val and Chet's Red Dog Saloon, Five Tickets to Hospital House from Norm Granger's Uni-Gas, Two Chinese Dinners at Frank Gee's Golden Stallion, a 1-Year Subscription to any of the four Desert Journal Publishing Company's papers, an Ironwood Pen Set from Roy and Margaret Jewett of Desert Lampmakers, Eight Tickets to Hospital House from Realtor and Contractor

Art Katje as well as a Case of Engine Additives which was donated by Francisco Laboratories in Los Angeles.

The winner was announced from a red and white checkered table inside the Red Dog Saloon at 6:3oPM on December 4th, 1958. Mrs. Fred Cliffe of Long Beach had submitted the name which won the vast majority of votes. Her submission, which arrived well before the extension on September 2oth, was the 14th one to be received of some 243 total entries. "Pioneer Pass" was the official name given to the Old Mormon Trail that went up from Pioneertown to Big Bear.

In June of 1958, a committee formed to study the annual winter problems that plagued the roads leading into the Big Bear area. The winter road conditions were typically summed up in less than a couple of words: "Closed". The committee was formed as a direct result of a meeting to address the same issues which had been held a week prior at the California State Chamber of Commerce building in Los Angeles. The first meeting was lead by James H. Hammond, Director of the Travel and Recreation Department of the State Chamber and H. H. "Bob" Roberts, chairman of the Southern Travel and Recreation Committee of the State Chamber.

The committee was represented by the U.S. Forest Service, California Highway Patrol, State Division of Highways, Southern California Ski Lift Operators Association and all of the villages, cities and counties affected, Highway Commissioner Martin A. Nicholas and Assistant Commissioner George P. Zimmerman of San Bernardino County as well as Director of the Travel and Recreation Department of the California Chamber of Commerce James H. Hammond. District VIII Engineer for the State Division of Highways, Clyde V. Kane, was adamant about the addition of plenty of public parking so that the new highways wouldn't turn into parking lots. But it was John H. Fairweather, the San Bernardino County Trade Manager, who suggested that more highways be made into loop-roads. Fairweather went on to mention that there were too many "dead ends" and suggested that areas like the Stockton Flats to Cajon Pass and Big Bear through Pioneertown would make for great through-ways down to lower areas of interest.

That committee was the precursor to the next wave of promoters for the new road. After the Pioneer Pass was named in December of 1958, an organization that called themselves the Pioneer Pass Pushers was established. The new organization was made up of just about everyone involved with previous improvements to the Pioneer Pass. Norman Granger of Uni-Gas in Yucca Valley is credited as the man who came up with the idea for the "Pioneer Pass Push" and was the first Acting Chairman of the project. The Pioneer Pass Push was another simple idea that gained a great deal of momentum. Volunteers were to gather and physically work together to make the Pioneer Pass more traversable.

The main event was to be a two day excursion where volunteers would work to level, widen and straighten the Pioneer Pass with good old fashioned elbow grease. A Button Sale was organized to help raise funds for the project. There were three main designations on the buttons: VIP, Pushers and Peons. San Bernardino County Supervisor Magda Lawson, Inspector Kendall Stone of the San Bernardino County Sheriff's Department and the Schmidt family were key promoters in the endeavor. Inspector Stone's family had owned land and used the Old Spanish Trail for cattle driving as far back as 1875. Mr. and Mrs. W. H. Schmidt lived near Baldwin Lake in Big Bear and their son, W. E. Schmidt, lived down in Rattlesnake Gulch.

On Sunday, September 31st, a Photo Trip up the Pioneer Pass was sponsored by the Pioneer Pass Pushers in an attempt to promote the Pioneer Pass Push. Attendants met at the Red Dog Saloon at 9AM and headed out from there. Inspector Kendall Stone left from Big Bear and met the group at Arrastre Creek, where he then took them on a tour of the Pioneer Pass's many famous sites, such as the Devil's Stool, the Needle's Eye, the Pipes, the Old Spanish Smelter, the Indian Grave and the Golden Stairs. This Photo Trip was the early start of the annual Pioneer Pass Camera Cavalcade.

On February 22nd, 1959, Civil Engineer for the Public Works office at the Marine Corps Base,

Pat Sullivan, joined the Pioneer Pass Pushers in a study of the problems along the route from Pioneertown to Big Bear as they readied for the Pioneer Pass Push Weekend. There were about 2o people in the group who also met at the Red Dog before they headed up and made it as far as Arrastre Creek, where the snow then stopped them from going any further. Sullivan walked the three mile stretch below the Rose Mine, across the Three Hells Hill, taking notes as he walked. He observed that the main problem the project would face was drainage.

Sullivan reported that the slide area where the Valle de las Vistas Club of Twentynine Palms had worked on the road in 1951 should be blasted with TNT so that the large rocks could be moved out of the way. He also said that they should cut and fill to help their situation. By "cut and fill", Sullivan meant that they should cut from the top of the hill and then use the harvested earth to fill in the sides and help cut the grade some. Sullivan suggested that the Pushers bring their heavy equipment to the site it where would be used at well before the actual Push, in case there were any unforeseen complications. Additionally, Sullivan suggested that the assigned Work Crews should be kept to teams of 21 men, 2o workers and a working foreman.

Another survey was conducted in March with equipment donated by the Bill Hatch. After both Pat Sullivan and San Bernardino National Forest Engineer Victor DeKalb suggested that the road go around the Three Hells Hill and skirt the side of the hill that Valle de las Vistas Club planned to take, the decision was made to bypass the Three Hells Hill. It was noted by Sullivan that if they took the suggested route, at no point would the grade exceed seven percent. Pat Sullivan drafted the road working plans which were approved by National Forest Engineer Victor DKalb, Chief Ranger Earl Nichols and Forest Supervisor Don Bauer. Heavy equipment was sent up after the survey to get ready for the Push and 15 Work Crews were signed up and ready shortly thereafter.

The Pioneer Pass Push was held on April 18th and 19th of 1959. Over 2oo men, women and children spent two long and hard days working with picks, shovels and their bare hands. Work teams were designated to specific work areas to limit the amount of traveling needed. Drinks and food were donated and served throughout the Push. After two very hard days of work, the road was widened, straightened and leveled from Burns Canyon up to within just one mile of the Rose Mine. The last mile to the mine was quite harder than expected and more work was needed on that last short stretch than could be completed during the Push. The USFS, aided by the 7th Engineers of the U.S. Marine Corps stationed at Twentynine Palms, continued to work on the road after the Push.

They were successful in replacing a stretch of the road along the south slope of Mineral Mountain that eliminated a bad stretch in the original trail which was commonly referred to as "Poop-out Hill" and shortened the whole trek by about a mile. They continued to work until the road was completed in May of 1959. It was around that time that, responding to the increase of activity in the area, that San Bernardino County filled the Rose Mine with cement to eliminate any threat of danger to nosy tourists. When Norman Granger, first Acting Chairman of the Pioneer Pass Pushers moved to Long Beach later that summer, Gene Albrecht from Sunfair village took his position. Albrecht had also been foremen of a labor crew during the Pioneer Pass Push. In August of 1959, the Pioneer Pass Pushers entered a float at the Old Miners Day Parade in Big Bear to promote their newly established dirt road to Pioneertown.

There were a very large number of visitors expected during the winter of 1959 - 196o. After President Eisenhower visited the High Desert, the number of people inquiring about desert vacationing had skyrocketed. In anticipation, the State Chamber of Commerce published a booklet titled *Southern California Deserts* and dubbed October of 1959 as "Desertland Month". Hundreds of desert activities were planned to keep the masses happy and entertained. The Pioneer Pass Pushers saw a chance to gain a great deal of attention and, in conjunction with the Desertland Month, they planned the Pioneer Pass Golf Challenge.

The 54 "holes" over some 4o miles of "golf course" that was originally planned out for the challenge was dubbed as the longest, ruggedest course in the world! The first 9 holes were to be played at the Hi-Desert Golf & Country Club, then 36 holes from Yucca Valley up the Pioneer Pass to Moonridge Golf Club at Big Bear Lake before the players had 9 more holes to play at the Moonridge course. While playing through the Pioneer Pass, the "holes" that players aimed for were actually chalk-marked circles, each 2o feet in diameter. The original course for the first challenge was set as a two day event and it was hyped that there was to be a massive 35 mile long 19th hole.

The original idea came about in April of 1959. After gaining approval by the San Bernardino National Forest and seeking support from the National Senior Golf Association, the plan was set. A contest to find a "Golf Girl" went underway and entries had to be in by September 1st. The Golf Girl would also reign over the third annual Hesperia Open Tournament the following week. This was the start of the annual Miss Pioneer Pass competition, where contestants were photographed during the summer time at the annual Pioneer Pass Cavalcade and then that winner was later crowned Miss Pioneer Pass.

A meeting was held on Tuesday, August 18th, to discuss the Pioneer Pass Golf Challenge. Among the topics discussed was the fact that the original proposal for a two day weekend event was expanded to include Friday, Saturday and Sunday. Also, even though it wasn't officially recognized by the Sportsman's Club, a request was submitted to see that all hunting be closed in that area during the proposed three day golf challenge. The following Sunday, August 3oth, a booth was set up to promote the PPGC at the Los Angeles County Fair in Pamona. The booth was run from September 18th through October 4th.

On October 2nd, 3rd and 4th of 1959, 13 men and two women competed in the first annual Pioneer Pass Golf Challenge. Friday, October 2nd, contestants played 9 holes of conventional golf in Yucca Valley. Players then tee'd off from the front of the Golden Stallion Restaurant on Saturday morning before they trekked through Pioneertown and up 8 checkpoints along the Pioneer Pass. Sunday, they wrapped up with 9 more holes of conventional golf in Big Bear. Though the route they took had been downsized since its original conception, it still proved to be an exceptional challenge. The Pioneer Pass Golf Challenge marked the start of the Desertland's Golf Week which ended with the $2o,ooo 3rd Annual Hesperia Open Tournament the following weekend. Five years later, a Travel-World production, *The 19th Hole*, depicted players trials and tribulations during the first few years of the PPGC.

Over the years the PPGC continued annually, as did the Pioneer Pass Cavalcade. While improvements to the road were not seen, plenty of activity was. One promotion to highlight both Pioneertown and Big Bear that didn't actually take advantage of the Pioneer Pass was the National Burro Derby of 1965. On August 5th, the 12th annual run of the National Burro Derby was held in conjunction with Big Bear's Old Miner Days. The two day race that began in Pioneertown and ended in Big Bear was the first traditional derby that did not start in Apple Valley.

The Burros were completely wild and were caught out in the Nevada desert the month before. Wranglers were paid $1o a day to bring in wild burros which were brought to the Pioneertown corals on July 31st to be well fed, watered, groomed and "branded". Branding for the competition was simply the act of painting a number on the burro's side. Riders drew for burros before saddling them and prepping for the trek. They left Pioneertown for Yucca Valley where they stopped for lunch before heading up to Lucerne Valley where they stayed overnight. They then headed up the mountain and arrived at Elks Lodge in Big Bear the following evening. Joe Spearman of Victorville, sponsored by Climate Control and the winner of the previous year's race, received the $5oo first place prize for his winning time of 7 hours, 54 minutes and 4o seconds. Three women entered, but Sherry Gridey was the only one to complete the race.

The interest for faster access from Pioneertown to Big Bear was palpable. On February 17th, 1966, 62 people voted, representing more than a dozen communities from San Bernardino and

Riverside Counties, to create the Pioneer Loop Association, dedicated to tourism and recreation. Over the next few months, they promoted their organization and held a number of meetings all throughout both Riverside and San Bernardino Counties. Howard Rees was appointed as the President and by August, there were so many members that they proposed to split the meetings into three groups and spread them out.

The idea was to create a 15o mile loop that would allow travelers to easily access the High Desert, the Low Desert and even the High Mountains. The Pioneer Pass was the last stretch of land that was unpaved and it was on Federal land, so it should have qualified for Federal and State Funding through the County. The proposed "Loop" would have connected Pioneertown to Big Bear, through to San Bernardino, down to Palm Springs and then through Desert Hot Springs and back up to Pioneertown. The Loop would have also granted travelers much easier access to sites like the Joshua Tree National Monument, the Salten Sea and the Aerial Tram in Palm Springs.

The County loved the idea but was not able to fund it directly and suggested that the Forestry Agencies would be most interested, as a portion of the road sat on National Park land. On December 11th, 1967, a resolution was approved by the Pioneer Loop Association which asked that State and Federal Forestry officials provide an estimated $2 million for road construction. The resolution was not met very well and in the process of incorporating the road into the State Highway System and the Master Plan for Scenic Highways, a step that needed to be taken before funds for the road could be provided through the County, the plan sadly fell through. This was the ultimate blow to the Pioneer Loop Association and all supporters of paving the Pioneer Pass as well as efforts to continue the fight for State approval and funding eventually ceased.

These days the idea of paving the Pioneer Pass is all but forgotten and quite a lot has been done most recently to keep the land exactly as it is. The Pioneer Pass still runs through the San Bernardino Mountains but is now very close to the newly established 154,ooo acre Sand to Snow National Monument. One also passes the 25,5oo acre Pioneertown Mountains Preserve on the way to the Pioneer Pass these days. The Preserve is operated by the Wildlands Conservancy who's adjacent 2o,ooo acre Pipes Canyon Wilderness is the largest nonprofit wilderness in California.

The Annual Pioneer Pass Golf Challenge is still held every year in September. The course has gone through extensive changes over the years. Though it is only a fraction of what it once was, the PPGC is still known as the world's longest, harshest and most unique golf challenge. The PPGC is sponsored by the Rotary Club of Yucca Valley and proceeds from the annual tournament go towards the Morongo Basin Historical Society and the Miracle League of Morongo Basin, which is a baseball field and league for kids with special needs.

The Pioneer Pass is open for automobiles to traverse and while off highway vehicles are not permitted on the road, a number of OHV trails run all along the way. A four wheel drive vehicle and at least one spare tire is definitely recommended for safe passage. Though still traversable, the winter months tend to leave the Pioneer Pass in less than ideal shape and a summer trip is strongly recommended for first time visitors. On a nice day, you are likely to see plenty of people driving along the Pass. While there are no posted speed limits, drivers should note that the road is only wide enough to accommodate two "lanes" of traffic about a quarter of the time.

The history and raw beauty of the Pioneer Pass is fiercely protected by all of those who call Pioneertown, the High Desert or the greater San Bernardino County their home. A strict carry-in carry-out law should be respected at all times. The vast majority of the land you'll see while visiting is wilderness area and there are a number of still active mineral claims all along the Pioneer Pass where one must avoid rock collecting of any kind. When visiting, please respect all of the rich history and lush beauty of the historic Pioneer Pass.

Chapter 9

Older Memories

Here is a collection of old advertisements, articles, documents, posters and pictures from Pioneertown's many years past. To try and include every picture, poster and advertisement of interest would be impossible, as there are simply too many for one single book. Included in this collection are some pictures of Pioneertown's heydays, some fun family memories, Hollywood highlights and plenty of true western American history. While there are surely plenty of common, even popular, images included - there are also quite a few which have never been published for the public before. They are presented in no particular order and every attempt was made to obtain the best quality images available.

Facing South in Pipes Country during the 193o's. The trail on the right side led down to Yucca Valley.

ABOVE: Margie Mattoon feeding the chickens at her Pipes Canyon farm in 194o.

BELOW: Dan Pekarovich clearing land at his family's homestead next to the Rimrock Motel.

ARTICLES OF INCORPORATION

OF

PIONEERTOWN

(A California corporation)

- - - - -

FILED
In the office of the Secretary of State
of the State of California

MAR 25 1946

FRANK M. JORDAN, Secretary of State

By _____
Assistant Secretary of State

KNOW ALL MEN BY THESE PRESENTS: That we, the undersigned, have this day voluntarily associated ourselves for the purpose of forming a corporation under and by virtue of the laws of the State of California.

WE DO HEREBY CERTIFY:

FIRST: That the name of the corporation shall be

PIONEERTOWN

SECOND: That the purposes for which the corporation is formed shall be as follows:

(a) To take, purchase, lease, hire or otherwise acquire, to hold, own, occupy, use and enjoy; to manage improve, develop, operate and work; to grant, sell, lease, let, sub-lease, demise, exchange and otherwise dispose of and generally to deal in and with real estate, buildings and improvements and any and every right, interest or estate therein, without limit as to the cost, amount or value thereof and wheresoever the same may be situated, outside of as well as within the State of California; to erect, construct, alter, repair, renew and equip buildings and other structures, and to make, enter into or assume any and every kind of contract, agreement and obligation by or with any person, firm, association or corporation for the erection, construction, alteration, repair, renewal, equipment, improvement, development, use, enjoyment, leasing, management, operation or control of any buildings or structures of any kind whatever and wheresoever the same may be situated: To improve develop and hold said real estate or any part thereof as a hotel, lodge or establishment for the housing, sleeping and serving food to natural persons.

(b) To engage in, conduct and carry on the business of making, producing, editing, leasing, utilizing and controlling picture films, negatives, cameras, camera equipment and all other appurtenances used in the making of motion pictures and without restriction importing trading, dealing and otherwise trafficing in and with motion picture film, camera and camera equipment, supplies, devices, articles of manufacture and parts for any of the same, and any and all things necessary or convenient for the carrying on of the business of producing, distributing and making pictures both moving and still.

IN WITNESS WHEREOF, we, the subscribed, and the persons hereinbefore named as directors for the first year, have hereunto set our hands and seals this _18th_ day of March, 1946.

Dick Curtis
Dick Curtis

Thomas Carr
Thomas Carr

Frank E Gray
Frank E. Gray

STATE OF CALIFORNIA   }   ss:
COUNTY OF LOS ANGELES   }

On this _18th_ day of March, 1946, before me, the undersigned authority, a notary public in and for the County of Los Angeles, State of California, residing therein, duly commissioned and sworn, personally appeared Dick Curtis, Thomas Carr, and Frank E. Gray, known to me to be the persons whose names are subscribed to the foregoing Articles of Incorporation, and acknowledged to me that they executed the same.

IN WITNESS WHEREOF, I have hereunto affixed my hand and seal.

John B Myers
Notary Public in and for the County of Los Angeles, State of California

LEFT & ABOVE: First and Last Pages of Pioneertown's 1946 Incorporation Documents.

Full Page Ad in the Desert Sun Newspaper on March 25th, 1947.

ABOVE: First Page of the First Edition of the Pioneertown Gazette from August 18th, 1947.

BELOW: Paid Advertising which ran in the Los Angeles Times Newspaper from 1947 - 1948.

ABOVE: Pioneertown Land Corporation's rock crusher was the very first machinery ever to be used in Pioneertown.

BELOW: Paid advertising that ran in numerous High Desert newspapers in 1967.

MEET ME AT THE

RED DOG

In Pioneertown, Calif.

THE ONLY PLACE WE KNOW OF WHERE YOU CAN SIT ON THE PORCH AND DRINK BY STARLIGHT.

Eatin - Drinkin - Dancin - an Carryin On

Bring Your Lunch And Stay All Day

Big Ed 'N His Red Doggers Makin' All The Music

ABOVE: Ground Breaking Ceremony on September 1st, 1946. Front row, from left to right, are David Bruce, Sally Patten, Adele Mara, Dick Curtis, Roy Rogers and George Tobias.

BELOW: Aerial View of Pioneertown before the majority of construction began in 1947. Note the completed Land Office in the center of Mane Street.

ABOVE: Early Pioneertown land owners draw straws for the first Rancho Sites in town, 1947.

BELOW: Aerial photo of Pioneertown in early development during 1948.

ABOVE: Building the Old Pioneer Trail Lodge in 1947. From right to left are Dick Curtis, Cliff & Glnny Priest, Jack Lunden on the ladder and an unknown worker.
BELOW: Mane Street in early development, facing west, from the roof of the Nickelodeon.

ABOVE LEFT: 1948 aerial shot facing south. Left to right are the Pioneertown Gazette, the Grubstake Cafe and the Red Dog Saloon.
ABOVE RIGHT: 1948 aerial shot facing west. This picture gives you an idea of how busy Mane Street was even while it was still just getting on its feet.
BELOW: Aerial shot facing south of the Pioneertown Gazette and the Grubstake Cafe.

ABOVE: 1950's advertisement from the side of Highway-99 which is now the I-10 Freeway.

BELOW: One of the very first signs which greeted visitors to Pioneertown.

ABOVE: Looking west down Mane Street in the 1950's.

BELOW: Aerial shot of Pioneertown as a parade of horses ride down Mane Street in the 1950's.

ABOVE: Looking west down Mane Street from the roof of the Golden Stallion.

BELOW: Resting in front of a false-front next door to the Pioneertown Land Office.

ABOVE: Maggie's Feed Barn in 1949. Note Cactus Kate is riding up on her white horse.

ABOVE: White's Grocery, formerly White's Hardware, in 1949. Note the still slightly visible "H" just to the left of the word "Grocery".

ABOVE: Nell's Ice Cream Palace in 1947.

ABOVE: George & Pee Wee Toal in front of the Frosted Pantry during the winter of 1948 - 1949.
BELOW: Maggie McDonald and her family in front of Maggie's Feed Barn as the sign is hung.

ABOVE: Some folks enjoying lunch at the Ole's Barbeque Corral in 1948.
BELOW: The Grubstake Cafe in its prime, during the 1950's.

The Pioneertown Gazette in its prime, during the 1950's.

The winter of 1948 - 1949 hit Pioneertown hard!

ABOVE: The Pioneer Townhouse in December of 1948.
BELOW: View of Mane Street from the roof of the Golden Stallion in December of 1948.

ABOVE: Winter of 1948 - 1949. The same wagon had been used in a parade only half a year earlier.
BELOW: Mary Ann and Louise Pekarovich early in 1949.

ABOVE: Henry Jew with his Cadillac standing in front of the newly completed Golden Stallion.
Frank Gee is standing at the entrance.
BOTTOM LEFT: Henry Jew BOTTOM RIGHT: Frank Gee

ABOVE: The rock watering trough where it originally sat in the center of Mane Street.

BELOW: Hanging out in front of the Althoof Furniture Store in the early 195o's.

ABOVE: View of the Red Dog Saloon from the front porch of the Wooden Indian.

ABOVE: Shorty Creswell resting in the back of the Red Dog Saloon.

ABOVE: Tommy and Lillian Thompson in the late 1940's.

BELOW: Don Kokx (right) and an unknown friend returning home from a fishing trip up to Big Bear. Kokx's plane reads: "RED DOG PIONEERTOWN"

ABOVE: Val Jones serves Cactus Kate and Faye Moon a beer inside the Red Dog Saloon.
BELOW: A typical crowd inside the Red Dog Saloon. Can you spot Shorty Creswell?

ABOVE: Val Jones reaches up to shake John Hamilton's hand in front of the Red Dog Saloon.

BELOW: The Red Dog typically operated at maximum capacity throughout the 1950's.

ABOVE: The Mounted Sheriffs Posse enjoying some beers inside the Red Dog Saloon.
CENTER: Some of the many crowds of people that frequented the Red Dog.
BOTTOM: The original Red Dog Saloon's wood bar was originally from a saloon in Oatman, AZ which burned down in 19o9.

ABOVE: The Sound Stage on Mane Street in the 1960's.

BELOW: One of the only pictures which shows Trigger Bill's Shooting Gallery in action.

ABOVE: Cactus Kate's horse gets some love from Vi Shade in front of the Pioneertown Nickelodeon.

CENTER: The Pioneer Bowl during the 1960's.

BOTTOM LEFT: Duncan Renaldo and Dick Curtis entertains some friends at the OK Corral.
BOTTOM RIGHT: Rodeo Show in Pioneertown. Shot from the roof of the Likker Barn facing east.

ABOVE: The Thompson family inside the Pioneer Bowl during its construction.
BOTTOM LEFT: Alice White, the first Post Master of Pioneertown, accepts a letter at the Post Office inside the Pioneer Bowl.
BOTTOM RIGHT: Roy Rogers rolling the very first ball at the Pioneer Bowl. Rogers was the only person who was ever allowed to wear his boots on the lanes.

ABOVE: The First Post Office in Pioneertown was in the back of the Pioneer Bowl.

BOTTOM: Alice White never had a shortage of customers!

ABOVE: A view from inside the Pioneertown's bowling alley.
© Kim Stringfellow 2018
BELOW: Art by Wallace Stark adorns every wall inside the Pioneer Bowl.

ABOVE: Six lovely lanes await you.
© Kim Stringfellow 2018
BELOW: These trophies are merely an homage to Mane Street's trophy, the Pioneer Bowl.

ABOVE: Jim Hester visits with Hester Guinan, Pioneertown's second Post Master, at Pioneertown's second Post Office, next door to the Land Office on Mane Street.

BELOW: The Jackass Mail was printed inside the old Nickelodeon building on Mane Street.

ABOVE: The Pioneertown Service Station and its two pumps in the late 1940's.

BELOW: The Cantina, formerly the Service Station, in the late 1970's.

ABOVE: The Likker barn was turned into the Gold Nugget Coffee Shop when Pioneertown Liquor went out of business in the late 1940's.

BELOW: The Likker Barn was originally home to Mrs. Pearl Seidl's Pioneertown Liquor.

ABOVE: The Likker Barn and Marshal's Office in the early 195o's.
BELOW: In the late 195o's, the Likker Barn was used as the Pioneertown Visitors Headquarters

ABOVE: The Golden Stallion sits in its prime during the 195o's.
BELOW: A cowboy's silhouette is seen against a view of Mane Street from the Golden Stallion.

Looking east towards the Pioneer Townhouse in the early 1950's.

ABOVE: The Studd Valley Trailer Park during the late 194o's.
BELOW: The first class of the Pioneertown Schoolhouse, 1947 - 1948

ABOVE: Early on Good Friday morning of 1966, the Red Dog Saloon burned to the ground.

BELOW: Just two days after the Red Dog burned to the ground, the same fate fell upon the Golden Stallion on Easter Sunday of 1966.

ABOVE: The Hayden Ranch in the early 196o's.
BELOW: The average attendance of the Sandra Hayden Memorial Foundation's July Barbecue.

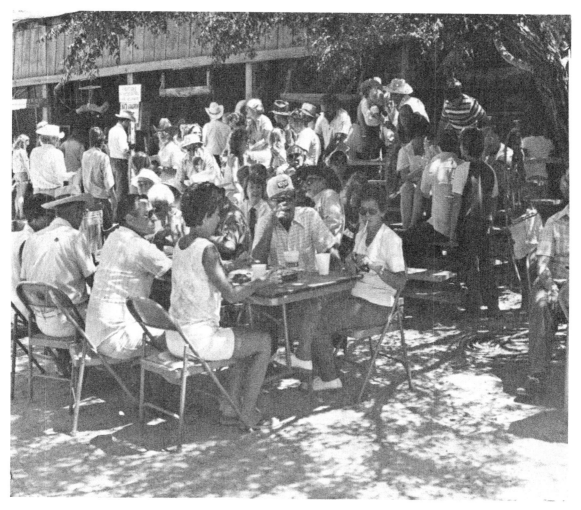

ABOVE: The Hayden Ranch was host to thousands of visitors each year during the Sandra Hayden Memorial Foundation's Annual July Barbecue.

BELOW: Just like Mane Street, the Hayden Ranch was also calm and quiet at times.

THE SCARLETT LADY

ABOVE: The Scarlett Lady being moved to the Hayden Ranch in 1983.

BOTTOM: The Scarlett Lady during the late 1980's.

ABOVE: Dale Evans dancing with Dick Curtis at one of many Pioneertown dances.
BOTTOM LEFT: The 1948 "Kan Kan" Girls, from left to right, are Jackie Bush, Candy Ammon, Patty Gathers, Frances Wiltse, Marilyn Moon and Joy Bush.
BOTTOM RIGHT: Korny Karnival cast members, from left to right, are Shorty Creswell, Pee Wee Toal and Julio Eisenbrook.

ABOVE: The Sons of the Pioneers in 1946. They are, from left to right, Tim Spencer, Bob Nolan, Roy Rogers, Ken Carson and Karl Farr.
BOTTOM LEFT: Tim Spencer, who wrote *Out in Pioneertown*, released in 1947.
BOTTOM RIGHT: Bob Nolan and Lloyd Perryman at the OK Corrals in the early 1950's.

THE SONS OF THE PIONEERS

ABOVE: The Sons of the Pioneers perform for fans on the front porch of the Land Office in December of 1947.
BELOW: A closer look at The Sons of the Pioneers performing on the front porch of the Land Office. Note Jack Lunden sitting to the far left as well as Pioneertown land promoters William Dennis and Gordon Brown standing in the far back.

ROY ROGERS & TRIGGER

GENE AUTRY
& CHAMPION

ABOVE: Duncan Renaldo as the Cisco Kid with his horse, Diablo.

CISCO & PANCHO

BELOW: Leo Carrillo as Pancho with his horse, Loco.

ABOVE: Duncan Renaldo having fun in costume and an old promo for *The Cisco Kid*.
BELOW: Pioneertown residents R. Tunstall, Pee Wee Toal and Gloria Eisenbruch attending the filming of *The Valiant Hombre* in 1948.

RUSSELL HAYDEN

ABOVE: Left to right are Russell Hayden, Tim Spencer, William Boyd and Roy Rogers in 1948.
BOTTOM LEFT: Sandra Hayden acting in *Judge Roy Bean*.
BOTTOM RIGHT: Sandra Hayden with her mother, stepfather and siblings.

LILIAN PORTER.

LEFT & ABOVE: Lilian Porter as a pinup model for the U.S. Troops during WWII.

LILIAN "MOUSIE" PORTER HAYDEN

ABOVE: Actress and Pioneertown resident Minna Gombell.
BELOW: Margie Mattoon Hamilton on her award winning bull. Margie and her first husband, Frank Mattoon, were early farmers in Pipes Canyon and old friends of the Curtis family.

TOP LEFT: Don Kokx was an original co-owner of the Red Dog Saloon.
TOP RIGHT: Marilyn Moon and Frank Gee were both original co-owners of the Golden Stallion.
BELOW: Grand opening celebration of Maggie's Feed Barn. Maggie McDonald is on the right.

ABOVE: Dazzlin' Dallas Morley entertaining inside the Red Dog Saloon.

BELOW: The famous lady on the Red Dog Saloon's barroom floor was actually a portrait of Dazzlin' Dallas Morley.

DAZZLIN' DALLAS
MORLEY

ABOVE: Left to right are Shorty Creswell, Tommy Thompson, Cactus Kate, unknown and Val Jones inside the Red Dog Saloon.
BELOW: A typical evening in Pioneertown during the 1950's.

ABOVE: Shorty Creswell and Cactus Kate performing for visitors on Mane Street.

BELOW: Left to right are Val Jones, Honey Fellers, and Paul Hammett in front of the Red Dog.

Cactus Kate and Gene Autry hanging out behind the Marshal's Office.

CACTUS KATE

Cactus Kate robbing Gene Autry in front of the old Pioneertown Photos building.

ABOVE: Director Frank McDonald, Gene Autry and Champion filming in 195o.
BELOW: Director Frank McDonald and Producer Louis Gray.

ABOVE: Gene Autry and Gail Davis in the late 1950's.

BELOW: Jimmy Hawkins and Gail Davis filming *Annie Oakley* in Pioneertown near Skyline Ranch Road. Note the buttes in the background.

ABOVE: Gene Autry and Pat Buttram in the late 1940's.

BELOW: Gene Autry visits Pat Buttram at the hospital. Buttram had suffered nearly fatal injuries from an accidental explosion while filming for the *Gene Autry Show* in Pioneertown.

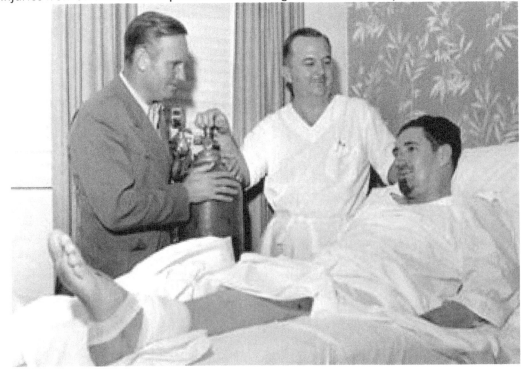

ABOVE: Pat Buttram and Assistant Director Rex Blair discuss a shoot in Pioneertown.
BELOW: Gene Autry filming for *The Gene Autry Show* near Skyline Ranch Road in 1951.

ABOVE: Gene Autry hanging out in front of the Sound Stage in 1951.

BELOW: Gene Autry gives the Kee brothers a $1oo check for recovering his runaway horse.

ABOVE: Despite what some might say, Gene Autry and Roy Rogers were very good friends.
BELOW: Chief Engineer Leonard Wikoff and Dick Curtis inside the Generator Building.

ABOVE: Filming *The Cisco Kid* in front of the Golden Stallion. Note Duncan & Leo on the far left.

BELOW: Filming in front of the Pioneertown Gazette for *Unusual Occupations* late in 1947.

ABOVE: Another view of *Unusual Occupations* in front of the Pioneertown Gazette.

BELOW: Filming the parade for *Unusual Occupations* in December of 1947.

Filming *The Gene Autry Show* near Skyline Ranch Road in 1951.

ABOVE: Filming the first episode of *The Gene Autry Show*.
BELOW: Bob Woodward and Gene Autry get ready to shoot a scene. Woodward was Autry's stunt double. Note the identical costume.

TOP: Roy Rogers with his daughter Cheryl, Dick Curtis and Dale Evans riding in the parade for *Unusual Occupations* shot in December of 1947.

CENTER: One of the first Stick Horse Rodeos in Pioneertown, in the late 194o's.

BOTTOM: Gail Davis and Jimmy Hawkins while filming *Annie Oakley*.

ABOVE: The Rawhide Riders on Mane Street in the early 1950's.
BELOW: 1950's cattle drive through the Chaparrosa Wash.

Pioneertown's wagon on the way to Palm Springs for the Palm Springs Western Week Parade in 1948. Note that the wagon actually says "1848".

The parade on Mane Street is filmed for *Unusual Occupations* by Robert Carlisle, the Jerry Fairbanks Company and Paramount Pictures in December of 1947.

ABOVE: Contestants and spotters compete in the first annual Pioneer Pass Golf Challenge.
CENTER: Hundreds of people attended the first PPGC in 1959. Note how nice the road looks!

PIONEER PASS GOLF CHALLANGE

BOTTOM: Contestants tee off at the start of the 35 Mile Long 19th Hole.

1965
Burro Race Route

Hwy 18 LUCERNE VALLEY

START SECOND DAY

OLD WOMAN'S SPRINGS ROAD

EL VAQUERO NOON STOP

SHAY RANCH END SECOND DAY

BIG BEAR LAKE   END

PIONEER PASS

FLAMING SHELL END OF FIRST DAY

Hwy 38

RACE ENDS AT ELK'S CLUB

START   PIONEER TOWN

COPPER ROOM NOON STOP

YUCCA VALLEY

FOLLOW THE BURRO RACE WITH

RADIO **KTOT** 1050 KC
BIG BEAR BROADCASTING CO.
P. O. BOX 155
BIG BEAR LAKE, CALIF.
Telephone UNiversity 6-3434

2

ABOVE: Map of the 1965 Burro Race which started in Pioneertown and ended in Big Bear.

BELOW: Contestants rode, pushed and pulled their randomly assigned wild burrow across the desert and up to Big Bear over the course of three days.

ABOVE: A family visits the Rose Mine on the Old Mormon Trail up to Big Bear.
BELOW: Russell Hayden, Karen Pekarovich and Mousie Hayden at the first annual Sandra
Hayden Memorial Foundation July Barbecue in 1977.

ABOVE: The historic Pioneertown duo, Pappy & Harriet, performing a duet in their Pioneertown Palace in the early 1980's.

PAPPY & HARRIET

BELOW: Everyone loved to listen to Pappy play!

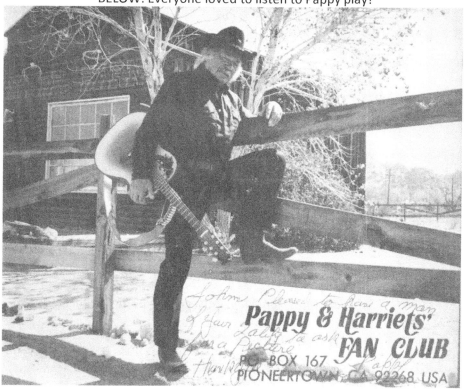

Sheet Music for *Out in Pioneertown* by Tim Spencer.

CHORUS

We'll build a lit-tle home where we can set-tle down, OUT IN PI-O-NEER -TOWN; A

peace-ful hide a-way to spend a la-zy day, OUT IN PI-O-NEER -TOWN, Where

sage in bloom and pine trees meet the wa-ter-fall, Where the moun-tains meet the sky, There we'll

while a-way the hours Through the pines and des-ert flow-ers When we set-tle down — OUT IN PI-O-NEER

-TOWN.   We'll -TOWN;

ABOVE: *The Valiant Hombre*, 1948
BELOW: *The Cowboy and the Indians*, 1949

Riders in the Sky, 1949

Satan's Cradle, 1949

The Daring Caballero, 1949

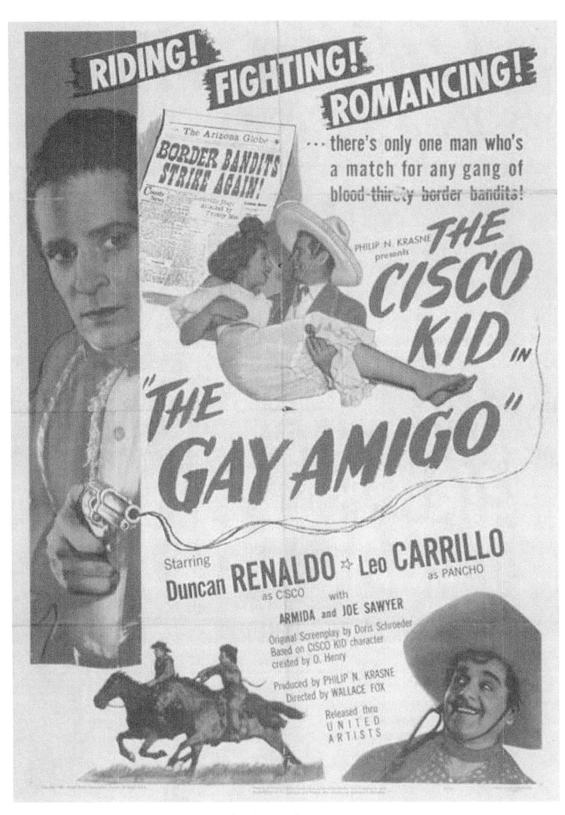

The Gay Amigo, 1949

Cody of the Pony Express, 1950

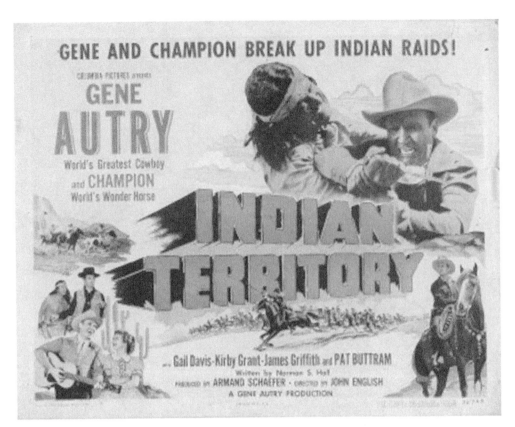

ABOVE: *Indian Territory*, 1950
BELOW: *The Capture*, 1950

ABOVE: *The Girl From San Lorenzo*, 1950
BELOW: *Silver Canyon*, 1951

ABOVE: *Whirlwind*, 1951
BELOW: *Jeopardy*, 1953

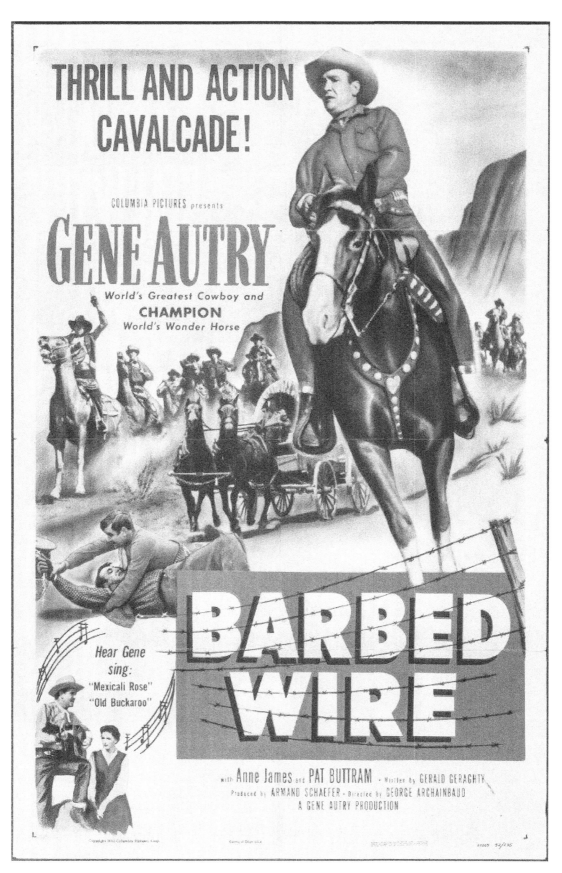

Barbed Wire, 1952

ABOVE: *Jeopardy,* 1953

ABOVE: *On Top of Old Smoky*, 1953

ABOVE: *Last of the Pony Riders*, 1953

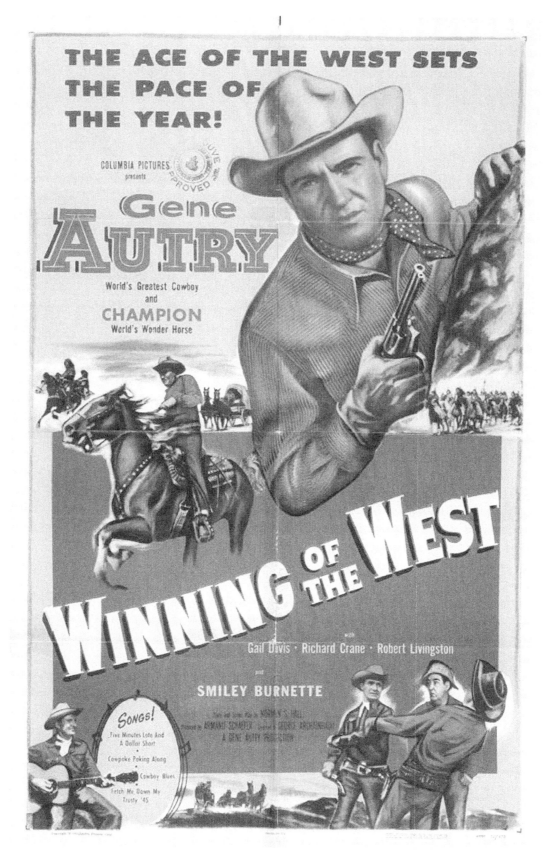

ABOVE: *Winning of the West*, 1953

Chapter 10

From Ghost Town, Back to High Desert Highlight

By the start of the 1990's, production companies had started to take an interest in Pioneertown once again. Director Alan Metzger chose to use Pioneertown, the surrounding wilderness and the long stretches of desert roads while filming *The China Lake Murders* which starred Tom Skerritt and Michael Parks. Released in 1990, the PG-13 title first aired on the USA Network and afterwards it held the record for the highest rated basic cable film for many years. For the first time in a long time, Pioneertown residents were able to enjoy watching cameras roll in their little town once again.

The deserts around Pioneertown also saw some big changes in the 1990's. In 1991, after four previous attempts at incorporation, Yucca Valley incorporated as a Town. The November 27th election was a historically close one when the majority vote was won by only 11 individual votes; 2,425 for and 2,414 against. Kindred Pederson was the first Mayor of the Town of Yucca Valley. Sadly, John Colin Hastie, the original Morongo Basin Bus Driver, died the same year. Old Betsy, Hastie's 1928 converted Chevrolet bus, complete with its wood burning heater, was still resting in his back yard until the day he died.

The following year, 1992, was the beginning of a very harsh period in the history of Pioneertown. As the town was beginning to get back on its feet, it was violently shaken back down to the ground. On April 23rd, 1992, a 6.1 magnitude earthquake rocked Joshua Tree. The High Desert saw a great deal of damage and recovered quickly. But no one was prepared for what came next. Just a few months later, at 4:57AM, on June 28th, 1992, the 7.3 magnitude Landers earthquake hit the High Desert like nothing ever had before. The rocking lasted some two to three minutes and sadly took three lives in its wake. Just three hours later, what was originally thought to be an aftershock of the Landers earthquake was in fact a 6.5 magnitude earthquake with an epicenter near Big Bear. Pioneertown residents and everyone else in the High Desert were hit hard and left unnerved for a long time to follow.

Veteran Pioneertown actor Pat Buttram died on January 8th, 1994, at the University of California Los Angeles Medical Center from kidney failure. In his later years, Buttram had lent his distinctive voice, which, in his own words "never quite made it through puberty", to a number of cartoons including *Who Framed Roger Rabbit*, *Garfield and Friends*, *Tiny Toon Adventures*, *A Goofy Movie,* and *Rugrats*. Buttram was even featured playing an endless game of poker inside the saloon in *Back to the Future III*. A month after Buttram passed, on February 28th, 1994, Pioneertown's Pappy, of Pappy & Harriet's, died of a heart attack at the age of 77. Hundreds of people attended his memorial, including singer Victoria Williams, who later wrote the song *"Happy to Have Known Pappy"*. Much like Mousie Hayden at the time of Russel's passing, tough-as-nails Harriet continued to run the family business after her husband's death.

The eye of the storm came later in 1994. On October 31st, Halloween Day of 1994, the Joshua Tree National Monument officially became a National Park. A new arrival also came in 1994 when Diamond Braverman, a Hollywood Art Director and Prop Maker, worked on the movie "*Shelter From the Storm*" in Pioneertown; a title that was very fitting for that time. Braverman enjoyed the area so much that he moved to Pioneertown and started a special effects and production design company that he named Diamond Location Services.

Diamond Braverman was around when The Gunfighters For Hire, a group of actors who perform on Mane Street, formed in 1995. It was for these Pioneertown performers that Braverman helped to design and construct the false fronts that are currently on Mane Street, like the Bath House, Jail and Bank. Residents celebrated Pioneertown's 5o'th Birthday on Saturday, October 12th, 1996. The new additions to Mane Street and the town's semi-centennial brought with them the overall gentrification of Pioneertown.

The short break in the storm then passed and the harsh period returned to Pioneertown. On February 1st, 1997, Lillian Mary Porter Hayden, "Mousie", died of undetermined causes. Mousie passed just three weeks shy of what would have been her 8oth birthday. She was buried alongside Russell and Sandra Hayden at Oakwood Memorial Park in Chatsworth, CA. Pioneertown had seen the loss of one of its original founders in 1997, but they would see even more the following year.

On July 6th, 1997, the "King of the Cowboys", Roy Rogers, died at his ranch in Apple Valley, CA, from congestive heart failure at the age of 86. Rogers was survived by his wife, Dale Evans, five children, 15 grandchildren and 33 great-grandchildren. The following month, on October 2nd, 1998, "America's Favorite Cowboy", Gene Autry, died of lymphoma at his home in Studio City, CA. Autry passed away just days after his 91st birthday and was buried at the Forest Lawn, Hollywood Hills Cemetery in Los Angeles. Gene Autry's epitaph reads: "America's Favorite Cowboy - American Hero, Philanthropist, Patriot and Veteran, Movie Star, Singer, Composer, Baseball Fan and Owner, 33rd Degree Mason, Media Entrepreneur, Loving Husband, Gentleman - A Believer In Our Western Heritage".

1998 also saw Ron Young leave the Pioneer Bowl after almost forty years of service. The following year, Pioneer Bowl, located at 53613 Mane Street in Pioneertown, was listed as California Historical Resource P36-o3oo77 in February of 1999. In its prime, Pioneer Bowl originally had shiplap siding which was covered in stucco in the late 198o's. The idea behind it being listed as a Historical Resource was to ensure that it would be preserved for future generations to enjoy. Until their doors closed for good in 2o1o, Pioneer Bowl was the oldest continually-operating bowling alley in southern California. Ron Young and his mother, Gladys, faithfully operated the Bowl from 1959 - 1998 and were followed by Stephanie, Valerie and friends, who all then tried to keep the Pioneer Bowl going.

On September 18th, 1999, "the man who saved Pioneertown", Philip N. Krasne, died at the age of 94 in West Los Angeles. He was buried at the Hillside Memorial Park in Culver City, CA. Later in his life, actor John Drew Barrymore was said to have disappeared to live in solitude after estranging himself from his family. During the late 199o's, while struggling with drugs and alcohol, Barrymore stayed at the Pioneertown Motel for prolonged periods of time and would always stay in room #1o. His daughter, Drew Barrymore, along with her dogs, would come stay in room #11 while they visited with him.

The Morongo Basin Historical Society, an amazing source of local history, was founded in 1999. That same year, the Shack Attack Program, a local effort to rid the area of blighted homesteads, began in the desert and continued for four years before ending in 2oo3. As a result, many of the jackrabbit homesteads and old ranches in the desert were lost. But the majority of properties which were effected saw positive results. Many residents were surprised to hear reports of a tornado in Joshua Tree which was recorded in 2ooo. That same year the historic Giant Rock split.

Right before the turn of the century, after the San Bernardino County Division of Environmental Health Services changed their testing procedures for water contaminate levels, it was announced that Pioneertown's water had high levels of both arsenic and uranium. A number of the supply wells which fed Pioneertown were shut off due to mineral pollution and a moratorium was set on new connections to the water system. The following was taken from a memorandum from Mike Farrell of the San Bernardino County Environmental Health Services to Bill Stone of the San Bernardino County Special Districts on September 11th, 1999: "Due to the lack of water quantity and sources producing water that exceeds primary and secondary maximum contaminant levels, there is a moratorium on any new connections to the Pioneertown water system."

On February 7th, 2oo1, the "Queen of the West", Dale Evans, died of congestive heart failure at her home in Apple Valley, CA. Evans was 88 years old when she passed and was interred next to Roy Rogers at Sunset Hills Memorial Park in Apple Valley. Later that year, the Palm Springs Walk of Stars dedicated a Golden Palm Star to both Dale Evans and Roy Rogers. Though her death marked the end of the harsh phase that hit the town, when Dale Evans passed away, the world lost the last remaining original investor in historic Pioneertown.

Later in 2oo1, California's 9th Welcome Center was established and opened in Yucca Valley. The same year saw the start of the annual HWY-62 Art Tours which showcases the High Desert's many unique artists and their studios. When Harriet entered into retirement, a retired United Airlines Pilot named Jay Hauk purchased Pappy & Harriet's Pioneertown Palace. Hauk and his partners constructed the Mercantile Shop and the Jack Cass Saloon on Mane Street in 2oo2. The Jack Cass, originally slated to be an additional bar, was mainly used for private parties and as a filming location while the Mercantile Shop was set up as retail and office space.

The Pioneertown Posse, the newest group of Western actors who put on free shows for visitors to Mane Street, was formed in 2oo2. That same year, the Morongo Basin Historical Society dedicated Warren's Well in Yucca Valley as a Historical Site. In a further attempt to preserve Pioneertown's historical highlights for future generations, in August of 2oo3, Mane Street in Pioneertown was listed as California Historical Resource P36-o11293. The following year, a Historical Marker, #117, was erected at the Pioneertown Post Office by the Billy Holcomb Chapter No. 1o69, E Clampus Vitus, in cooperation with the Pioneertown Post Office. Around this time, the Hayden Ranch also became registered as a California Historical Resource.

In 2oo3, Jay Hauk sold Pappy & Harriet's Pioneertown Palace to the current owners, New York natives Linda Krantz and Robyn Celia. When the sale was recorded by the County of San Bernardino in May of 2oo4, Krantz and Celia quickly went to work sprucing up the place and the patrons responded by multiplying quite steadily. That same year, Ernie and Carol Kester sold the Pioneertown Motel to Scott and Stacie Samuels. 2oo5 saw another High Desert tornado recorded; this time in Twentynine Palms. There were also a record number of wild flowers that spring. Unfortunately, the following year would not prove to be as pretty. On July 12th, 2oo6, the Sawtooth Complex fire tore through the area.

The Sawtooth Complex fire was the result of three separate wildfires which burned independently until merging into one large fire. Originally started by lightning around 8:3oAM on July 9th, it burned a total of 61,7oo acres by the time it was contained 1o days later. Sadly, in Pioneertown alone, it burned around 26,ooo acres, totaled 3o homes and buildings and also claimed the life of one man. Although the fire burned on both the south and north side of Pioneertown Road, the brave and courageous efforts of hundreds of Fire Personnel, some 861 in total, saved all the buildings on Mane Street. The Hayden Ranch was hit hard. Sadly, a number of the sites there were all but lost, including the Scarlett Lady, which was severely damaged inside and out as well as the old Pioneertown School House, which had been moved to the Hayden Ranch years earlier and burned down to the foundation.

Pioneertown, and all of Pipes Country for that matter, was never the same again and damage from the fire can still be seen till this day. Gene Autry once had a friend by the name of Madeline Beatty who lived in Rimrock and professionally trained horses. It was reported that one of her favorite horses could do over 15o tricks. Sadly, Beatty, like so many others, was burned out during the Sawtooth fire. The sign that greets visitors entering Pioneertown from Yucca Valley was saved, but one side of it did burn quite badly and the Joshua Trees that once rested directly next to it were completely lost. One will never be able to view Pioneertown again without seeing a scar in its beauty that was the Sawtooth Complex fire.

In a further attempt to preserve history and also to bring new life into Pioneertown, the County of San Bernardino decided to change the downtown zoning of Pioneertown from Special Development Residential to Commercial, late in 2oo8. The idea was to help make it easier for more businesses to move onto Pioneertown's Mane Street. New arrivals to Pioneertown around that time were John Ironsnake Jefferies & Gary Suppes of the Chaparrosa Outfitters, who set up their operations in the General Mercantile shop. The reintroduction of quality hand made leather goods to Pioneertown's Mane Street was well overdue and the Chaparrosa Outfitters quickly became very familiar faces around town.

The last owners of the bowling alley to keep it in operation were John and Valerie Lee who closed the doors for good around 2o1o. Pioneer Bowl currently sits in the center of Mane Street in dire need of restoration. The fact that it isn't currently open to the public is quite a sore subject with all of Pioneertown's residents. In direct contrast to one of the most jeopardized structures in Pioneertown, directly next door, Trigger Bill's Shooting Gallery is the most original, untouched, structure on Mane Street. The outside has suffered from the typical weathering any structure experiences while sitting in the desert for seventy years. But the inside of the building has remained untouched since it closed in the early 196o's and might very well be the best preserved arcade-type .22 caliber shooting gallery in southern California.

In December of 2o1o, Thomas and Amara Alban of MazAmar Art Pottery, moved their amazing business into the old Nickelodeon building on Mane Street. The sign on their wall now reads "Fine Ware For Fine Folks - Cracked Pots For The Rest Of Y'all". Starting around 2o11, Pioneertown residents Christy and Roger Anderson began purchasing the majority of the businesses on the north side of Mane Street, including everything from the Jack Cass Saloon to the Land Office and the Pioneertown Corrals in the back. The Andersons quickly set to work improving the town and reintroducing old traditions. Christy and Roger Anderson are responsible for a vast majority of the renovations and beautification on Mane Street in the past decade.

The Pioneertown Posse disbanded in 2o11 and was succeeded by the Mane Street Stampede Reenactors who continue to offer free wild west shows on Mane Street. Bands continue to flow to Pappy & Harriet's and the once little hole-in-the-wall restaurant continues to grow in both fame and success. After the motel switched owners a couple of times, Mike and Matt French purchased it in 2o14. Around the same time, Tim Blankman purchased the old Sound Stage on the opposite end of Mane Street. Just like the Andersons, Celia and Krantz - the French brothers and Blankman set to work improving the historical Pioneertown relics.

Both the Hayden Ranch and the Red Dog Saloon are independently under new ownership. The exact plans for each of Pioneertown's historical relics are still to be determined. But while researching for this book, it was noted that the current owners of both the Red Dog Saloon and Hayden Ranch have definite intentions of renovating and reopening in the very near future. The past decade has seen the creation of a non-profit organization called the "Friends of Pioneertown", which is dedicated to preserving the historical splendor that is Pioneertown.

The non-profit organization, which is headed by long time Pioneertown residents Jack and Sandy Dugan, is also in charge of setting up the holiday and annual celebrations in town. The Friends of Pioneertown are responsible for a great deal of the improvements and general maintenance which is done in Pioneertown and they are currently working hard to see the completion of the Pioneertown Museum. The museum is designated to be completed in memory of Ernie Kester who sadly passed away in 2o16.

Today, the Pioneertown Motel's most recent renovations have left it in great condition, both inside and out. These days it is very common to see the Motel running at full capacity. In recent years, a great deal of the Pioneertown Motel's original furniture, antique decorations and landscaping has been replaced in an attempt to keep up with today's high volume of guests. But while new amenities like Wi-Fi and online booking are now available, a great deal of work also went into decorating the Pioneertown Motel in the traditional old western theme.

The recent renovations to Mane Street's Sound Stage were done with diligent respect to the history of Pioneertown. The building currently stands in absolute prime condition for its age. Tim Blankman operates the Sound Stage as the Mane Street Book Store, as well as a unique venue where bands play live music, celebrations are held and couples are married quite often. Thanks to Blankman's hard work, the Sound Stage is once again host to holiday parties and get-togethers for Pioneertown locals, just as it was back in the 194o's.

Mane Street, though old and weathered by the stresses of time, looks better than ever, due strongly to the efforts of the new local owners and business operators. The proof is clear when one reviews the list of recent productions in Pioneertown. Starting at the turn of the century, production companies have once again started to film in Pioneertown on a steady basis. While keeping with the original charm and sticking to the original rules laid out by Dick Curtis and his Pioneertown Corporation back in the 194o's, the new residents, owners and operators of Pioneertown have truly brought new life to an already amazing town.

Pappy and Harriet's continues to get more and more popular with just about every crowd. Drinks are served in mason jars, the kitchen cooks great food and the cooked-to-order barbecue is out of this world. But the musicians that perform there really make the place pop! To list the names of famous bands and musicians who have played at Pappy & Harriet's throughout the years would probably require an additional chapter to this book. Over the years, new visitors and fans of Pioneertown have brought with them music festivals and art tours, such as the Desert Stars festival and the annual HWY-62 Open Studio Art Tours. Weather permitting; it is common to see thousands of attendees per day, as well as hundreds of campers at the Pioneertown Corrals per night, during these events.

Pioneertown was once a place that was hard to sell. It was hard enough to get people to visit the area at times; let alone sell land there. But as the public eye has begun to stare at Pioneertown's thriving new life, it has become increasingly harder to purchase property in the area as the majority of the current land owners have no intentions of selling. Additionally, no more new attachments to the current water system will be permitted and the new water system which will bring safe water to Pioneertown, proposed to be started in 2o18, will only service 3oo homes. With all that said, it is safe to say that Pioneertown won't see a large increase in population anytime soon. A fact that is quite cherished by Pioneertown's current residents, business owners and operators.

For anyone who hasn't visited Pioneertown since the 198o's, or even the early 2ooo's, the night and day difference is easy to see from the second you pass through the granite boulders leading into town. The world famous Pappy & Harriet's Pioneertown Palace greets visitors as they approach Pioneertown from the Yucca Valley entrance to the east and the Pioneertown & Pipes Canyon Preserves greet visitors as they enter from Pipes Canyon to the west. Upon entering the town, especially on the weekends, you will find a handful of stores open on Mane Street and likely a handful of people enjoying the town. Just as they did back in the 194o's, the scents of barbecue and horses still adorn Pioneertown both day and night and the good times are still found all year long.

Chapter 11

Today's Mane Idea: Visiting Information

DIRECTIONS & PARKING:

From Palm Springs take the I-1o Freeway West for about 6 Miles. Head North onto California Highway 62 Towards Twentynine Palms for about 2o Miles. Turn Left onto Pioneertown Road and continue for 5 miles. Downtown Pioneertown will be on your right-hand side.

From Los Angeles take the I-1o Freeway East for about 1oo Miles. Head North onto California Highway 62 Towards Twentynine Palms for about 2o Miles. Turn Left onto Pioneertown Road and continue for 5 miles. Downtown Pioneertown will be on your right-hand side.

From Joshua Tree National Park take California Highway 62 West for about 6 Miles. Turn Right onto Pioneertown Road and continue for about 5 Miles. Downtown Pioneertown will be on your right-hand side.

From Big Bear take the California Highway 18 North for about 12 Miles. Turn Right onto Camp Rock Road and continue for about 5 Miles. Turn Right onto California Highway 247 South and continue for about 35 Miles. Turn Right onto Pipes Canyon Road and continue for about 7 Miles. Turn Left onto Pioneertown Road and continue for another 3 Miles. Downtown Pioneertown will be on your left-hand side.

From Barstow take California Highway 247 South for about 4o Miles. Turn Right onto Pipes Canyon Road and continue for about 7 Miles. Turn Left onto Pioneertown Road and continue for about 3 Miles. Downtown Pioneertown will be on your left-hand side.

Please Don't Park On Pioneertown Road. There are plenty of parking spaces for Pappy & Harriet's surrounding the entire building, including a multiple acre parking lot just to the west, before Pioneer Bowl. The Pioneertown Motel has their own parking lot. There is also plenty of parking on the east side of Mane Street, accessible via Curtis Road. You should have no trouble finding off street parking and can take comfort in knowing that everything is within a short walking distance in Pioneertown. All parking in Pioneertown is free of charge.

COMMERCIAL FILMING/PHOTOGRAPHY:

Pioneertown is still a living breathing production set. All commercial filming or photography is restricted by permit only. If you are interested in obtaining a permit to shoot in Pioneertown, please contact the Pioneertown Corrals at 760.365.7580

HOURS & SCHEDULE:

Mane Street in Downtown Pioneertown is open and free to the public 365 days a year. You'll find that the majority of the action in town happens during the weekends. Businesses in Pioneertown don't tend to keep to a strict schedule and are typically open from mid-day until sundown. A weekend visit is highly recommended for first time visitors to Pioneertown.

RULES & GUIDELINES:

- No Cars Or Automobiles Are Permitted On Downtown Mane Street. The pedestrian-walking and horse-riding only areas are clearly marked "Hoof and Foot Only" and there is easy access to Rawhide Road from Roy Rogers Road to the west and Curtis Road to the east.
- All animals of all shapes and sizes are allowed in Pioneertown and inside just about every business. But there is a Strict Leash Law In Effect - All Animals, of all shapes and sizes, Are Required To Be On A Leash Inside Pioneertown.
- Half of Pioneertown's beauty and charm is experienced at night, when the stars are bright. Unnecessary Light & Noise Pollution is Highly Frowned Upon in Pioneertown. Of course, everyone needs light to see and people tend to make noise when they are enjoying themselves. Use Common Sense and Please Refrain From Using Any Bright Lights Or Producing Any Unnecessary Noise When At All Possible and help us keep the nights in Pioneertown as dark, quiet and beautiful as they were back in the good old 1880's.
- There are Trash Barrels located up and down Mane Street. Please Keep All Trash Inside Those Trash Barrels and help us keep the beauty and charm of Pioneertown intact.
- There Are Limited Public Restrooms In Town. The only indoor restrooms are available at Pappy & Harriet's and the Pioneertown Corals provides outhouses for campers.
- The use of Drones or any other controlled flying device is strictly prohibited in Pioneertown and may be operated in town by permit only.
- Commercial filming and photography in Pioneertown is authorized by permit only.
- Pioneertown's 1880's theme is expressed through just about the entire zip code and around Mane Street in particular. While the vast majority of Mane Street is open to the public, there are a handful of private residences right in the heart of the town. Please Respect All Signs, Fences, Rules and Guidelines.

SHOPPING:

General Mercantile Shop
The General Mercantile Shop on Mane Street is actually an art studio and gift shop. In addition to a variety of art from a handful of local artists, this shop also offers a wide range of crystals and minerals, vintage western clothes and cowboy boots, handmade jewelry as well as authentic Pioneertown merchandise.
Generally Open Thursdays - Sundays, from Midday to Sundown or whenever we happen to be there.
www.TrailerTags.com
www.HighDesertVarnish.com

Pioneertown General Store
The Pioneertown General Store is located in the old Likker Barn at 53635 Mane St in Pioneertown. The General Store offers handmade art and jewelry from the High Desert, awesome vintage and antique treasures along with hand-picked desert provisions; all within the historic Likker Barn! Generally Open Thursdays - Mondays, from 11AM to 6PM or whenever they happen to be there.
www.PioneertownGeneralStore.com

Jessie Keylon's Art Studio & Shop
Come check out Jessie's unique and amazing art work! Located on Mane Street in the Pioneertown Land Office which is directly next door to the Pottery Shop. Come watch as Jessie works away at putting her dreams onto paper or browse through her already completed selection of awesome art. Jessie's Studio is Open Thursdays - Mondays, from Midday to Sundown.
www.JessieKeylon.com

The Pottery Shop and Mazamar Art Pottery
The Pottery Shop offers
"High Fired Functional Art Pottery - Servin' it Up in the Morongo Basin Since 2ooo".
Come take a look at their amazing handmade art, much of which is made right inside Pioneertown's old Nickelodeon. And be sure to check out the amazing work of local artist Geoffrey Fennell, on permanent display in the showroom.
The Pottery Shop is Open Every Weekend and Most Weekdays, from Midday to Sundown.
www.MazAmar.com

Soap Goats Shop
The Soap Goats Shop is really JoAnne's Simply Soap and Bill & JoAnne's Pipes Canyon Pygoras. Come meet Bill and all of the friendly goats. Be sure to check out JoAnne's shop where you can get freshly handmade soap plus a variety of different items which are all made from hand-spun goat wool.
You can even watch JoAnne spin some goat wool right there on the front porch!
The Soap Goat Shop is Open Saturday and Sunday Afternoons, Weather Permitting.
www.PipesCanyonPygoras.weebly.com

Arrow & Bear
A new addition to Pioneertown is this misfit mercantile on Mane Street which offers handmade art and treasures to their friends and visitors to the wild west. Arrow & Bear opened in the winter of 2o17 and is operated by Lorenzo and Jolyn.
They are located directly next door to the Chaparosa Outfitters Leather Shop on Mane Street.
Arrow Bear is Open Most Weekends from Midday to Sundown.

Chaparrosa Outfitters in the Pioneertown Saddlery Shop
Stop on by the Saddle Shop on Mane Street where John and Gary do custom saddle and leather work. Check out their detailed, high quality western saddles, leather cowboy accessories and Native American art or browse through their selection of fine leather care goods. Located inside of the old Land Office, the first building completed in Pioneertown, on the west end of Downtown Mane Street. Pioneertown Saddlery is Generally Open Every Day of the Week from Midday to Sundown.
www.facebook.com/ChaparrosaOutfitters

Sound Stage & Book Store
Pioneertown's historic Sound Stage on Mane Street has been beautifully restored by owner Tim Howard. The massive Sound Stage is available for private parties, weddings, band rehearsals and much more! When the Sound Stage isn't being rented out for a private event, Tim opens up the Book Store, where visitors can browse through a wide selection of vintage books, records and movies. The Sound Stage is also host to a number of different live, free events, like live music and holiday parties. Check out their website for more information.
The Sound Stage is Generally Open to the Public on Weekends from Midday to Sundown.
www.facebook.com/PioneertownSoundStage

LODGING:

The Pioneertown Corrals (Campground)
Located in the center of Pioneertown at 53626 Mane Street, Pioneertown.
Pioneertown Corrals offers campers a place to pop a tent or an RV that is just a stones throw away from Mane Street and Pappy & Harriet's. Some of the cheapest camping in the USA!
Corrals for your four legged friends are available.
Hosted by Camp Master John, rates are $10 A Night, Per Person or Horse.
Access the campground via the north entrance off of Curtis Road.
760.365.7580
www.PioneertownCorrals.com

The Pioneertown Motel
If you don't prefer to sleep under the stars, come stay at the cozy and historic Pioneertown Motel.
Located just to the east of the Pioneertown Corrals at 5240 Curtis Road in Pioneertown, with very easy walking access to Mane Street as well as Pappy & Harriet's. Recently restored and charming as ever, each room is host to over seventy years of High Desert History!
Call or check their website for rates and availability.
760.365.7001
www.Pioneertown-Motel.com

Desert Willow Ranch
The Desert Willow Ranch was privately purchased in 1969 from none other than Russell Hayden and is located at 53722 Pioneertown Road in Pioneertown, right across Curtis Road from Pappy & Harriet's. The Ranch hosts a 3-Bed Cabin Rental with a Kitchen, and multiple Patios. Bring your horses! They have two Corrals, a Round Pin, Arena and Tack Room available as well.
Check their website for rates and availability.
760.369.2211
www.DesertWillowRanch.com

Rimrock Ranch
The historic Rimrock Motel, established an entire year before Pioneertown, is still alive today! Now known as the Rimrock Ranch - this 11 acre ranch includes four cabins, retro-fitted Airstream trailers, a Lodge and the world famous Hatch House.
The Rimrock Ranch is a perfect location for a weekend getaway, weddings, last minute retreats, film and photography shoots or celebrations of any kind.
760.228.0130
www.RimrockRanchPioneertown.com

FOOD & ENTERTAINMENT:

Pappy & Harriet's Pioneertown Palace
To sum it up in just one word: "BBQ"! Pappy & Harriet's Pioneertown Palace is home to some of the best Barbecue in the High Desert! Stop in for some Lunch, Dinner or Drinks. P&H's is also an exceptional music venue that hosts live shows each week. A famous hangout for many world famous musicians - You never know who might stop in and pick up a guitar.
Pappy & Harriet's is open for Lunch and Dinner, Thursdays - Mondays. They are the only place to get a hot meal or an alcoholic beverage in Pioneertown and can fill up really quick! Check out their website for a Schedule of upcoming shows or to take a look at their Menu.
760.365.5956
www.PappyAndHarriets.com

Wild West Shows and Shootouts on Mane Street
Two groups currently perform free live action wild west reenactments on Mane Street: the Gun Fighters For Hire and The Mane Street Stampede. The Seasonal Shows are Saturdays, Starting at 2:3oPM, Weather Permitting, in front of the Pioneer Bowl.
Check their websites for show schedules and special events.
www.GunFightersForHire.com
www.ManeStreetStampede.com

The Pioneertown Wild West Theater at the Desert Willow Ranch
The newest live-action addition to Pioneertown is the Wild West Theater, located right next door to Pappy & Harriet's inside of the Desert Willow Ranch. In addition to life performances, the Wild West Theater also hosts weekly Line Dancing parties.
Check their website for information and showtimes.
www.facebook.com/Pioneertown-Wild-West-Theater-929995077116698

COMING SOON: THE PIONEERTOWN MUSEUM, IN MEMORY OF ERNIE KESTER
The Pioneertown Museum organized in 2o17 and at the time of this book's publication, was still in the process of being completed. The Museum will open sometime in 2o18 and will be located inside of the Jack Cass Saloon & Kester Trading Post on Mane Street.

The Church in Pioneertown
Active to this very day, The Church in Pioneertown is a non denominational Church which offers weekly Sunday Service at 1o:oo AM. The Church is located across from the Red Dog Saloon on Mane Street. Members of The Church in Pioneertown are active in local and nationwide charity and even go caroling to many High Desert locations each Christmas.
www.facebook.com/pages/The-Church-in-Pioneertown/141698982606479?fref=ts

The Pioneertown Mountains Preserve
Some Of Southern California's Best Hiking Is Just A Quick Drive From Downtown Pioneertown! The 25,5oo Acre Wildlands Conservancy's Pioneertown Mountains & Pipes Canyon Preserve Visitor Facilities Include Trailhead Parking, a Kiosk, a Shade Ramada and Public Restrooms. They offer free Interpretive Programs, host numerous Outdoor Educational Events and are Open Daily From Dawn to Dusk. They are located at 51010 Pipes Canyon Road in Pioneertown.
760.369.71o5
www.WildlandsConservancy.org/Preserve_Pioneertown.html

The Wildlands Conservancy

Pioneertown Mountains Preserve

51010 B Pipes Canyon Road
Pioneertown, CA 92268
(760) 369-7105

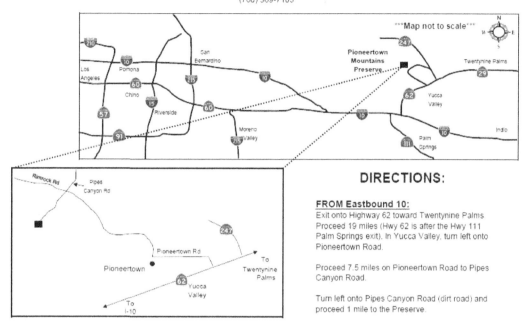

DIRECTIONS:

FROM Eastbound 10:
Exit onto Highway 62 toward Twentynine Palms
Proceed 19 miles (Hwy 62 is after the Hwy 111
Palm Springs exit). In Yucca Valley, turn left onto
Pioneertown Road.

Proceed 7.5 miles on Pioneertown Road to Pipes
Canyon Road.

Turn left onto Pipes Canyon Road (dirt road) and
proceed 1 mile to the Preserve.

The Wildlands Conservancy
Pioneertown Mountains Preserve
51010 Pipes Canyon Road | Pioneertown, CA | 92268

(760) 369-7105
wildlandsconservancy.org

*Pioneertown Mountains Preserve is a wilderness preserve. Many areas that are open to hiking are remote
and may not be frequented by staff. Be advised of the possible presence of bears, mountain lions, and rattlesnakes.
For your safety, please sign in at the Ranger Station kiosk or the trailhead.*

Sawtooth Loop	9.5 miles	Moderate—Difficult

Designed primarily as a horseback-riding loop, the Sawtooth Loop trail can also be traversed on foot. This trail is better suited to experienced hikers due to frequent, sharp changes in elevation and the relative length of the trail. The loop offers scenic views of the Sawtooth Mountains as well as glimpses of Southern California's second-tallest peak, Mt. San Jacinto.

Indian Loop	6 Miles	Varies (see below)

The Indian Loop trail is comprised of three separate trails: the Pipes Canyon, Indian Springs, and Chaparrosa Peak Trails. Points of interest along the trail include a wetlands area—particularly beautiful in fall, winter, and early spring—and the Olsen homestead ruins. Chaparrosa Peak can be summited via a ¼ mile spur trail from the intersection of the Indian Loop and Chaparrosa Peak Trails.

The Indian Loop Trail has two starting points. The Pipes Canyon trailhead can be reached by walking up the service road towards a white gate just to the west of the ranger station. The Chaparrosa Peak trailhead is located along the East side of the upper parking lot, just up the hill from the Ranger Station.

Pipes Canyon Trail	Easy—Moderate

With shady rest stops along the length of the trail, this trail gently winds its way up Pipes Canyon for several miles before ending at the junction with the Indian Springs trail. The area beyond this junction has been closed due to the July 2015 Lake Fire.

Indian Springs Trail	Moderate-Difficult

This trail runs up a steep, narrow drainage south from the Pipes Canyon Trail before connecting with the Chaparrosa Peak Trail. This trail is only accessible from the Pipes Canyon Trail or Chaparrosa Peak Trail.

Chaparrosa Peak Trail	Moderate-Difficult

This trail gains 1000 ft. over 3.3 miles on its way up to Chaparrosa Peak. Most of this occurs within the first mile of the trail. Once you reach the top you are rewarded with majestic views of Pioneertown and Flat Top Mesa to the west and the Morongo Basin and Mt. San Jacinto to the South.

Chapter 12

What's Where & Who's Who

      The next two pages contain a map and key to the past and present sites in Pioneertown. While it is not drawn to scale, this map should help to provide you with a good idea of just how busy Mane Street has been over the years.

      Following the map of Pioneertown you will find a alphabetized list of names which indexes the people who were a part of Pioneertown's history. This is obviously not a complete list, but rather a means of helping to identify key figures in the early history and continuing development of Pioneertown.

Past & Present Map of Pioneertown

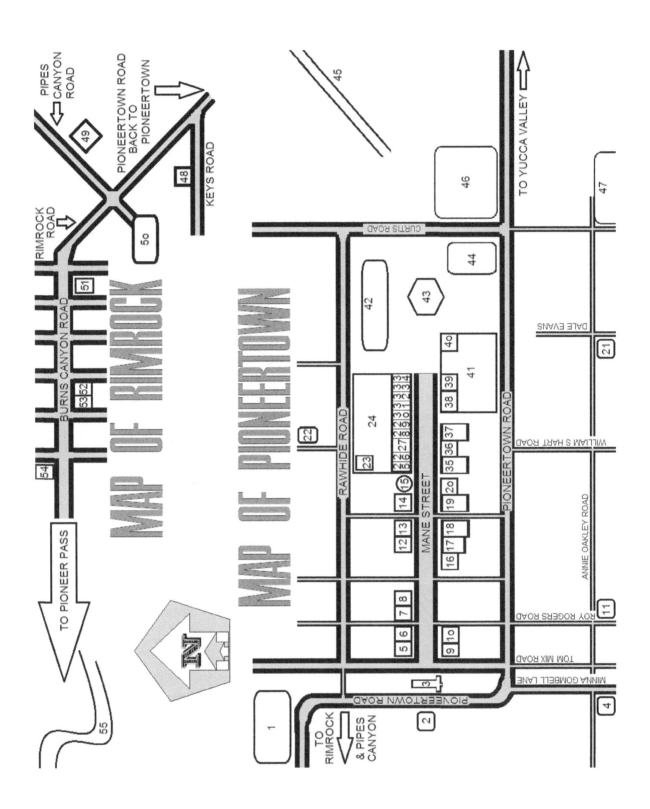

1. Site of the **Studd Valley Trailer Park**, Pioneertown's First Well & the "**Laun-dromat**" Laundry Facilities   (Private Residence)
2. Site of the **Pioneertown School House**
3. Pioneertown's **O.K. Corral**
4. Site of **Minna Gombell's Home** (Private Property)
5. Site of **Maggie's Feed Barn**
6. **White's Grocery**, formerly **White's Hardware** (Now Private Property)
7. Site of **Nell's Ice Cream Palace**
8. Site of **The Chuckwagon Cafe**
9. The **Sheriff's Office**, original site of **The Frosted Pantry** (Closed to the Public)
10. **Pioneertown Post Office** & site of a California Historical Marker, originally **Marble's Electronics**
11. **Roy Rogers' Old Property** (Private Property)
12. Site of **Gem Trader, Toll Mine** and **The Wooden Indian** (Newer Private Residence)
13. **The Church in Pioneertown**, originally **Althoof's Furniture Store**
14. **The Open Air Dance Floor**
15. **The Rock Watering Trough** that originally sat in the center of Mane Street
16. Site of **The Barber Shop and Beauty Corral** with **Cecil the Barber**, then Sam's Grocery, then Antiques & Junk (Private Residence)
17. Site of **The Ole's Barbeque Corral** (Original structure was replaced and the site is currently Private Property)
18. Pioneertown's **Red Dog Saloon** (Currently Closed to the Public)
19. Site of the **Grubstake Cafe** (Private Property)
20. **The Pioneertown Gazette** (Private Residence)
21. **Dale Evans' Old Property** (Private Property)
22. **Old Home of Tommy Thompson and Cactus Kate** as well as Buzz Gamble (Private Property)
23. **The Pioneertown Generator House** (Now Private Property)
24. **The Pioneertown Corrals Campground** (Open 365 Days A Year)
25. **Pioneertown Saddlery**, originally **The Pioneertown Land Office** and the first building to be completed in Pioneertown
26. **Arrow and Bear**, Originally **Pioneertown Duds and Saddlery** as well as the **Second Post Office** in Pioneertown
27. **Fun False Fronts** that were added to Mane Street in 1998 - 1999
28. **Schnald Mining Corporation**, Originally **Pioneertown Photos** (Private Residence)
29. **The Soap Goats Shop**, Originally the Mane Street Utility Shed
30. **Pioneertown Pottery**, originally **The Pioneertown Nickelodeon**
31. **The Pioneertown Land Office** & home of artist Jessie Keylon (Added to Mane Street in 2o15)
32. **The Pioneertown Bell House** (Another storage shed that was added to Mane Street in 2o15)
33. **The General Mercantile Shop** (Added to Mane Street in 2oo2)
34. **The Jack Cass Saloon** aka **The Kester Trading Post** (Added to Pioneertown in 2oo2)
35. **The Pioneertown Sound Stage**, originally **The Silver Dollar**
36. **Trigger Bill's Shooting Gallery** (Currently Closed to the Public)
37. **Pioneer Bowl**, The Pioneertown Bowling Alley (Currently Closed to the Public)
38. **The Likker Barn**, currently the **Pioneertown General Store**, originally **Pioneertown Likker**, then **The Golden Nugget Coffee Shop** and then **The Pioneertown Visitor Center**
39. **The Marshall's Office**, originally **Carol Burgess' Gift Shop** (Closed to the Public)
40. **The Klip n' Kurl Hair Saloon** & the Office of **Dr. R. E. Guenther, D. C.** (Private Residence)
41. **Pioneertown Public Parking** (Free)
42. **The Pioneertown Motel**, originally **The Pioneer Townhouse**, then **The Golden Stallion Lodge**
43. Site of **The Golden Stallion Restaurant** which burned down in 1966 and was never rebuilt
44. **Pappy & Harriet's Pioneertown Palace**, formerly the **Cantina** and originally the **Pioneertown Service Station & Pony Express** (Open Thursday-Monday)
45. Site of **Pioneertown's Second Landing Strip** (Private Property)
46. **The Desert Willow Ranch** and home of the **Wild West Stunt Show**
47. **The Historic Hayden Ranch** (Private Property)
48. Site of the old **Kee's Ranch and Homestead** (Now Private Property)
49. The **Mattoon Chicken Farm** (Private Property)
50. **Pioneertown Mountains & Pipes Canyon Preserve** (Open Daily From Dawn Till Dusk)
51. **Maggie McDonald's Ranch** (Private Property)
52. **Rimrock Ranch**, originally **The Rimrock Motel**
53. Site of the old **Pekarovich Ranch and Homestead** (Now Private Property)
54. **Dick Curtis' Old Property** (Private Property)
55. **The Pioneer Pass** (Back Road to Big Bear)

Who's Who in the History of Pioneertown
A Comprehensive List of the People Involved With the History of Pioneertown

- **Adele Mara** — Actress, Singer, Dancer and Pinup Girl who was a friend of Roy Rogers and Dick Curtis, attended the Ground Breaking Ceremony and was a frequent guest to Pioneertown

- **Al Lipps** — Original Co-Owner of the Red Dog Saloon

- **Alexander Bradner** — Original Architect and Planning Commissioner for the Pioneertown Corporation

- **Alice "Honey" Fellers** — Pioneertown Realtor who worked out of the Likker Barn

- **Alice White-Creswell** — The first Postmaster of Pioneertown and Lillian and Tommy Thompson's Daughter

- **Althoff, Harry & Nell** — Some of the very first people to buy land in Pioneertown and the owners of Althoof's Furniture Store

- **Anderson, Roger & Christy** — Most recent owners of the majority of Mane Street and the people responsible for Pioneertown's most recent renovations

- **Art Baker** — Famous Radio and Television Personality and one of the very first people to buy land in Pioneertown

- **Art Daly** — Public Relations & Advertising Counselor to the Pioneertown Corporation and Co-Owner of the advertising firm Daly-Strong

- **Barbara Billingley** — Actress who starred in the first movie filmed in Pioneertown, *The Valiant Hombre* filmed in 1947 and released in 1948

- **Barbara Stanwick** — Actress who starred in *Jeopardy* which was filmed in Pioneertown during 1952 and then released in 1953

- **BeeBe Kline** — Paramount Studios publicity representative and author of the Studd Valley News for the Pioneertown Gazette

- **Benton Lefton** — Head of the California Golden Empire and previous owner of Pioneertown from the 1960's through the 1970's

- **Beverly Moninger** — Named the "Queen of Pioneertown" - She represented Pioneertown at the 1948 Circus Parade in Palm Springs

- **Bill Kramer** — An old man from Iowa who moved way up the Mormon Trail in the 1920's to find health and solitude

- **Bill Dennis** — Land Promoter and Co-Head of the Pioneertown Land Corporation - Arguments between Dick Curtis, Bill Dennis and his partner, Gordon Brown, lead to Curtis stepping down from President of the Pioneertown Corporation in 1948

- **Bill Wolfe** — Private Contractor who built the original Red Dog Saloon

- **Bob Nolan** — A Founding Member of The Sons of the Pioneers, Friend of Dick Curtis' and one of the first land owners in Pioneertown

- **Bryan Johnson** — Ran Maggie's Feed Barn on Mane Street with Shorty Creswell

- **Bud Abbot** — Famous Comedian, Actor, "Abbot" of *Abbot & Costello* as well as a very old friend of Dick Curtis'

- **Burns, Bruce & Jean** — One of the first families to buy land in Pioneertown and the largest private land owners at one time, owning 320 Acres off Skyline Ranch Road. In 1972 they deeded 265 acres to the University of CA which established the Burns Pinon Ridge Reserve

- **Buzz Gamble**　　　　Long time resident of Pioneertown, a singer who frequently played at Pappy & Harriet's Pioneertown Palace and who also renovated the bar at Pappy & Harriet's

- **"Cactus Jim"**　　　　Tended the bar along with Val Jones at the Red Dog Saloon

- **"Cactus Kate"**　　　　Was actually Lillian Thompson, the Manager of the Pioneertown Townhouse and co-owner of the Bowling Alley

- **Carol Burgess**　　　　Ran Carol Burgess' Gift Shop in the Marshall's Office, next door to the Likker Barn

- **Cecil Sly**　　　　Manager of the SPS Corporation and former president of the Pioneertown Businessman's Association

- **Cecil the Barber**　　　　Head Barber at the Barber Shop & Beauty Corral on Mane Street

- **Champion**　　　　Gene Autry's famous Wonder Horse

- **Charles L. Nichols**　　　　Original Member of the Pioneertown Board of Directors

- **Charles M. Baker**　　　　Pioneertown Land Sales Agent

- **Charles V. McClure**　　　　Old-timer and local prospector from Yucca Valley who discovered a large vein of gold that stretched through the north west tip of Pioneertown

- **Charles Starrett**　　　　Famous Western actor that worked alongside Dick Curtis in over two dozen films

- **Claude Guinan**　　　　One of the first people to buy land in Pioneertown

- **Claude "Pappy" Allen**　　　　"Pappy" of Pappy & Harriet's Pioneertown Palace

- **Claudine A. Wilson**　　　　Former owner of the Red Dog Saloon

- **Clyde Biddle**　　　　One of the First Two School Teachers in Pioneertown

- **Curt Bush**　　　　An Original Board Member of the Pioneertown Corporation

- **Curtis, John & Phyllis**　　　　Dick Curtis' son and daughter

- **Dale Evans**　　　　Western Actress, Married Roy Rogers and was one of the First Promoters and Land Owners in Pioneertown

- **Daniel Keohane**　　　　Original Secretary for the Pioneertown Corporation

- **Danny Sall**　　　　Also known as "Danny Boy" - First baby resident of Pioneertown

- **David Bruce**　　　　Actor who was a friend of Dick Curtis, attended the Ground Breaking Ceremony and was a frequent guest to Pioneertown

- **Davenport, "A" & "E"**　　　　Owned and operated the Pioneer Gem Trader on Mane Street

- **Dazzlin' Dallas Morley**　　　　Town celebrity and bar maiden at the Red Dog Saloon who came to Pioneertown in 1949 and stayed until her retirement in 1977

- **De Churchill**　　　　One of the first people to buy and develop land in Pioneertown and Minna Gombell's longtime business partner

- **Dick Curtis**　　　　The Infamous Dick Curtis! Famous actor, the Sole Founder and the "Father of Pioneertown". The First President and one of the three Original Directors of the Pioneertown Corporation

- **Don Imus**　　　　Early visitor to Pioneertown who painted the mural of Dazzlin' Dallas Morley on the original Red Dog Saloon's Floor

- **Don Julio Eisenbruch**　　　　Pioneertown Land Sales Agent who was also known as "The Happy Gringo"

- **Don Kokx**　　　　Original co-owner of the Red Dog Saloon

- **Dr. R. E. Guenther, D.C.**　　　　First doctor (Chiropractor) to set up a medical practice in Pioneertown. Worked out of the Klip n' Kurl on Mane Street

- **Duncan Renaldo** — Actor who played the Cisco Kid in all of *The Cisco Kid* titles that were filmed in Pioneertown, including the first production filmed in town, *The Valiant Hombre* in 1948

- **Elwood Hutcheson** — Owned Nell's Ice Cream Palace which was managed by Mrs. "Mac" MacKinnon

- **Erkine Johnson** — One of the first people to buy land in Pioneertown, Radio and Television Personality and Syndicated Columnist

- **Ernie Kester** — Local Historian & Previous Owner of Pioneertown Motel

- **Father John Lima M.M.** — Conducted the first religious service in Pioneertown on 7.26.1947 and was an old friend of Dick and Ruth Curtis'

- **Fletcher Jones** — Original Pioneertown Corporation Board Member who became a Co-owner of Pioneertown in 1954 with William Murphy

- **Flora B. Stone** — Known as "The Girl Sign Painter" who worked on Mane Street

- **Floyd McDonald** — Co-owned Maggie's Feed Barn along with his brother and sister, Lloyd and Maggie

- **Frances Aleba** — Original Owner of the Cantina which later became Pappy & Harriet's Pioneertown Palace - Frances was Harriet's mother

- **Francis Livingston** — Ran Pioneertown Freighters with Jack Duckett

- **Frank E. Gray** — Unknown Investor and one of the only three people listed in Pioneertown's California Business Incorporation Documents other than Dick Curtis & Thomas Carr

- **Frank Gee** — One of three original investors and owners of The Golden Stallion Restaurant

- **Frank Kara** — Designed the first promotional Pioneertown Bumper Sticker

- **Frank Mattoon** — First husband of Margie Mattoon-Hamilton, Co-owner of the largest chicken farm in the High Desert and a very old friend of Dick Curtis'

- **Frank McDonald** — Famous Western director, original Second Vice President of Pioneertown Corporation and old friend of Dick Curtis'

- **Fred Marble** — Owned and operated Marble's Electric Shop on Mane Street

- **Fred Moninger** — Architect and Planning Engineer for the Pioneertown Corporation and Assistant to the Original Architect and Planning Commissioner, Alexander Bradner

- **Gail Davis** — Actress who played Annie Oakley which was filmed entirely in Pioneertown

- **Gloria Henry** — Western Actress and Gene Autry's Lead Lady in many productions

- **George Sinclair** — Built the adobe Pony Express and Gas Station in Pioneertown which later became Pappy & Harriet's Pioneertown Palace

- **George Tobias** — Film and Television Actor who was a friend of Dick Curtis', attended the Ground Breaking Ceremony and was a frequent guest to Pioneertown

- **Gene Autry** — Radio, Television and Movie Star known around the world as the "Singing Cowboy" and a Pioneertown promoter who filmed and produced hundreds of productions in Pioneertown

- **Gene Lester** — Famous Hollywood Photographer who was a friend to many of Pioneertown's founding members, attended the Ground Breaking Ceremony and was a frequent guest to Pioneertown

- **Gordon Brown** — Land Promoter and co-head of the Pioneertown Land Corporation - Arguments between Dick Curtis, Gordon Brown and his partner, Bill Dennis, lead to Curtis stepping down from President of the Pioneertown Corporation in 1948

- **Harold Church** — Owned and operated Pioneertown Photos on Mane Street

- **Harriet Allen**   "Harriet" of Pappy & Harriet's Pioneertown Palace
- **Harry Schaad**   Owned and operated the Nickelodeon on Mane Street
- **Hazel Strong**   Public Relations & Advertising Counselor to the Pioneertown Corporation and co-owner of the advertising firm Daly-Strong
- **Hedda Hopper**   One of the first people to buy land in Pioneertown, gossip columnist and a longtime rival of Louella Parsons
- **Henry Jew**   One of three original investors and owners of The Golden Stallion restaurant
- **Hugh Farr**   Member of The Sons of the Pioneers During 1945 - 1946 and a friend of Dick Curtis but didn't own any land in Pioneertown
- **J. B. Webb**   General Sales Manager for the Pioneertown Land Corporation
- **Jack Bailey**   Television celebrity & former owner of The Golden Stallion restaurant and the Pioneertown Lodge, which he named "The Golden Stallion Lodge"
- **Jack Duckett**   Ran Pioneertown Freighters with Francis Livingston
- **Jack Lunden**   Actor who was a friend of Dick Curtis', attended the Ground Breaking Ceremony and was a frequent guest to Pioneertown
- **Jake Price**   Constructed the OK Corral rodeo grounds at the end of Mane Street
- **Janis Page**   Film, Musical Theater and Television Actress who was a friend of Dick Curtis', attended the Ground Breaking Ceremony and was a frequent guest to Pioneertown
- **Jerry Fairbanks**   Filmed "Unusual Occupations" for Paramount Pictures at Pioneertown in December of 1947
- **Jim Sullivan**   Managed the Althoof's Furniture Store for his Parents, Harry & Nell Althoff
- **Jimmy Fidler**   Radio and Television Personality, Syndicated Columnist and one of the first people to buy land in Pioneertown
- **Jimmy Starr**   Screen Writer, Hollywood Columnist and one of the very first people to buy land in Pioneertown
- **John Carroll**   Actor and Singer who was an old friend of Dick Curtis', attended the Ground Breaking Ceremony and was a frequent guest to Pioneertown
- **John Hamilton**   Married to Margie Mattoon, equestrian enthusiast and founder of the Rawhide Riding Club in Pioneertown
- **John James**   Actor who starred in the first movie filmed in Pioneertown, *The Valiant Hombre*, released in 1948
- **John Litel**   Actor who starred in the first movie filmed in Pioneertown, *The Valiant Hombre*, released in 1948
- **Johnnie Kee**   Local homesteader from before the days of Pioneertown who constructed the watering trough in the center of Mane Street and was President of the Pioneertown School Building Board
- **Karl Farr**   Member of The Sons of the Pioneers During 1945 - 1946 and a friend of Dick Curtis but didn't own any land in Pioneertown
- **Katherine Newton**   Second owner of the Likker Barn and manager of the Golden Nugget Coffee Shop
- **Ken Carson**   Western Actor and Singer as well as an old friend of Dick Curtis'
- **Ken Maynard**   Western Actor and an old friend of Dick Curtis'

- **KENNETH B. GENTRY** — Your Author!
- **Kurt Bush** — Pioneertown Land Sales Agent who specialized in selling desert land to residents of Big Bear, CA
- **Lillian Porter Hayden** — Actress, known as "Mousie", married Russell "Lucky" Hayden, helped develop Pioneertown Road and was a very well known resident of Pioneertown
- **Lillian Thompson** — Also known as Cactus Kate, Manager of the Pioneertown Townhouse and co-owner of the Bowling Alley with her husband, Tommy Thompson
- **Leo Carrillo** — Actor who played Pancho, the Cisco Kid's sidekick, in all of *The Cisco Kid* titles that were filmed in Pioneertown including the very first production filmed in town
- **Leonard P. Wikof** — President of the Pioneertown Utilities Company
- **Lloyd McDonald** — Co-owned Maggie's Feed Barn along with his brother and sister, Floyd and Maggie
- **Lloyd Perryman** — A Member of the Sons of the Pioneers, Friend of Curtis' and one of the First Land Owners in Pioneertown
- **Lois Elaine** — Daughter of Margie Mattoon-Hamilton and a very early resident of Pioneertown
- **Lou Costello** — Famous comedian, Actor, "Costello" of *Abbott & Costello* and friend of Dick Curtis'
- **Louella Parsons** — One of the first people to buy land in Pioneertown, "Queen of Hollywood" and the very first gossip columnist in the U.S.
- **"Mac" Mackinnon** — She managed Nell's Ice Cream Palace along with the owner, Mrs. Elwood Hutcheson. She was also a Pioneertown Land Sales Agent
- **Maggie McDonald** — Also known as "Rud Rud" - Co-owned Maggie's Feed Barn on Mane Street along with her brothers, Lloyd and Floyd
- **Mallette, Rene & Mabel** — Some of the first people to buy land in Pioneertown
- **Marie Bush** — Ran the Chuck Wagon in Pioneertown along with Toodles Senn
- **Marilyn Moon** — One of three original investors and owners of The Golden Stallion Restaurant
- **Martha Vickers** — Model and Actress who was a friend of Dick Curtis', attended the Ground Breaking Ceremony and was a frequent guest to Pioneertown
- **Marvel Lind** — Managed the Pioneer Townhouse after Lilly Thompson
- **Maude Ransom** — Original Assistant Secretary-Treasurer for the Pioneertown Corporation
- **McCluer Senn** — Owner and Operator of Pioneertown Plumbers
- **Minna Gombell** — Famous Movie Actress, Friend of Dick Curtis' and one of the First Land Owners as well as the Only Celebrity to live in Pioneertown besides Russell and Mousie Hayden
- **Nicholas "Nick" Treosti** — Pioneertown Land Sales Agent
- **Norman Granger** — Ran the Uni-Gas propane plant in Yucca Valley until it was sold to the Union Oil Company. Credited as the Creator of the "Push" portion of the Pioneer Pass Pushers as well as the First Chairman of Pioneer Pass Pushers
- **Pat Brady** — Member of The Sons of the Pioneers During 1945 - 1946, friend of Dick Curtis' but didn't own any land in Pioneertown
- **Pattrick Buttram** — Famous Actor and good friend of Gene Autry's who was severely injured in an accident when a prop cannon exploded while filming in Pioneertown
- **Pearl Jones** — One of the First Two School Teachers in Pioneertown and was also married to Val Jones of the Red Dog Saloon

- **Pearl Seidl**   First owner of the Likker Barn and manager of Pioneertown Likker, Pioneertown's very first liquor store
- **Phillip N. Krasne**   Produced *The Cisco Kid* Serial and Movies, known as the "Savior of Pioneertown" and the man responsible for converting the Silver Dollar into Pioneertown's famous Sound Stage
- **Philo J. Harvey**   An Original Board Member of the Pioneertown Corporation
- **Priest, Cliff & Glnny**   Built the Old Pioneer Trail Lodge, also known as the Pioneertown Lodge, the Pioneer Townhouse and the Pioneertown Motel
- **Ralph Dawson**   Three Time Academy Award Winning Film Editor and an old fiend of Dick Curtis'
- **Ralph O' Neil**   Engineer for the Pioneertown Development Corporation
- **Richard M. Wambsgans**   Registered Accountant and Original Auditor for the Pioneertown Corporation
- **Rick Wolfe**   Helped build the original Red Dog Saloon with his brother Bill
- **Robert Carlisle**   Directed "Unusual Occupations" for Paramount Pictures at Pioneertown in December of 1947
- **Robert Mitchum**   Actor, Director, Author, Composer and Singer who was an old friend of Dick Curtis', attended the Ground Breaking Ceremony and was a frequent guest to Pioneertown
- **Roy Brown**   Owned and operated the Pioneertown Gazette on Mane Street
- **Ron Young**   Ran the Pioneer Bowl for Almost 4o Years, From 1961 - 1998
- **Roy Rogers**   Western Actor, A Founding Member of The Sons of the Pioneers, One of the First Land Owners in Pioneertown, Married to Dale Evans and an Original Pioneertown Corporation Board Member
- **Russell "Lucky" Hayden**   Actor, original Pioneertown Corporation Treasurer and former President, Married to Mousie Hayden and was one of the only actors who not only purchased land, but also built a house and lived in Pioneertown
- **Ruth M. Sullivan-Curtis**   Actress and Dick Curtis' second wife
- **R. W. O'Neil**   Took over Russell Hayden's position on the Pioneertown Board of Directors in 1948 and engineered the Diversion Dam in Burns Canyon the same year
- **Sall, Daniel & Dorothy**   Some of the first people to buy land in Pioneertown and the parents of "Danny Boy" Sall, the first child born in Pioneertown
- **Shorty Creswell**   Ran Maggie's Feed Barn with Bryan Johnson, named Studd Valley and also worked along with Trigger Bill to improve the roads around Pioneertown
- **Shug Fisher**   A Member of the Sons of the Pioneers, Friend of Curtis' and One of the First Land Owners in Pioneertown
- **Skare, Mr. & Mrs. Ole**   Owners of the Barbeque Corral and some of the very first people to buy and develop land in Pioneertown
- **Smiley Burnette**   Famous Western Actor, friend and partner of both Roy Rogers and Gene Autry
- **Stanley Andrews**   Actor who starred in the very first movie filmed in Pioneertown, *The Valiant Hombre*, released in 1948
- **Teresa Wright**   Actress, an old friend of Dick Curtis' and a frequent guest to Pioneertown
- **Terry Frost**   A Member of The Sons of the Pioneers who was named as an Original Pioneertown Investor independently from The Sons of the Pioneers on multiple accounts and who was also a very old friend of Dick Curtis'

- **Thomas Carr** — A Member of The Sons of the Pioneers, Old Friend of Curtis', First Vice President and one of three Original Directors of the Pioneertown Corporation
- **Tim Spencer** — Member of The Sons of the Pioneers During 1945 - 1946, a friend of Dick Curtis', wrote the song *Out in Pioneertown* but didn't actually own any land in Pioneertown
- **Toal, George & Pee Wee** — Owned and operated the Frosted Pantry on Mane Street
- **Tom McIntosh** — Pioneertown Land Sales Agent and first "Sheriff" of Pioneertown
- **Tom Mix** — Famous Western actor and an old friend of Dick Curtis'
- **Tommy Thompson** — Personally built the Pioneer Bowl by hand and co-owned it with his wife, Lillian Thompson, a.k.a. Cactus Kate
- **Toodles Senn** — Ran the Chuck Wagon in Pioneertown along with Marie Bush
- **Trigger** — Roy Rogers' famous palomino Horse
- **Trigger Bill** — Owner of Trigger Bill's Shooting Gallery who also worked along with Shorty Creswell to improve the roads around Pioneertown - His real name is unknown
- **Val Jones** — Tended the bar along with "Cactus Jim" at the Red Dog Saloon and later purchased the Red Dog Saloon along with his wife, Pearl, who was one of Pioneertown's first teachers
- **Victoria Williams** — Musician who wrote the song *Happy to Have Known Pappy* after Claude "Pappy" Allen died
- **Wallace Roland Starx** — The artist who painted the inside of Pioneertown Bowl with pictures of Pioneertown's early history and founders
- **Walt Giles** — An Original Board Member of the Pioneertown Corporation
- **Wayne Mills** — Pioneertown's First local Farrier
- **White, Ray & Marge** — Former Owner of the Golden Stallion restaurant in Pioneertown
- **William Boyd** — Famous Western Actor who portrayed Hopalong Cassidy
- **William E. Grigsby** — Land Surveyor and Appraiser for the Pioneertown Corporation
- **William Murphy** — Original Pioneertown Corporation Board Member who became co-owner of Pioneertown in 1954 along with Fletcher Jones
- **William S. Hart** — Veteran Western Actor and idol of Dick Curtis and Roy Rogers
- **Wm. Rogers** — Delivered the first gas services to Pioneertown from Rock Gas
- **Yvonne De Carlo** — Actress, Dancer and Singer who was a friend of Dick Curtis', attended the Ground Breaking Ceremony and was a frequent guest to Pioneertown

Chapter 13

All Titles Filmed in Pioneertown

The next two pages contain a comprehensive list of every film and television production that has ever been filmed in Pioneertown. The list does include a couple music videos, but it does not fully detail the tremendous number of commercials, still photography and other music videos that have been produced in town.

The Valiant Hombre (1948)

Unusual Occupations L-7-3 Modern Pioneers (1948)

The Gay Amigo (1949)

The Daring Caballero (1949)

The Cowboy and the Indians (1949)

Satan's Cradle (1949)

Riders in the Sky (1949)

Beyond the Purple Hills (1950)

The Girl from San Lorenzo (1950)

The Cisco Kid (1950–1956) 6 SEASONS of HALF-HOUR EPISODES - 156 EPISODES IN TOTAL
ALL FILMED or FRAMED IN PIONEERTOWN

Cody of the Pony Express (1950)

The Capture (1950)

The Gene Autry Show (1950–1955) 5 SEASONS of 25-MINUTE EPISODES - 91 EPISODES IN TOTAL
ALL FILMED or FRAMED IN PIONEERTOWN

Indian Territory (1950)

Whirlwind (1951)

Silver Canyon (1951)

The Range Rider ('51–'53) 3 SEASONS of 26 1/2 HOUR EPISODES +1 SPECIAL - 79 EPISODES IN TOTAL
ALL FILMED or FRAMED IN PIONEERTOWN

Barbed Wire (1952)

Winning of the West (1953)

On Top of Old Smoky (1953)

Jeopardy (1953)

Last of the Pony Riders (1953)

Cowboy G-Men, Episode: Silver Fraud (1953)

Annie Oakley (1954–1957) 3 SEASONS of 25-MINUTE EPISODES - 81 EPISODES IN TOTAL
ALL FILMED or FRAMED IN PIONEERTOWN

Buffalo Bill, Jr. (1955–1956) 2 SEASONS of 21 HALF-HOUR EPISODES - 42 EPISODES IN TOTAL
ALL FILMED or FRAMED IN PIONEERTOWN

Judge Roy Bean (1955-1956) 1 SEASON of 24-MINUTE EPISODES - 39 EPISODES IN TOTAL
ALL FILMED or FRAMED IN PIONEERTOWN

The Rainmaker (1956)

26 Men (1957–1959) 2 SEASONS of 25-MINUTE EPISODES - 78 EPISODES IN TOTAL
AN UNKNOWN NUMBER OF EPISODES WERE FRAMED or FILMED IN PIONEERTOWN

The 19th Hole (1964)

Cain's Cutthroats (1971)

The Life and Times of Judge Roy Bean (1972)

The China Lake Murders (1990)

Shelter from the Storm (1994)

Desert Cross (1994)

The Howling: New Moon Rising (1995)

Last Chance (1999)

Fabulous Shiksa in Distress (2003)

Cracker & Camper Van Beethoven: First Annual Camp Out Live (2006)

CYXORK 7 (2006)

The Last Western (2007)

God's Way Love (2007)

Remembering Nigel (2009)

Desert Gold (2010)

The Oregon Trail (2010)

Ice Cube: I Rep That West Music Video (2010)

The Scarlet Worm (2011)

Seven Psychopaths (2012)

Tales of the Frontier   Episode: Redemption (2012)

Bulletproof (2012)

Western Bells: Projection 1 (2013)

Blown Speaker Gospel: Pioneertown Music Video (2013)

Becoming Bulletproof (2014)

The Gambler (2014)

Of Dust and Bones (2016)

Cyndi Lauper: Funnel of Love Music Video (2016)

Best F(r)iends (2017)

Ingrid Goes West (2017)

Chapter 14

Straight From the Heart

Poetry and prayers pertaining to Pioneertown:

The Desert's Ten Commandments
(Published in the Pioneertown Gazette by an unknown writer):

Thou shalt love the Desert, but not loose patience with those who say it's bleak and ornery (even when the wind is blowing).

Thou shalt speak of the Desert with great reverence, and lie about it with great showmanship, adding zest to tall tales and legends.

Thou shalt not admit other Deserts have more color than the one on which you have staked your claim.

Thou shalt on the Sabbath look to the mountain peaks so's to know better your whereabouts, so's you can help others to know the Desert, dotting on the map the places where you have camped.

Honor the Pioneers, Explorers and Desert Rats who found and marked the water holes; and stop shooting the road signs full of holes - they tell you about the next water hole and try to help you live in the Desert.

Thou shalt not shoot the antelope chipmunk, kangaroo rat or other harmless Desert friends.

Thou shalt not adulterate the water holes nor leave the campsite messed up. Be sure to take 1o gallons of water with you. Don't have to ask the other fellow on the road for a quart, but be able to help the tenderfoot by giving him some water.

Thou shalt not steal (from the prospectors shack), nor forget to fill the wood box and water pail.

Thous shalt not bear false witness against thy neighbor; you know the mining laws; you know the whereabouts of his monuments.

Thy shalt not covet thy neighbor's sleeping bag, his gun nor the contents of his canteen.

Studd Valley Serenade by Beebe Kline:

Well, it was down to Studd Valley
That I went
Took some blankets
And a good ole Army tent
Took my trusted forty-four
'Cause on that tent
There warn't no door
Down in Studd Valley.

Oh, there was an artist feller
Down there
Wanted to sketch my figger
In the rare,
Said, no sir I do not choose
To take off even my shoes
Down in Studd Valley.

Had about a week of
Good ole desert air
And I seemed tuh lose all
Thought of time and ker
Took lots of them cold showers
Felt just like a desert flower
Down in Studd Valley.

Soon I threw away
My trusted fourty-four
And I'm glad that on my tent
Thar warn't no door.
Gess I knowed right from the start
Them bearded men
Would win my heart
Down in Studd Valley.

Poem about the Red Dog Saloon by Bruce Cranston, Dedicated to Jonesy & Don:

I dropped into the Red Dog Rest
      To get a ginger ale.
"Come in," said Jonesy, "to our nest,
      Step right up to the rail.
Just tell us what you like to drink,
      We've everything in here;
We'll serve you quicker than a wink
      A soda pop or beer.
We folks out here in Pioneertown
Extend our hands to you,
This is a place of great renown
      Where neighbors are true blue.
Our hearts are light, our welcome strong,
      We greet you with a smile,
And join together in a song
      That makes your trip worthwhile."
I thanked the man who took my hand,
      Said, "Buddy, you're all right,
You bet I'll come back to your land;
      Good luck, my friend. Good night!"

Cactus Kate, by Bruce Cranston:

O! ridin' down the desert trail
       An' through the purple sage,
Aheadin' fer old Pioneertown,
       To meet the Twin Palms stage.
Singin' as they loped along,
       "Pony, we've a date,
Popsie Brown's awaitin' there
       To greet his Cactus Kate.

O! flap yer ears an' swish yer tail
       An keep on goin' right.
We've got to foller this yere trail,
       E'en tough the dust we bite.
In Pioneertown we'll find Ol' Pops
       A lookin' fer his mate.
You bet that he'll be feelin' tops,
       Fer he loves his Cactus Kate."

As Cactus Kate rode into town,
       Folks came from near an' far.
They whooped it up, fer her renown
       Reached to the farthest star.
A "45" strapped to her side,
       She looked a queen of state,
A smilin', cooin' like a bride,
       The dashin' Cactus Kate.

Pioneertown Hitching Rails, by Dazzlin' Dallas Morley:

Way back a while, in Pioneertown
'ere horse and cowboy were obsolete-
Hitching rails adorned the fronts
Of every building on our "Mane Street".

Hitching rails were made of wood-
Posts or crossbars all gave service.
When cowboys staged their "shoot-outs",
They held the horses if they got nervous.

There was no charge for parking then-
The cowboys "drinking" in the bars,
No worries about "parking tickets",
No worries, then, about motor cars!

The "day of the horse" is returning here-
A lot of folks have two or three.
The hitching rails must appear again,
When all the tourists come back to see

The horses standing patiently-
At hitching rails along the street.
They take us back in memory-
To happier days, that can't be beat!

We loved our town the way it was.
Fires took both ends in 'sixty-four.
Now "Time" and "Progress" aid the cause
Of ruining our wondrous "Lore"!

And now that horses have returned,
And hitching rails are back in style-
Please build them back, so folks can learn
How it used to be-way back a while!

Gene Autry's Guide:

1. The Cowboy must never shoot first, hit a smaller man, or take unfair advantage.
2. He must never go back on his word, or a trust confided in him.
3. He must always tell the truth.
4. He must be gentle with children, the elderly, and animals.
5. He must not advocate or possess racially or religiously intolerant ideas.
6. He must help people in distress.
7. He must be a good worker.
8. He must keep himself clean in thought, speech, action, and personal habits.
9. He must respect women, parents, and his nation's laws.
1o. The Cowboy is a patriot.

Roy Rogers Rider's Rules:

1. Be neat and clean.
2. Be courteous and polite.
3. Always obey your parents.
4. Protect the weak and help them.
5. Be brave but never take chances.
6. Study hard and learn all you can.
7. Be kind to animals and take care of them.
8. Eat all your food and never waste any.
9. Love God and go to Sunday school regularly.
10. Always respect our flag and our country.

Roy Rogers' Prayer

Lord, I reckon I'm not much just by myself,
I fail to do a lot of things I ought to do.
But Lord, when trails are steep and passes high,
Help me ride it straight the whole way through.

And when in the falling dusk I get that final call,
I do not care how many flowers they send,
Above all else, the happiest trail would be,
For YOU to say to me, "Let's ride, My Friend."

Chapter 15

Newer Memories

Here is a collection of newer advertisements, articles, documents, posters and pictures from Pioneertown's more recent years. Just as Chapter 9 mentioned: to try and include every picture, poster and advertisement of interest would truly be impossible because there are simply too many for one single book. Included in this chapter are some pictures of Pioneertown's more recent shops and renovations, more fun family memories and a glimpse of the modern western American lifestyle. The vast majority of these pictures were taken specifically for this book. All others have been credited. These are presented in no particular order and every attempt was made to present the best quality images available.

Entering Pioneertown from Yucca Valley in 2o18,

Road sign on the west end of Mane Street in 2o18, facing east.

ABOVE: The Jack Cass Saloon shortly after completion.

BELOW: Newer additions to the Jack Cass sign. Picture from 2o18.

ABOVE: Gary enjoys the winter view from the front porch of the General Mercantile Shop.

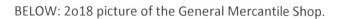

BELOW: 2o18 picture of the General Mercantile Shop.

ABOVE: View of the Pioneertown Gazette's printing press in the early 2ooo's.

BELOW: 2o18 location of the Pioneertown Gazette's printing press.

ABOVE: Riders enjoying Mane Street in February of 2o18.

BELOW: The Pioneertown Bell House (storage shed) in 2o18.

ABOVE: Pioneertown Pottery and the Pioneertown Land Office in 2o18.

BELOW: The signs which adorn Pioneertown Pottery. The signs read: "FINE WARE FOR FINE FOLKS - CRACKED POTS FOR THE REST OF Y'ALL" & "THE POTTER SAID UNTO THE CLAY 'BE WARE' AND SO IT WAS - WHERE? HERE! IN PIONEERTOWN, CA - TAKE HOME A SOUVENIR"

Font of Pioneertown Pottery in February of 2o18. The majority of the shops on Mane Street run by the same schedule that's posted in front of Pioneertown Pottery. The sign reads: "POTTERY HOURS - OPEN MOST WEEKENDS AND SOME OTHER DAYS - If the door is unlocked, we're open!"

ABOVE: The Law Office (storage shed) on Mane Street in the late 199o's.

BELOW: The Soap Goats shop, formerly the Law Office, on Mane Street in February of 2o18.

JoAnne Gosen and a native Pioneertown Reindeer in front of the Soap Goats shop in December of 2o17.

ABOVE: The Likker Barn in a very cold winter during the 199o's.

BELOW: Likker Barn at night during the winter of 2o17 - 2o18.

Sarah Tabbush (above) in front of the Likker Barn with a new Pioneertown General Store sign in February of 2o18.

ABOVE: View of the Pioneertown Gunfighters For Hire performing on Mane Street early in 2o18. Photo taken from the front porch of the General Mercantile Shop.

BELOW: Shot from in front of the Pioneertown Saddlery as the crowd gathers in front of the Pioneer Bowl for the same Saturday afternoon show in 2o18 that is shown above.

A bright and beautiful sky above Mane Street. Photo shot in front of the Pioneertown Sound Stage in the summer of 2o17.

ABOVE: The Pioneertown Bank (false front) in the early 2ooo's.

BELOW: The Pioneertown Bank and Bath House (false fronts) in January of 2o18.

ABOVE: The Pioneertown Bank, Bath House and Livery (false fronts) in January of 2o18.

BELOW: A handful of Mane Street residents enjoying breakfast in February of 2o18.

ABOVE: The Schnald Mining Corporation (originally Pioneertown Photos) in February of 2o18.

BELOW: The Pioneer Bowl road sign silently sits in wait late in February of 2o18.

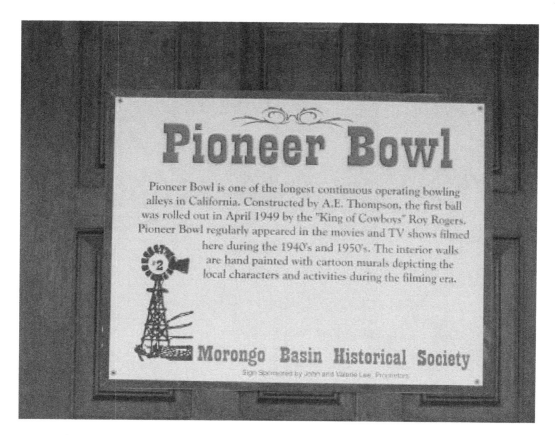

ABOVE: Morongo Basin Historical Society sign on the Pioneertown Bowl in 2o15.

BELOW: The Pioneer Bowl sign stands out like a sore thumb while driving down Pioneertown Road.

ABOVE: A crowd gathers in front of the Pioneer Bowl for a Mane Street Stampede performance in the summer of 2o17. There would be twice as many people inside if the Pioneer Bowl was open!

BELOW: The Pioneer Bowl sits, waiting to see new life late in February of 2o18.

ABOVE: The sign that currently greets all visitors to the Pioneer Bowl. Even if *they are there*, they're still closed.

BELOW: Trigger Bill's, next door to the Pioneer Bowl in the center of Mane Street, also sits waiting to be brought back to life. Picture from February of 2o18.

Pioneertown Saddlery (originally the Pioneertown Land Office) and Arrow & Bear (the original site of Pioneertown Duds and Saddlery) in February of 2o18.

ABOVE: Left to right are John Ironsnake Jefferies and Gary Suppes of the Chaparrosa Outfitters in February of 2o18.

BELOW: Pioneertown Saddlery, present day home of the Chaparrosa Outfitters, on the same day in February of 2o18.

ABOVE: The Pioneertown Sound Stage in December of 2o17.

BELOW: Inside the Pioneertown Sound Stage in February of 2o18.

ABOVE: The Pioneertown Sound Stage lit up at night for a party in October of 2o17.

BELOW: Inside a Pioneertown Sound Stage holiday party in December of 2o17.

ABOVE: The present location of the Rock Watering Trough on Mane Street. In 2o18.

BELOW: Damage done when the Rock Trough was pushed to the side of Mane Street.

ABOVE: The Pioneertown Gazette in January of 2o18.

BELOW: The Open Air Dance Floor and the Red Dog Saloon in February of 2o18.

ABOVE: Looking north from Mane Street at the land which was originally slated to be the site of the Pioneertown Public Pool.

BELOW: The Church in Pioneertown, originally the site of Althoof Furniture, during February of 2o18.

ABOVE: The Church in Pioneertown during the winter of 2o1o - 2o11.

BELOW: A view from inside The Church in Pioneertown.

Top to bottom are the east and west interior walls of The Church in Pioneertown.

ABOVE: The Red Dog Saloon in February of 2o18.

BELOW: The bar inside the Red Dog Saloon is still intact and includes the hand-carved names from many of Pioneertown's historical figures. Photo from February of 2o18.

ABOVE: The original site of the Beauty Corral on Mane Street, now a private residence, in 2o18.

BELOW: Facing west from in front of The Church in Pioneertown looking at the original site of the Wooden Indian which is now a private residence. Photo from February of 2o18.

ABOVE: Sign on the west end of Mane Street to keep Pioneertown visitors out of private property.

BELOW: Looking at the Pioneertown Post Office from the site of Nell's Ice Cream Palace in 2o18.

Inside and outside views of White's Hardware, originally White's Grocery, in February of 2o18.

ABOVE: Looking at the site of Maggie's Feed Barn from the front porch of White's Hardware in 2o18.

BELOW: Facing north towards the foundation from Maggie's Feed Barn in February of 2o18.

Pioneertown's OK Corral in February of 2o18.

ABOVE: Facing north from Pioneertown Road in February of 2o18.

BELOW: Left to right are the Pioneertown Post Office and Sheriff's Office in 2o18.

Front door and inside view of the Pioneertown Sheriff's Office in February of 2o18.

Pictures from the 2o14 (below) and 2o17 (above) Mane Street Parades in Pioneertown.

ABOVE: The Pioneertown Corrals sees an equal ratio of four-legged and two-legged visitors.

BELOW: The east entrance to the Pioneertown Corrals from Rawhide Road.

ABOVE: The Barbecue Pit at the Pioneertown Corrals in February of 2o18.

BELOW: A big celebration at the Barbecue Pit in the Pioneertown Corrals in 2o14.

ABOVE: Roger Anderson hanging out at the Pioneertown Corrals in 2o14.

BELOW: Christy and Pickle Anderson in 2o15.

Campers enjoy some good conversation on a cold day at the Pioneertown Corrals as their horses enjoy some lunch. Photos taken in February of 2o18.

ABOVE: John Ironsnake Jefferies playing a harmonica for one very curious and entertained fan.

BELOW: Christy Anderson and Josh Landon in the BBQ Pit at the Pioneertown Corrals in 2o14.

The present day Kilp n' Kurl on Mane Street in February of 2o18.

ABOVE: The former site of Pioneertown's Golden Stallion restaurant which is now public parking. Photo from February of 2o18.

BOTTOM LEFT: August 2o1o ad in the Los Angeles Times for Pappy & Harriet's Pioneertown Palace.

The asking price was $1,89o,ooo.

BOTTOM RIGHT: March 1992 ad in the Los Angeles Times for the historic Pioneer Bowl.

The asking price was $335,ooo.

PIONEERTOWN $1,890,000
Yucca Valley
Unbelievable investor/owner/user oppty! Best muisc,
steak & ribs W of Mississippi. www.PappyandHarriets.com

ABOVE: The Pioneertown Motel's office around 2oo8.

BELOW: The Pioneertown Motel's present day office in 2o18.

ABOVE: The Pioneertown Motel while Ernie and Carol Kester owned it in the late 2ooo's.

BELOW: A view of the Pioneertown Motel from Mane Street in January of 2o18.

ABOVE: The inside of the Pioneertown Motel's covered patio in 2o17.

BELOW: The vintage Parking Sign for Pioneertown's free public parking.

ABOVE: A 2oo5 postcard from Pappy & Harriet's Pioneertown Palace in Pioneertown, CA.
© anotherplanet, LLC art/design - Bingo

BELOW: The entrance to Pappy & Harriet's Pioneertown Palace in 2o17.

ABOVE: The stage at Pappy & Harriet's Pioneertown Palace in 2o17.

BELOW: The stage at Pappy & Harriet's Pioneertown Palace in 2o18.

ABOVE: A view inside of Pappy & Harriet's from the back door in 2o17.

BELOW: The first level of the back patio at Pappy & Harriet's in 2o18.

ABOVE: The Pioneertown Cantina in the early 1980's.

BELOW: Pappy & Harriet's Pioneertown Palace , formerly the Cantina, in 2o17.

ABOVE: A quite afternoon inside Pappy & Harriet's Pioneertown Palace in January of 2o18.

BELOW: The signs on Pappy & Harriet's back door.

ABOVE: Pioneertown Pottery during the early 2o1o's.

BELOW: Pioneertown Pottery's new sign.

ABOVE: A view of the Wild West Theater entrance from Curtis Road in January of 2018.

BELOW: A view of the Desert Willow Ranch's stage for the Pioneertown Wild West Theater.

ABOVE: A view of the Desert Willow Ranch from Pioneertown Road in January of 2o18.

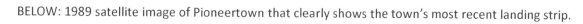

BELOW: 1989 satellite image of Pioneertown that clearly shows the town's most recent landing strip.

ABOVE: A view of present day Hayden Ranch in Pioneertown.

BELOW: Facing west at the Hayden Ranch in the fall of 2o17.

ABOVE: The Scarlett Lady as she stands at the Hayden Ranch in 2o18.

BELOW: The inside of the Scarlett Lady still tells the hellish story of the Sawtooth Complex Fire.

ABOVE: Fire Fighters and work fearlessly to stop the Sawtooth Complex Fire in 2oo6.

BELOW: What looks like a fun looking prop on Mane Street is actually one of many legitimate emergency fire hydrants recently installed in Pioneertown.

SUNDAY
July 23, 2006

The Desert Sun
SERVING THE COACHELLA VALLEY SINCE 1927

$1.25

thedesertsun.com updated throughout the day

'CAP, ARE WE GOING TO DIE?'

Firefighters barely avoided tragedy in Pioneertown firestorm

By Keith Matheny
THE DESERT SUN

PIONEERTOWN — As a blanket of fire surrounded them, the four Twentynine Palms firefighters made a risky decision: Their only chance to escape the fury of the fast-approaching blaze was to jump from the open-cab fire engine and race to a nearby garage.

They shielded themselves from the heat and smoke, dodging flames and burning debris, as they axed their way inside.

But now the structure was being consumed.

Fire danced on all sides and atop the roof. Flames were licking below the garage door.

From a rear window shattered by the heat, they saw the unbelievable ferocity of the Sawtooth fire: orange-red flames, burning embers and smoke that roared horizontally.

They were surrounded.

Desperate for a way out, firefighter Chris Giertz cracked a side door to look outside. He was met with flames and quickly pulled back.

"All I can see is smoke and fire, Cap," Giertz told his crew leader, Capt. Jesse Quinalty.

The garage was filling with smoke, choking the firefighters, who lacked air tanks.

There was no apparent escape.

Karissa Boyce, the newest firefighter on the crew, began to panic.

"Cap, are we going to die?" the 21-year-old asked Quinalty.

The captain, a 14-year veteran, reassured her: "It may hurt a little, it may even hurt a lot, but we are not going to die here."

Boyce

The crew began taking shorter breaths, trying to limit the amount of deadly smoke inhaled into their lungs.

Quinalty radioed for air support, asking that helicopters or airplanes swoop in and drop water or fire retardant on the garage.

There's too much smoke, came the response. Aircraft could not see the structure, nor was it safe enough to send in the aerial calvary, Quinalty was told.

"We're going to have to sit it out," he told his crew.

The flames intensified.

The smoke grew thicker.

Giertz, 21, reflected on his young life and those he loved.

Boyce huddled in firefighter Scott Pilon's arms.

She began to pray.

The Twentynine Palms fire crew had been assigned to pro-

Twentynine Palms Fire Department firefighters (from left) Chris Giertz, 21, Scott Pilon, 24, and Capt. Jesse Quinalty, 32, are framed by the collapsed roof of a Pioneertown garage in which they took refuge on July 11 as the Sawtooth blaze became a firestorm around them. They and firefighter Karissa Boyce waited until after the ignition point of the fire blew over the garage, and then they crawled out of a window while the garage burned. **See more wildfire photos at thedesertsun.com.**

WADE BYARS, THE DESERT SUN

The Sawtooth Complex fire was part of a monster wildfire that became the largest so far this year in California. It burned for more than a week, charring nearly 90,000 acres. It is blamed for one death. On July 11, four Twentynine Palms firefighters unexpectedly met the wrath of Sawtooth and all its fury. This is their story.

tect structures — homes and garages, primarily — that July 11 morning on the off-chance Sawtooth spread into residential areas.

Lightning ignited the fire Sunday, July 9. The next day, officials said they had it about 75 percent contained.

But on July 11, firefighters were surprised by high winds, triple-digit temperatures and very low humidity. The key ingredients to a runaway wildfire.

Please see ESCAPE, A4

FIRE COVERAGE

■ More harrowing stories from firefighters, residents. **A5**

■ Lightning sparks a new fire near Joshua Tree National Park. **B1**

■ Go to thedesertsun.com and see nearly 450 photos and more than 30 videos of the wildfires that scored nearly 90,000 acres

■ Picking up the pieces, coping with loss in the fire's aftermath. **E1**

PHOTO COURTESY OF WARNER TRUMP

Pioneertown firefighter Scott Pilon gazes at a foreboding scene: Black fire clouds and fast-approaching flames from the massive Sawtooth Complex fire. This was the view July 11 on Lariat Trail in Pioneertown. Pilon and three other firefighters narrowly escaped tragedy when the out-of-control fire overwhelmed them.

The Desert Sun, July 23rd, 2006 edition, highlighting the Sawtooth Complex Fire.

ABOVE: A view of Mane Street facing north east in 2oo8.

BELOW: The sculpture garden on Mane Street in February of 2o18.

ABOVE: Thomas and Amara Alban of of Mazamar Art Pottery in Pioneertown.

BELOW: Thomas Alban and Christy Anderson inside the General Mercantile Shop in February of 2o18.

Geoffrey Fennell (above) and the inside of Pioneertown Pottery (Mazamar Art Pottery) in 2o18.

ABOVE: The Pioneertown Pottery showroom from inside the stone archway.

BELOW: Jessie Keylon and her art studio inside the Pioneertown Land Office in summer of 2o17.

The magical smell that typically haunts the many carnivores in Pioneertown comes from the Pappy & Harriet's Pioneertown Palace outdoor barbecue.

ABOVE: A typical scene on Pioneertown's Mane Street.

BELOW: The 2o16 cast of Pioneertown's Gun Fighters For Hire.

A view from Mane Street on a cold December evening in 2o17. Pappy & Harriet's Pioneertown Palace is on the right side.

ABOVE: Christmas Party at Pappy & Harriet's Pioneertown Palace in 2o17.

BELOW: Jack & Sandy Dugan giving out the Christmas presents at the 2o17 party.

ABOVE: A pair of wild cows along Burns Canyon Road in the summer of 2o16.

BELOW: Headed towards Big Bear on the Pioneer Pass in the summer of 2o17.

ABOVE: A view of the trees that begin to cover the Pioneer Pass the closer you get to Big Bear.

BELOW: A view of Baldwin Lake while facing north west on the Pioneer Pass in the summer of 2o18.

Players start off at the First Hole of the 2o17 annual Pioneer Pass Golf Challenge in Big Bear.

ABOVE: Trucks, Jeeps and 2o17 PPGC contestants make their way down the Pioneer Pass.

BELOW: The Arastre Creek Hole near the center of the Pioneer Pass in 2o17.

ABOVE: Lets see how well you would do in the PPGC. Can you spot the Forth Hole, Eddie's Meadows, a Par 6? Hint: It's near the center.

BELOW: The PPGC is fun for golfers, spotters, spectators and outdoor enthusiasts alike!

ABOVE: A shot of Mane Street facing east around the time that the Andersons purchased the north half of Mane Street. Note how deep the newly formed creek bed, known locally as the "Mane Street River", cuts into Mane Street.

BELOW: Check out Mane Street facing west in 2o18. The long, hard and expensive work of the Andersons can clearly be seen all the way across Pioneertown!

ABOVE: A crowd gathers to see a performance on Mane Street in summer of 2o17.

BELOW: A Wanted Ad for Pioneertown's Mane Street Stampede.

ABOVE: Bill Gosen and some very happy goats at the Soap Goats Shop in February of 2o18.

BELOW: Resident Spanky Schnald in front of his Mane Street home in February of 2o18.

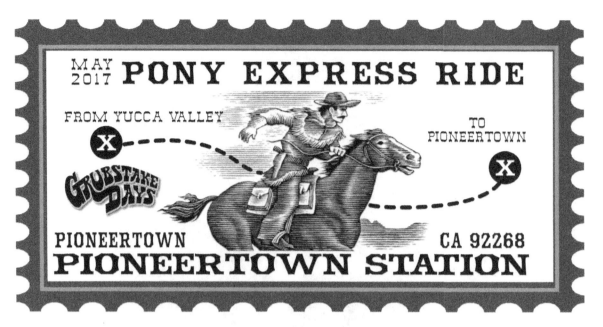

ABOVE: Advertisement for the 2o17 annual Pony Express Ride up to Pioneertown from Yucca Valley as part of the annual Grubstake Days in Yucca Valley.

BELOW: Advertisement for the annual Pioneertown Shodeo Rodeo and Chili Throwdown.

ABOVE: Ray Wise in a scene from *CYXORK 7* (2oo6)
BOTTOM LEFT: *CYXORK 7* (2oo6) BOTTOM RIGHT: Advertisement for the 1st Cracker & Camper Van Beethoven Campout in Pioneertown.

Advertisement for the annual Cracker & Camper Van Beethoven Campout in Pioneertown.

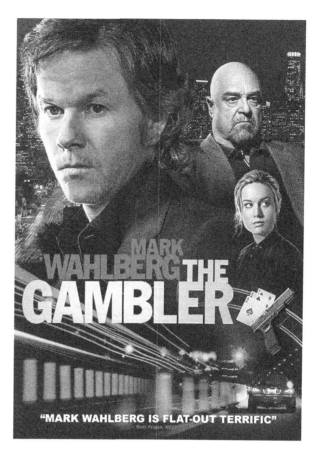

TOP LEFT: *The Howling: New Moon Rising* (1995) TOP RIGHT: *The Gambler* (2014)

BOTTOM: *Seven Psychopaths* (2012)

TOP LEFT: *The Scarlet Worm* (2011) TOP RIGHT: *Shelter from the Storm* (1994)

BOTTOM LEFT: *The Last Western* (2007) BOTTOM RIGHT: *The China Lake Murders* (1990)

ABOVE: Scene from *The China Lake Murders* (1990,) shot on Pioneertown Road.

CENTER: Scenes from *The Howling: New Moon Rising* (1995,) shot inside Pappy & Harriet's and starring a handful of Pioneertown residents.

BOTTOM: Scene from *Seven Psychopaths* (2012,) shot near Skyline Ranch Road in Pioneertown. Left to right are Colin Farrell, Sam Rockwell and Christopher Walken.

TOP & CENTER: Scenes from Cyndi Lauper's *Funnel of Love* Music Video (2016).

BOTTOM: Scene from the movie *Ingrid Goes West*, (2017,) shot inside Pappy & Harriet's. Left to right are Elizabeth Olsen and Aubrey Plaza.

ABOVE: Desert Stars Festival at Pappy & Harriet's in September of 2015.

BOTTOM LEFT: *Ingrid Goes Westl* (2o17)   BOTTOM RIGHT: *Best F(r)iends (*2o17)

Road sign on the west side of Mane Street in January of 2o18. Happy trails, friends!